MICROSOFT® Access 2000

NITA RUTKOSKY
Pierce College at Puyallup
Puyallup, Washington

DENISE SEGUIN
Fanshawe College
London, Ontario

CONTENTS

The Marquee Series Team: Sonja Brown, Senior Editor; Michael Sander, Developmental Editor; Joan D'Onofrio, Art Director; Jennifer Wreisner, Cover Designer; Leslie Anderson and Bill Connell, Desktop Production Specialists; Susan Capecchi and Desiree Faulkner, Testers; Sharon O'Donnell, Proofreader; and Nancy Fulton, Indexer.

Acknowledgments: The Publisher, Authors, and Editors would like to thank the following instructors for their valuable contributions to the development of this textbook: Angela Ambrosia, Rio Salado College; Patty Anderson, Lake City Community College; Beverly Bilshausen, College of DuPage; Jerry Booher, Scottsdale Community College; Deborah C. Clear, Virginia Highlands Community College; Tony Davila, Houston Community College; Elaine Denham, Macon Tech; Mike Feiler, Merritt College; Charles Finkbeiner, Washtenaw Community College; David Laxton, Southern Ohio College; Dan Maguire, Brevard Community College; Virginia Melvin, State Technical Institute of Memphis; Kay Newton, Commonwealth Business College

Library of Congress Cataloging-in-Publication Data
Rutkosky, Nita Hewitt.
Microsoft Access 2000 / Nita Rutkosky, Denise Seguin.
p. cm. — (Marquee series)
Includes index.
ISBN 0-7638-0368-5
1. Microsoft Access. 2. Database management. I. Seguin, Denise
II. Title. III. Series

QA76.9.D3 R87 2000
005.75'65—dc21 **99-057581**

Published by EMCParadigm (800) 535-6865
875 Montreal Way E-mail: educate@emcp.com
St. Paul, MN 55102 Web Site: www.emcp.com

Printed in the United States of America

10 9 8 7 6 5 4 3 2

Access

Maintaining Data in Access Tables

Managing business information effectively is a vital activity, since data forms the basis upon which transactions are conducted or strategic decisions are made. Microsoft Access is a database management system that is used to store, retrieve, and manage information. The type of information stored in an Access database can include such items as customer lists, inventory articles, human resources, and supplier lists. Activities that are routinely performed with a database include adding, editing, deleting, finding, sorting, querying, and reporting information. In this section you will learn the skills and complete the projects listed below.

Skills

- Define field, record, table, datasheet, and database
- Start and exit Access
- Identify features in the Access window
- Open and close a database
- Open and close tables
- Adjust column widths
- Navigate in Datasheet view
- Find and edit records
- Add records
- Delete records
- Sort records
- Move columns in Datasheet view
- Preview and print a table
- Change the page orientation
- Use the Clipboard toolbar
- Use the online help
- Compact and repair a database

Projects

Add, delete, find, and sort records, preview and print tables, and compact the Distributors database. Find, edit, add, delete, and sort records, and preview and print the Employees database.

Find student records and input grades into the Grades database. Compact the Grades database.

Maintain Inventory database by adding and deleting records.

Delete records, sort, and print two reports from the Costume Inventory database.

Exploring Database Fundamentals

A *database* contains information logically organized into related units for easy retrieval. You access a database when you open a telephone book to look up a friend's telephone number, or browse the yellow pages looking for a restaurant. Microsoft Access is an application that is used to manage databases electronically. Information stored in an Access database is organized into *tables*. A table contains information for related items such as customers, suppliers, inventory, or human resources.

PROJECT: You will examine a table in the Distributors database for Worldwide Enterprises to define and identify: field, record, table, and datasheet.

steps

1. At the Windows desktop, click the Start button on the Taskbar.

   This causes a pop-up menu to display.

2. Point to Programs.

   Pointing to an option on the Start pop-up menu that displays with a right-pointing triangle after it causes a cascading side menu to appear.

3. Click *Microsoft Access.*

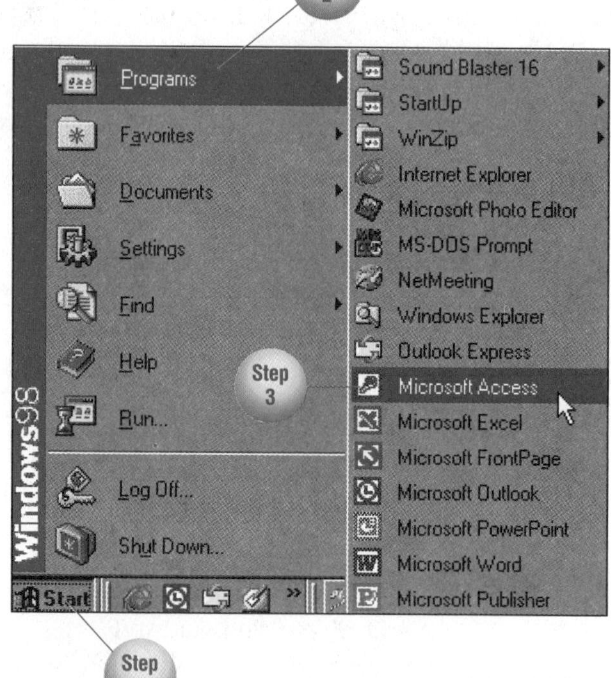

Problem

Depending on your system configuration, the steps you complete to open Access may vary. Check with your instructor if necessary.

4. With Open an existing file already selected in the Microsoft Access dialog box, click OK.

5. If necessary, when the Open dialog box appears, change to the location where the student data files are located.

   To change to a different drive, click the down-pointing triangle to the right of the Look in text box and select the correct drive from the drop-down list.

6. Double-click *WE Distributors1.mdb.*

   Access databases end with the file name extension mdb.

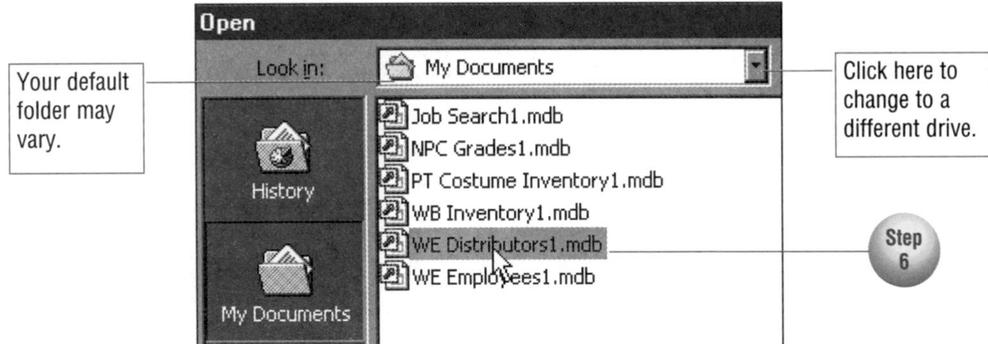

7. Double-click *Canadian Distributors* in the WE Distributors1 Database window.

   The Database window will be explored in more detail in the next topic. For now, you are opening a table in Datasheet view to see how data is organized. Datasheets display the contents of a table in a column/row format.

8. Compare your screen with the one shown in Figure A1.1 and examine the identified elements.

   The identified elements are further described in Table A1.1.

FIGURE A1.1 Canadian Distributors Datasheet

Canadian Distributors : Table

Name	Street Address1	Street Address2	City	Province	Postal Code	Telephone	Fa
EastCoast Cine	62 Mountbatten Driv		St.John's	NF	A1A 3X9	709-555-8349	709-555-
Millennium Movi	4126 Yonge Street	Suite 302	Toronto	ON	M2P 2B8	416-555-9335	416-555-
MountainView M	5417 RoyalMount A		Montreal	PQ	H4P 1H8	514-555-3584	514-555-
New Age Movie	73 Killarney Road		Moncton	NB	E1B 2Z9	506-555-8376	506-555-
Northern Reach	P. O. Box 34		Yellowknife	NW	X1A 2N9	867-555-6314	867-555-
Northern Stars I	811 Cook Street		Whitehorse	YK	Y1A 2S4	867-555-6598	867-555-
Olypmic Cinem	P. O. Box 1439	188 Riverbrook R	Calgary	AB	T2C 3P7	403-651-4587	403-651-
Plains Cinema I	P. O. Box 209	46 Prospect Plac	Regina	SK	S4S 5Y9	306-555-1247	305-555-
Riverview Cinem	1011-848 Sheppard		Winnipeg	MB	R2P 0N6	204-555-6538	204-555-
Seaboard Movie	P. O. Box 1005	696 Colby Drive	Dartmouth	NS	B2V 1Y8	902-555-3948	902-555-
Waterdown Cine	575 Notre Dame Str		Summerside	PE	C1N 1T8	902-555-8374	902-555-
West Coast Mo	P. O. Box 298	7348 Granville Dr	Vancouver	BC	V6Y 1N9	604-555-3548	604-555-

Table Name

Each row is one record in the table.

Each column represents a field in the table.

(continued)

9 Identify the fields and the field names in the Canadian Distributors table. Notice each field contains only one unit of information.

The field names Name, Street Address1, Street Address2, and so on, are displayed in bold in the gray header row in Datasheet view.

10 Identify the records in the Canadian Distributors table. Each record is one row in the table.

The right-pointing triangle to the left of EastCoast Cinemas identifies the active record.

11 Press the down arrow key four times to move the active record.

The right-pointing triangle moves down as you move the insertion point and the Record number at the bottom of the window changes to indicate you are viewing record 5 of a total of 12 records.

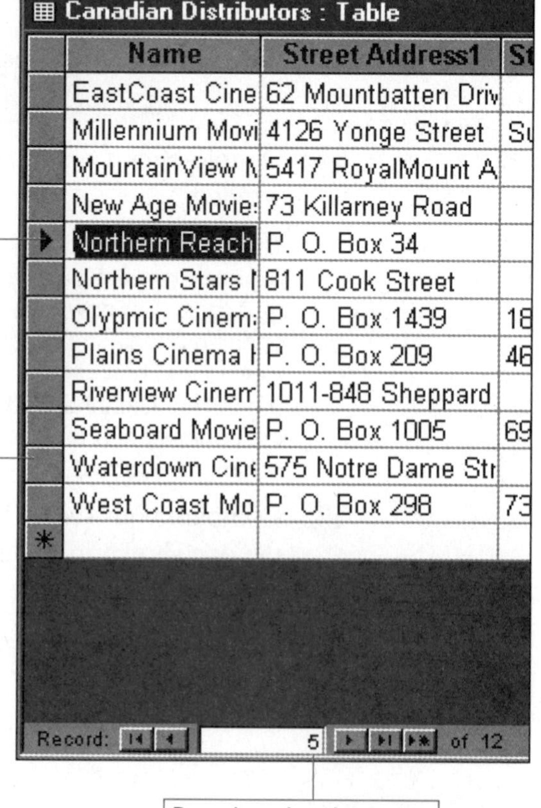

12 Click the Close button ✕ at the right edge of the Canadian Distributors Table Title bar.

The Canadian Distributors table closes and you are returned to the WE Distributors1 Database window.

13 Click File and then Exit.

TABLE A1.1 Elements of a Database

Element	Description
Field	A single component of information about a person, place, item, or object
Record	All of the fields for one unit, such as a customer, supplier, or inventory item
Table	All of the records for one logical group
Datasheet view	Data for a table displayed in columns (fields) and rows (records)
Database	A file containing related tables

Planning and Designing a Database

One of the first steps in designing a new database is to look at the format from which the input will originate. For example, look at an existing file card for a customer to see how the information is currently organized. Determine how you will break down all of the information into fields. Discuss with others what the future needs of the company will be for both input and output. Include extra fields for future use. For example, add a field for a Web site address even if you do not currently have URLs for your customers. Refer to Performance Plus Activity 5 at the end of this section for an exercise in the steps included in designing a new database.

Start Access

1 Click Start.
2 Point to Programs.
3 Click *Microsoft Access.*
4 Open an existing file or create a new database.

Selecting and Opening Objects in Access

The Microsoft Access application window contains the same elements as other Office application windows—Title bar, Menu bar, Toolbar, and Status bar. An open database file displays in a Database window. The Database window contains the various objects in the active database that can be created or opened. Objects in an Access database include tables, queries, forms, reports, pages, macros, and modules.

PROJECT: Using the WE Distributors1 database you will select, open, and close objects.

steps

1. Start Access.
2. Double-click *WE Distributors1* in the file list in the Microsoft Access dialog box.

   Access displays the last nine opened database file names in the Open an existing file list box. *More Files* is selected by default and will display the Open dialog box, where you can navigate to a database not in the file list.

3. At the Access screen, identify the various features by comparing your screen with the one shown in Figure A1.2.

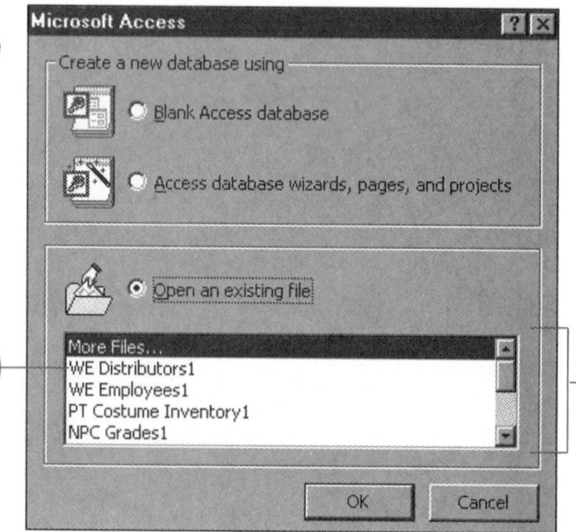

FIGURE A1.2 The Access Screen

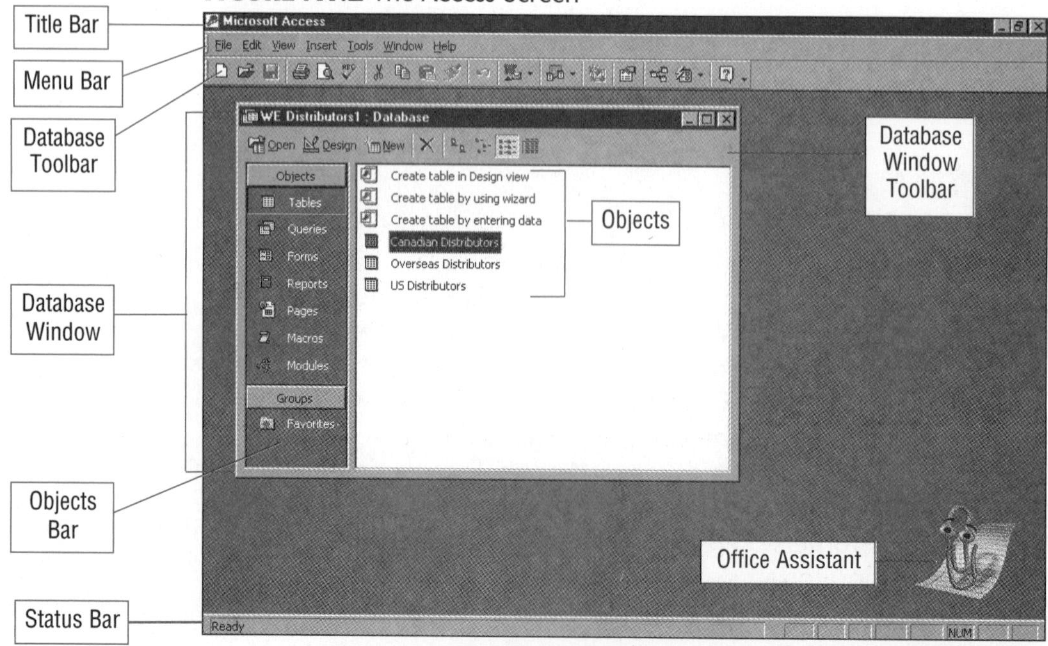

4. Position the mouse pointer over the table named *US Distributors* and then click the mouse to select the object.

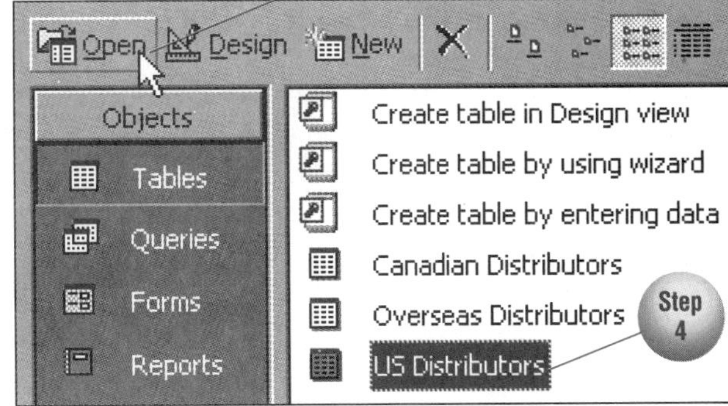

5. Click Open in the Database window toolbar.

   The US Distributors table will open in Datasheet view.

6. Click the Close button on the US Distributors Table Title bar.

7. Click *Forms* in the Objects bar.

8. Double-click *Overseas Distributors*.

   The Overseas Distributors form opens in Form view. A form is used to view and edit data one record at a time. Forms will be discussed in the section titled *Modifying Tables, Creating Forms, and Viewing Data.*

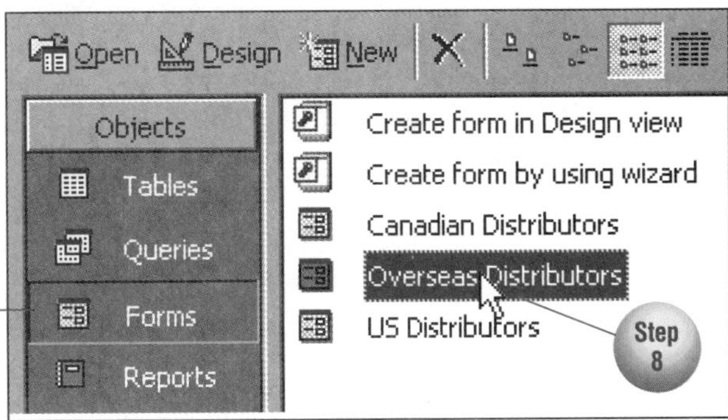

9. Click the Close button on the Overseas Distributors Title bar.

   A description of database objects is presented in Table A1.2.

TABLE A1.2 Database Objects

Object	Description
Tables	Organize data in fields (columns) and rows (records). A database must contain at least one table. The table is the base upon which other objects are created.
Queries	Use to display data from a table that meets a conditional statement and/or perform calculations. For example, display only those records in which the city is Toronto.
Forms	Allow fields and records to be presented in a different layout than the datasheet. Use to facilitate data entry and maintenance.
Reports	Print data from tables or queries. Calculations can be performed in a report.
Pages	Web pages designed for working with data from the Internet or an intranet.
Macros	Automate repetitive tasks.
Modules	Advanced automation through programming using Visual Basic for Applications.

Open Objects
1 Open database file.
2 Select object type from Objects bar.
3 Click object name.
4 Click Open.

Adjusting Columns and Scrolling in Datasheet View

A table opened in Datasheet view displays data in a manner similar to a spreadsheet, with a grid of columns and rows. Columns contain the field values, with the field names in bold text in column headings. Records are represented in rows. A gray record selector bar is positioned at the left edge of the window. The record navigation bar displays along the bottom of the window with record selector buttons. Horizontal and/or vertical scroll bars appear if the entire table is not visible in the current window.

PROJECT: You will adjust column widths and practice scrolling through records using the US Distributors table.

steps

1. With the WE Distributors1 database open, click *Tables* in the Objects bar and then double-click *US Distributors*.

   The US Distributors table opens in Datasheet view.

2. Click the Maximize button in the US Distributors Table Title bar.

   Notice that some columns contain data that is not entirely visible. In steps 3–5 you will learn how to adjust the column widths using two methods.

Problem

If the table window is already maximized, the Maximize button is replaced with the Restore Window button. Skip step 2.

3. With the insertion point positioned in the first record in the *Name* field, click F<u>o</u>rmat and then <u>C</u>olumn Width.

4. Click <u>B</u>est Fit in the Column Width dialog box.

   The column is automatically widened to accommodate the width of the longest entry. In the next step you will widen a column using the mouse in the column headings row.

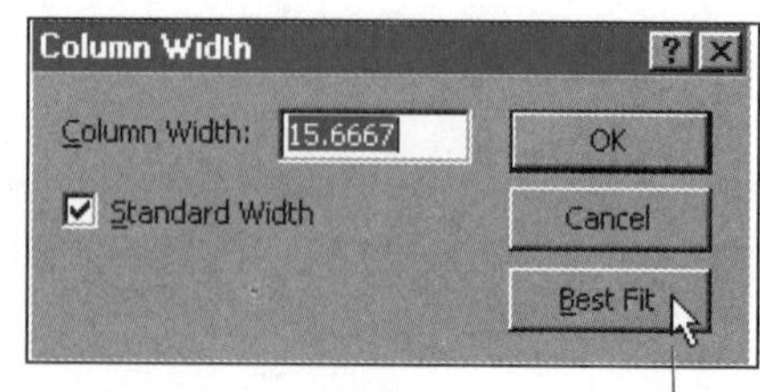

Step 4

5. Position the mouse pointer on the vertical line between columns two and three *(Street Address)* until the pointer changes to a vertical line with a left- and right-pointing arrow, and then double-click the left mouse button.

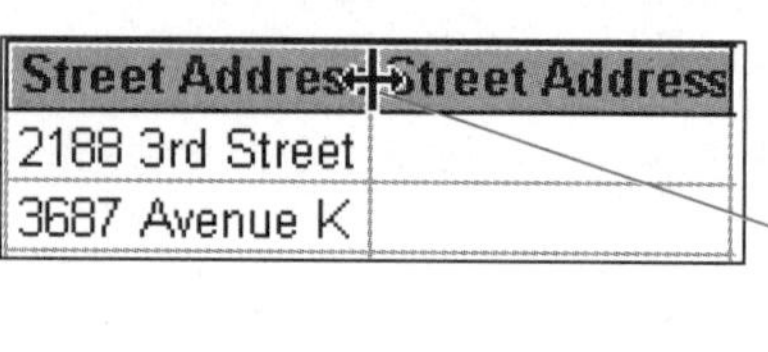

Step 5

Double-clicking the column boundary performs the Best Fit command.

6. Click the right-pointing horizontal scroll arrow two times to scroll the datasheet to the right and view the remaining columns. (Scrolling can also be performed using keyboard commands, as shown in Table A1.3.)
7. Best Fit the *E-Mail Address* column.
8. Drag the horizontal scroll box to the left edge of the horizontal scroll bar.

   This scrolls the screen to the left until the first column is visible.

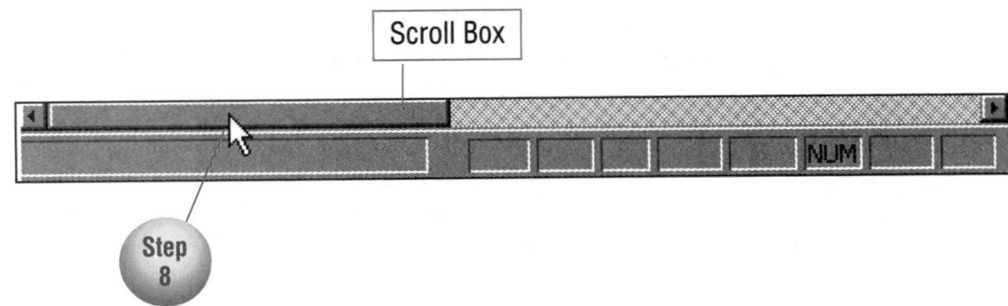

9. Best Fit column three *(Street Address2)*.
10. Click the Save button on the Database toolbar.

TABLE A1.3 Scrolling Techniques Using the Keyboard

Press	To Move to
Home	First field in the current record
End	Last field in the current record
Tab	Next field in the current record
Shift + Tab	Previous field in the current record
Ctrl + Home	First field in the first record
Ctrl + End	Last field in the last record
Page Down	Same field one screen down
Page Up	Same field one screen up

Saving Data

Microsoft Access differs from other Office applications in that data is *automatically* saved as soon as you move to the next record or close the table. Database management systems are such a critical component of business activities that saving is not left to chance. The Save button on the Database toolbar was used in this topic to save the layout changes that were made when the column widths were enlarged before moving on to the next topic.

Open Table in Datasheet View
1. Open database file.
2. Select *Tables* in Objects bar.
3. Double-click table name.

Finding and Editing Records

The Find command can be used to quickly move the insertion point to a specific record in a table. This is a time-saving feature when the table contains several records that are not all visible in one screen. Once a record has been located, click the insertion point within a field and insert or delete text as required to edit the record.

PROJECT: You have received a note from Sam Vestering that Waterfront Cinemas has changed its fax number and Eastown Movie House has a new P.O. Box number. You will use the Find feature to locate the records and make the changes.

steps

1. With the US Distributors table open and the insertion point positioned in the *Name* column, click the Find button on the Database toolbar.

   This displays the Find and Replace dialog box.

2. Key **Waterfront Cinemas** in the Find What text box and then click the Find Next button.

   The insertion point moves to record 17.

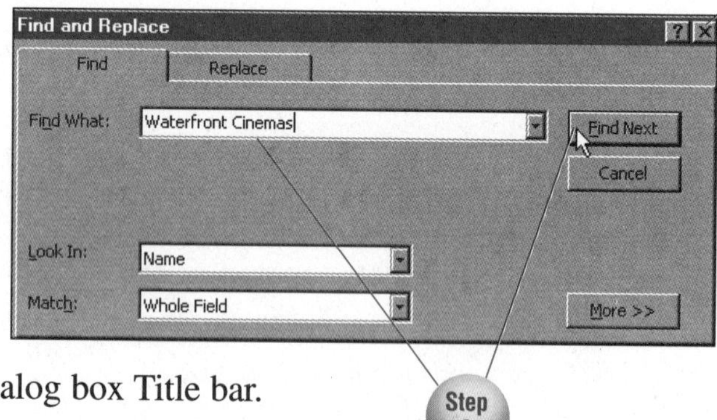

3. Click the Close button in the Find and Replace dialog box Title bar.

4. Press Tab or Enter seven times to move to the *Fax* column.

   The entire field value is selected when you move from column to column using Tab or Enter. If you need to edit only a few characters within the field you will want to use Edit mode. As an alternative, you could scroll and click the insertion point within the field to avoid having to turn on Edit mode.

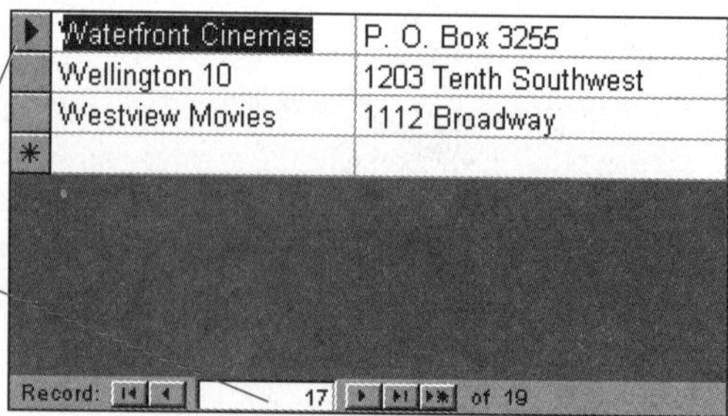

5. Press F2 to turn on Edit mode.

6. Press the left arrow key four times, delete *3947,* and then key **4860**.

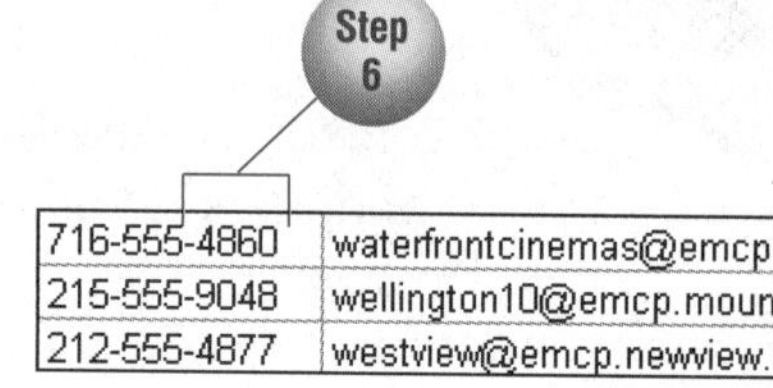

7. Look in the record selector bar for record 17 at the pencil icon that is displayed.

   The pencil icon indicates the current record is being edited and the changes have not yet been saved.

Step 7

Pencil indicates record is being edited.

✎		Buffalo
		Philadelphia
		New York
*		

8. Press Enter twice to move to the next record in the table.

   The pencil icon disappears, indicating the changes have now been saved.

9. Click in any record in the *Street Address1* column and then click the Find button.

10. Key **P. O. Box 722** and then click the Find Next button.

    The insertion point moves to record 5.

If no records are found, check your entry in the Find What text box—you may have missed keying a period or space, or keyed an incorrect letter or number.

11. Close the Find and Replace dialog box.

12. Edit the field to display *P.O. Box 429*.

13. Click in any other record to save the changes to record 5.

Replace Command

Use the Replace tab in the Find and Replace dialog box to automatically change a field entry to something else. For example, in steps 9–12 you searched for P.O. Box 722 and then edited the field to change the box number to 429. The Replace command could have been used to change the text automatically. To do this, display the Find and Replace dialog box, key **P.O. Box 722** in the Find What text box, key **P.O. Box 429** in the Replace With text box, and then click the Find Next button. Click the Replace button when the record is found.

Find a Record

1. Click in any row in the field by which you want to search.
2. Click Edit, Find or click the Find button.
3. Key the search text.
4. Click Find Next.

Adding Records in Datasheet View

New records can be added to a table in either Datasheet view or Form view. To add a record in Datasheet view, open the table, click the New Record button on either the Table Datasheet toolbar or the Record Navigation bar, and then key the data. Press Tab or Enter to move from field to field. When you press Tab or Enter after keying the last field, the record is automatically saved. Initially, the new record will appear at the bottom of the datasheet until the table is closed. When the table is reopened, the records are rearranged to display alphabetically sorted by the field that has been defined as the primary key.

PROJECT: Worldwide Enterprises has signed two new distributors in the United States. You will add the information in the US Distributors table.

steps

1. With the US Distributors table open, click the New Record button on the Table Datasheet toolbar.

   The insertion point moves to the first column in the blank row at the bottom of the datasheet and the record navigation box indicates you are editing record 20.

2. Key **Dockside Movies** and then press Tab.

3. Key **P. O. Box 224** and then press Tab.
4. Key **155 S. Central Avenue** and then press Tab.
5. Key **Baltimore** and then press Tab.

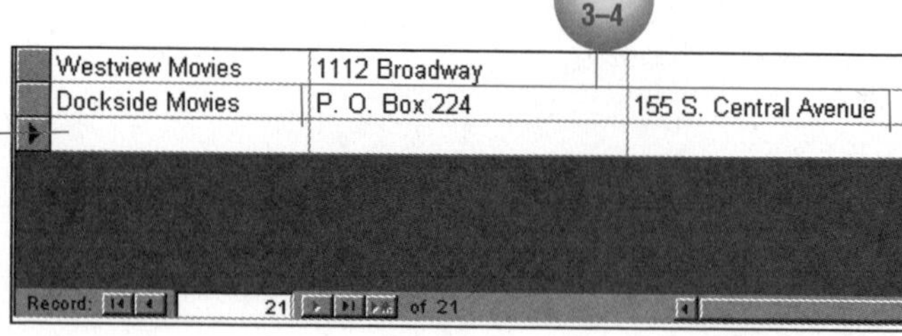

Insertion point moves to the first field in the next record automatically when you press Tab or Enter after the last field.

6. Key **MD** and then press Tab.
7. Key **21203** and then press Tab.

Problem ? Press Enter to move to the next field if you are using the numeric keypad to input numbers—it will be more comfortable.

8. Key **301-555-7732** and then press Tab.
9. Key **301-555-9836** and then press Tab.

10 Key **dockside@emcp.mdwt.net** and then press Tab.

The insertion point moves to a new row when you press Tab or Enter after the last field in a new record to allow you to continue typing the next new record in the table.

11 Key the following information in the next row:

Renaissance Cinemas
3599 Woodward Avenue
Detroit, MI 48211
313-555-1693
313-555-1699
renaissance-cinemas@emcp.worldnet.com

12 Expand the *E-Mail Address* column to view all of the data.

Step 12

State	Zip Code	Telephone	Fax	E-Mail Address
KY	40201	502-555-4238	502-555-4240	allnite@emcp.mountain.com
TX	76013	817-555-2116	817-555-2119	centurycinemas@emcp.sworg.com
VT	05201	802-555-1469	802-555-1470	countryside@emcp.nenet.com
SC	29201	803-555-3487	803-555-3421	danforth@emcp.ns.com
MA	02142	413-555-0981	413-555-0226	eastown@emcp.camnet.com
NJ	07920	201-555-1147	201-555-1143	hillman@emcp.njnet.com
AZ	86355-6014	602-555-6231	602-555-6233	lavista@emcp.southnet.com
GA	73125	404-555-8113	404-555-2349	libertycinemas@emcp.agnet.com
WA	98220-2791	206-555-3269	206-555-3270	mainstream@emcp.ws.com
CA	90045	612-555-2398	612-555-2377	marqueemovies@emcp.westcoast.net
KS	66801	316-555-7013	316-555-7022	midtown@emcp.ksnet.com
OH	43107	614-555-8134	614-555-8339	mooretown@emcp.newview.com
IL	60302	312-555-7719	312-555-7381	oshea@emcp.midtown.com
OR	97466-3359	503-555-8641	503-555-8633	redwoodcinemas@emcp.northwest.net
FL	33562	813-555-3185	813-555-3177	sunfest@emcp.cinemaorg.net
CA	97432-1567	619-555-8746	619-555-8748	victory@emcp.skygroup.com
NY	14288	716-555-3845	716-555-4860	waterfrontcinemas@emcp.virtual.com
PA	19178	215-555-9045	215-555-9048	wellington10@emcp.mountainview.net
NY	10119	212-555-4875	212-555-4877	westview@emcp.newview.com
MD	21203	301-555-7732	301-555-9836	dockside@emcp.mdwt.net
MI	48211	313-555-1693	313-555-1699	renaissance-cinemas@emcp.worldnet.com

New records initially appear at the bottom of the datasheet.

Step 11

13 Close the US Distributors table. Click Yes when prompted to save changes to the layout of the table.

14 Reopen the US Distributors table to view where the new records are now positioned.

Name	Street Address1
All Nite Cinemas	2188 3rd Street
Century Cinemas	3687 Avenue K
Countryside Cinemas	22 Hillside Street
Danforth Cinemas	P. O. Box 22
Dockside Movies	P. O. Box 224
Eastown Movie House	P. O. Box 429
Hillman Cinemas	55 Kemble Avenue
LaVista Cinemas	111 Vista Road
Liberty Cinemas	P. O. Box 998
Mainstream Movies	P. O. Box 33
Marquee Movies	1011 South Alameda Street
Midtown Moviehouse	1033 Commercial Street
Mooretown Movies	P. O. Box 11
O'Shea Movies	59 Erie
Redwood Cinemas	P. O. Box 112F
Renaissance Cinemas	3599 Woodward Avenue
Sunfest Cinemas	
Victory Cinemas	12119 South 23rd
Waterfront Cinemas	P. O. Box 3255
Wellington 10	1203 Tenth Southwest
Westview Movies	1112 Broadway

New records have now been rearranged alphabetically by name.

Take 2

Primary Key Field

When a table is created, one field is defined as the *primary key*. A primary key is the field by which the table is automatically sorted whenever the table is opened. The primary key field must contain unique data for each record. When a new record is being added to the table, Access checks to ensure there is no existing record with the same data in the primary key. If there is, Access will display an error message indicating there are duplicate values and will not allow the record to be saved. The primary key field cannot be left blank when a new record is being added, since it is the field that is used to sort and check for duplicates.

Add a Record
1 Open table.
2 Click New Record button.
3 Key data in fields.

Deleting Records in Datasheet View

Records can be deleted in either Datasheet view or Form view. To delete a record in Datasheet view, open the table, click in any field in the row or select the entire row by clicking in the record selector bar for the record you want to delete, and then click the Delete Record button on the Table Datasheet toolbar. Access will display a message indicating the selected record will be permanently removed from the table. Click Yes to confirm the record deletion.

PROJECT: The Countryside Cinemas and Victory Cinemas distributor agreements have lapsed and you have just been informed that they have signed agreements with another movie distributing company. You will delete their records from the US Distributors table.

steps

1. With the US Distributors table open, click the insertion point in any field in the row for Countryside Cinemas.

   This selects record 3 as indicated in the record navigation bar.

2. Click the Delete Record button on the Table Datasheet toolbar.

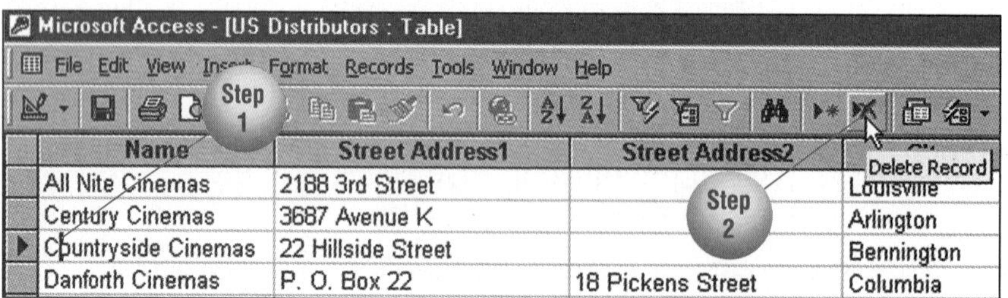

3. Access will display a message box indicating you are about to delete 1 record and that the undo operation is not available after this action. Click Yes to confirm the deletion.

Check that you are deleting the correct record before clicking Yes. Click No if you selected the wrong record by mistake.

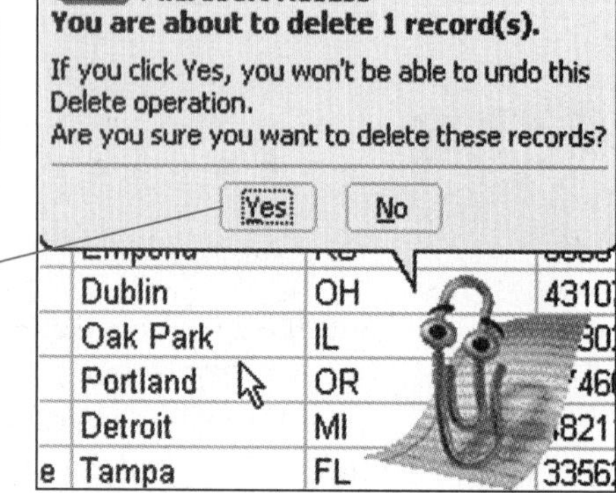

4. Position the mouse pointer in the record selector bar for Victory Cinemas until the pointer changes to a black right-pointing arrow and then click the left mouse button.

   This selects the entire row.

5. Click the Delete Record button on the Table Datasheet toolbar.

6. Click Yes to confirm the deletion.

	Renaissance Cinemas	3599 Woodward Avenue
	Sunfest Cinemas	
⇨	Victory Cinemas	12119 South 23rd
	Waterfront Cinemas	P. O. Box 3255
	Wellington 10	1203 Tenth Southwest
	Westview Movies	1112 Broadway
*		

Step 4

7. Use the Find command to move the active record to LaVista Cinemas.

8. Close the Find and Replace dialog box.

9. Click the Delete Record button on the Table Datasheet toolbar.

10. Click No when prompted to confirm the deletion.

    The LaVista Cinemas record is restored to the table.

11. Click in any field in the table to remove the selection from record 7.

Take 2

Backing Up and Restoring Access Data

Deleting records is a procedure that should be performed only by authorized personnel; once the record is deleted, crucial data can be lost. Always back up the database file before deleting records. To do this, close the database. In a multi-user environment, ensure that all other users have closed the database. Launch Windows Explorer and use the Copy and Paste commands to copy the database to a secure area. If restoring a database becomes necessary, follow the same routine and copy the backup file from the secure area back to the folder in which the database normally resides. Any changes made to the database since the backup was performed will have to be redone.

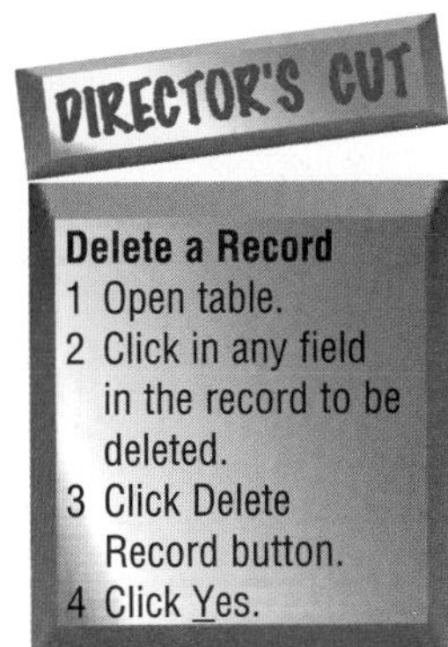

Sorting Records

Records in a table are displayed alphabetically in ascending order by the primary key field. To rearrange the order of the records, click in any field in the column you want to sort by and then click the Sort Ascending or Sort Descending button on the Table Datasheet toolbar. To sort on more than one column, select the columns first and then click the Sort Ascending or Sort Descending button. Access will sort first by the leftmost column in the selection, then by the next column, and so on. Columns can be moved in the datasheet if necessary to facilitate a multiple-column sort. Access will save the sort order when the table is closed.

PROJECT: You will perform one sort routine using a single field and then perform a multiple-column sort. To do the multiple-column sort you will have to move columns in the datasheet.

steps

1. With the US Distributors table open, click in any row in the *City* column.
2. Click the Sort Ascending button on the Table Datasheet toolbar.

   The records are rearranged to display the cities starting with A through Z.
3. Click the Sort Descending button on the Table Datasheet toolbar.

   The records are rearranged to display the cities starting with Z through A. In steps 4–7 you will move the State column to the left of the Name column to perform a multiple-column sort.

Sort Ascending

Step 2

Street Address2	City
	Louisville
	Arlington
18 Pickens Street	Columbia
155 S. Central Avenue	Baltimore

Click in any row in the *City* column.

4. Position the mouse pointer in the *State* column heading until the pointer changes to a downward-pointing black arrow and then click the left mouse button.

   The State column is now selected and can be moved by dragging the heading to another position in the datasheet.

Click when you see this icon.

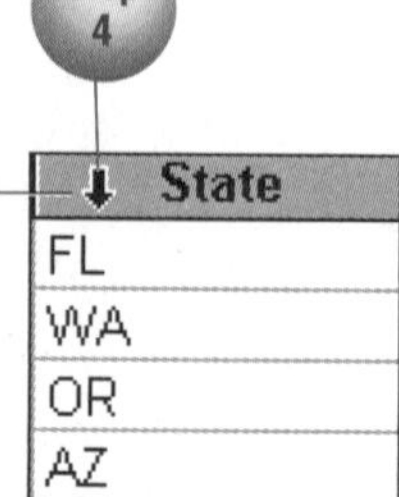

5. With the *State* column selected, move the pointer to the column heading *State* until the white arrow pointer appears.

Step 5

City	State	Zip Code
Tampa	FL	33562
Seattle	WA	98220-2791
Portland	OR	97466-3359
Phoenix	AZ	86355-6014

6. Hold down the left mouse button, drag to the left of the *Name* column, and then release the left mouse button.

   As you drag the mouse a thick black line will appear between columns, indicating the position to which the column will be moved when you release the mouse button. In addition, the mouse pointer displays with a gray box attached to it, indicating you are performing a move operation.

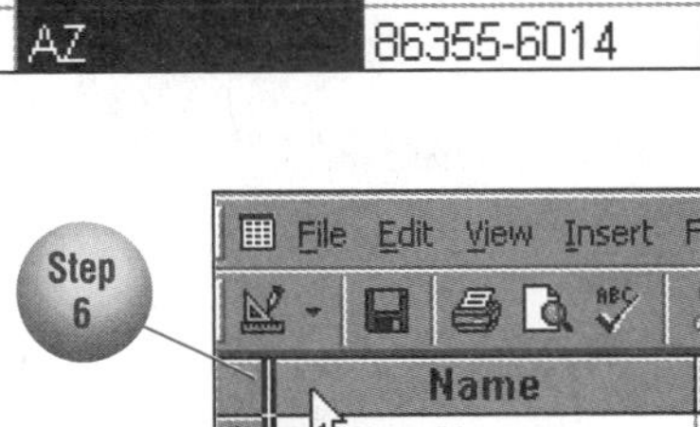

7. Click in any field in the table to deselect the *State* column.
8. Position the mouse pointer in the *State* column heading until the pointer changes to a downward-pointing black arrow, hold down the left mouse button, drag to the right until both the *State* and *Name* columns are selected, and then release the left mouse button.

9. Click the Sort Ascending button.

   The records are sorted first by State and then by Name.

10. Look at the two records for the state of New York. Notice that Waterfront Cinemas has been placed before Westview Movies.
11. Close the table. Click Yes when prompted to save the design changes.

More about Sorting

When you are ready to conduct a sort in a table, consider the following:

- records in which the selected field is empty are listed first.
- numbers are sorted before letters.
- numbers stored in fields that are not defined as numeric (e.g., Social Security Number or telephone number) are sorted as characters (not numeric values). To sort them as if they were numbers, all field values must be the same length.

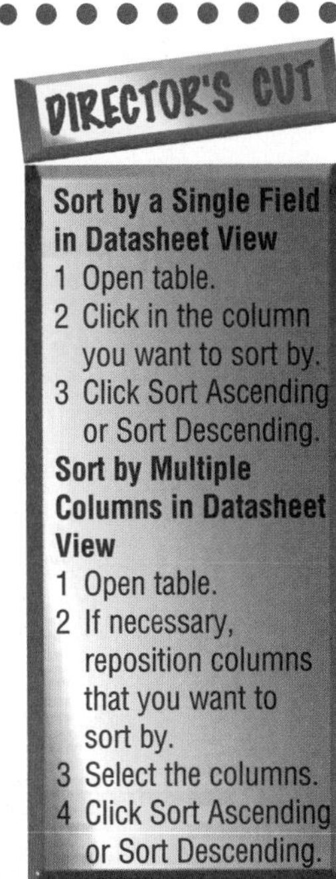

Previewing and Printing

Click the Print button on the Table Datasheet toolbar to print the table in Datasheet view. To avoid wasting paper, use Print Preview to view how the datasheet will appear on the page before you print a table. Change the margins or page orientation in the Page Setup dialog box.

PROJECT: Sam Vestering has requested a list of the US Distributors. You will open the table, preview the printout, change the page orientation, and then print the datasheet.

steps

1. Open the US Distributors table.
2. Click the Print Preview button on the Table Datasheet toolbar.

   The table is displayed in the Print Preview window as shown in Figure A1.3.

FIGURE A1.3 Print Preview Window

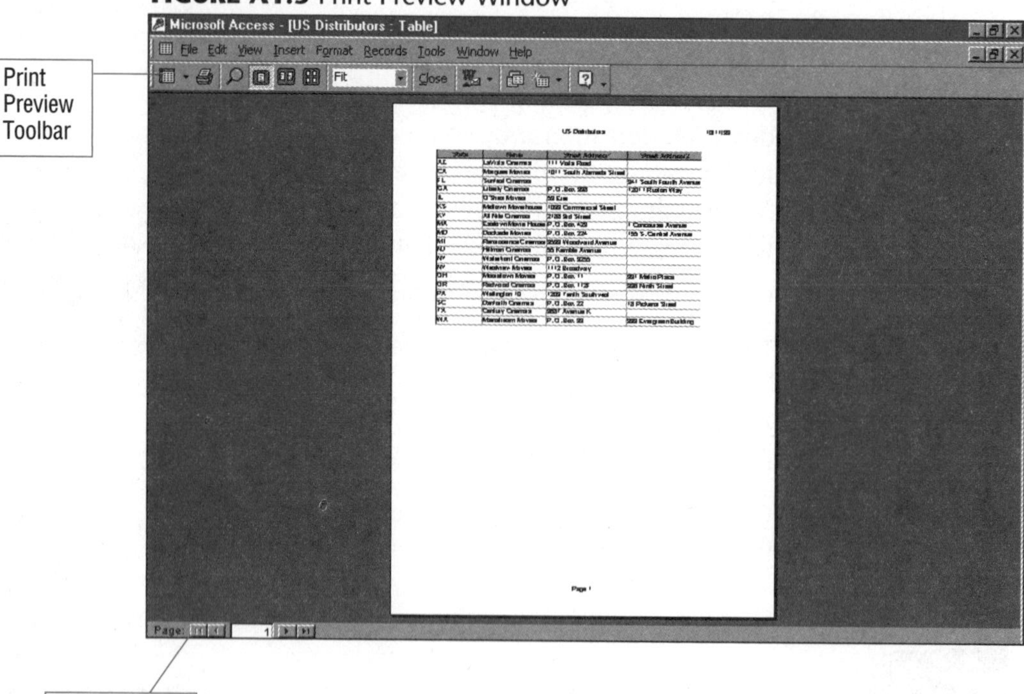

3. Move the mouse pointer (displays as a magnifying glass) over the body of the table and then click the left mouse button.

   The Zoom changes to 100% magnification.
4. Click the left mouse button again.

   The Zoom changes back to Fit.
5. Click File and then Page Setup.

6. Click the Page tab in the Page Setup dialog box.
7. Click Landscape and then click OK.

   Landscape orientation rotates the printout to print wider than it is taller. Changing to landscape will allow more columns to fit on a page.

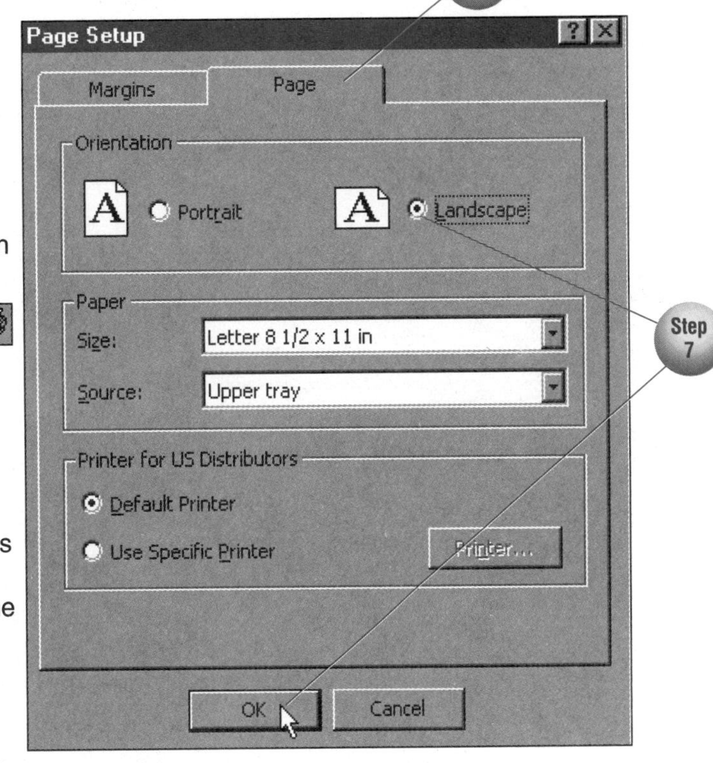

8. Click the Print button on the Print Preview toolbar.

   In a few seconds the table will print. The printout will require two pages, since there are too many columns to fit on one page even in landscape orientation. In the section titled Creating Queries and Reports you will learn how to create a report for a table that will give you more control over the layout of the page.
9. Click Close on the Print Preview toolbar.
10. Close the US Distributors table.

Changing the Margins

The margins on the page are initially set to 1 inch Top, Bottom, Left, and Right. Display the Margins tab in the Page Setup dialog box to change the margins. Changing the left and right margins is another strategy that can be used to try to fit more columns on a page.

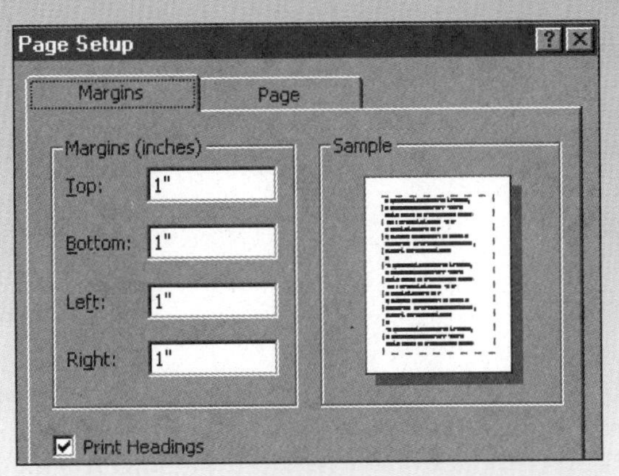

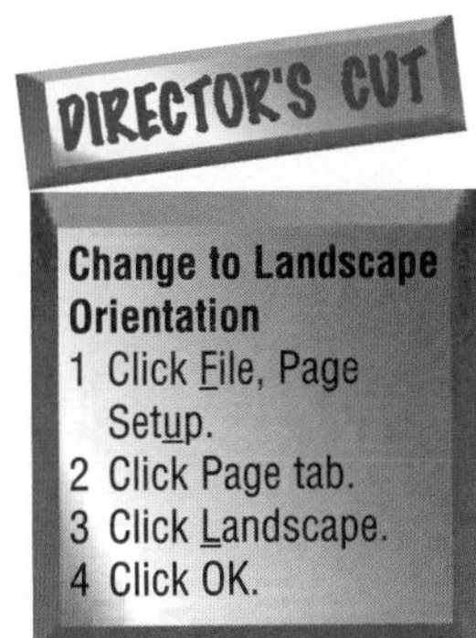

Change to Landscape Orientation

1. Click File, Page Setup.
2. Click Page tab.
3. Click Landscape.
4. Click OK.

Using the Office Clipboard

Use the Clipboard toolbar to copy several different items and paste them in various locations. Up to 12 different items can be stored in the Clipboard. The Clipboard toolbar can facilitate data entry in a table where there is repetitive text, or it can be used to copy and paste entries from other Office applications to Access tables. Initially the Clipboard toolbar automatically appears when you cut or copy any two consecutive items. If you close the Clipboard toolbar three times in a row without clicking any buttons on the toolbar, the Clipboard toolbar will no longer appear. Click View, point to Toolbars, and click Clipboard to redisplay the toolbar.

PROJECT: You will use the Clipboard toolbar to store city names to facilitate entering new records in the Canadian Distributors table.

steps

1. Open the Canadian Distributors table.
2. Click View, point to Toolbars, and then click Clipboard.

   This causes the Clipboard toolbar shown in Figure A1.4 to open. Once opened, the Clipboard toolbar is active in all Office application windows.

FIGURE A1.4 Clipboard Toolbar

If icons display in the gray cornered pages at the bottom of the Clipboard toolbar, click the Clear Clipboard button before beginning step 3.

3. Select the text *Toronto* in the *City* field in record 2. To do this, position the mouse pointer over the *T* in *Toronto* until the pointer changes to an I-beam pointer, hold down the left mouse button, and then drag to the right until the entire field value is selected.
4. Click the Copy button on the Clipboard toolbar.

   This places one icon in the Clipboard toolbar as shown below.

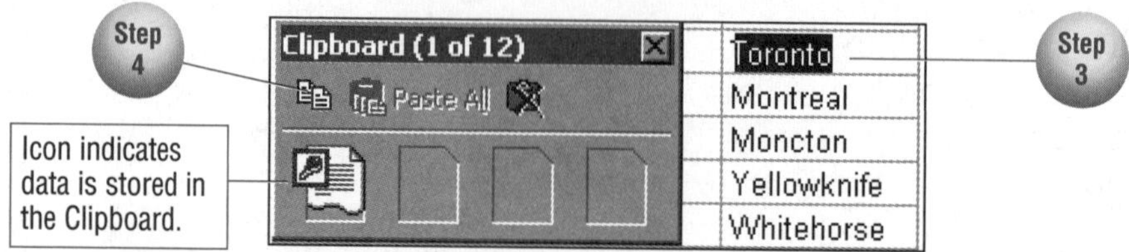

5. Select the text *Calgary* in the *City* field for record 7 and then click the Copy button on the Clipboard toolbar.

Drag the Clipboard Toolbar Title bar to the edge of the screen if it is obscuring the *City* column.

6. Select the text *Vancouver* in the *City* field for record 12 and then click the Copy button on the Clipboard toolbar.
7. Click the New Record button on the Table Datasheet toolbar.
8. Key **Canadian Cinemas Plus** and then press Tab.
9. Key **305 Dundas Street West** and then press Tab twice.
10. With the insertion point positioned in the *City* field, click the icon on the Clipboard toolbar representing Toronto (first icon at the left), and then press Tab.

Position the mouse pointer over an icon to display a Tooltip illustrating the contents of the clipboard entry.

11. Key the remaining field values as follows:
    ON
    M5T 1G8
    416-555-7736
    416-555-9022
    cinemasplus@emcp.entertain.com
12. Key the following data in two new records in the table. Use the Clipboard toolbar to input the city names Calgary and Vancouver.

Hildebrand Movies	**Coastal Cinemas**
100 Oakwood Place SW	**6207 Summit Drive**
Calgary, AB T2V 7Y5	**Vancouver, BC V7W 1Y9**
403-555-4492	**604-555-3419**
403-555-4494	**604-555-3421**
hildebrand@emcp.westnet.ca	**coastal@emcp.islandnet.com**

13. Best Fit columns that are not displaying the entire field values.
14. Change the page orientation to landscape and then print the table.
15. Close the Clipboard toolbar.

Take 2

Managing the Office Clipboard

The Office Clipboard can hold up to 12 items. If you select a thirteenth item and then click the Copy button, a message displays asking if you want the first item removed from the clipboard or if you want to copy the current item. The items collected remain in the Clipboard until you click the Clear Clipboard button or you exit all Office programs. Unlike many other toolbars, the Clipboard toolbar cannot be customized.

Display Clipboard Toolbar
1 Click View.
2 Point to Toolbars.
3 Click Clipboard.

Using the Office Assistant

An extensive online help resource, including information from the Microsoft Office 2000 Web site, is available whenever you are working in Access by clicking the animated Office Assistant. The Office Assistant will sometimes provide tips while you are working based on the action you have just performed—available tips are indicated when the yellow light bulb appears over the Office Assistant. Click the light bulb to read the tip and then click OK.

PROJECT: After printing the Canadian Distributors table you decide it would look better if the row heights were increased. You will use the Office Assistant to learn how to do this.

steps

1. With the Canadian Distributors table open, click the animated Office Assistant.

Problem

Office Assistant not visible? Click Help and then Show the Office Assistant to turn it on.

2. Key **How do I increase the row height?** and then click the Search button.

   A list of categories that are relevant to keywords within your question text will appear above the question text box.

3. Click *Resize rows in Datasheet view.*

   The pointer changes to a hand with the index finger pointing upward when you position the pointer over a help topic. Click the topic to display a separate Microsoft Access Help window beside the Office Assistant containing information about the selected topic. You can continue clicking topics and reading information in the Help window until you have found what you are looking for.

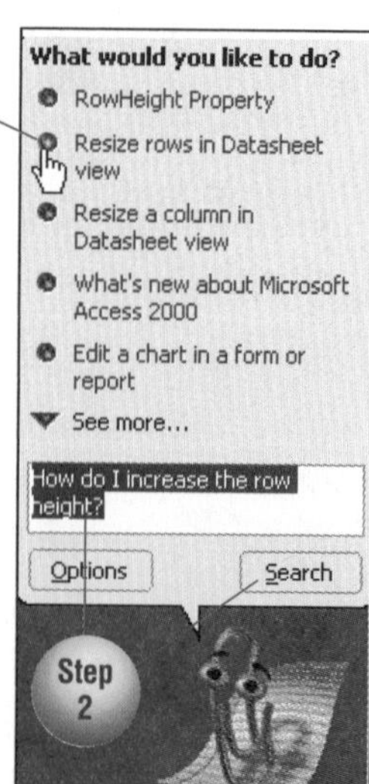

4 Read the steps under *Resize rows in Datasheet view* in the Microsoft Access Help window. If you would like a hard copy of the information, click the Print button on the Microsoft Access Help toolbar.

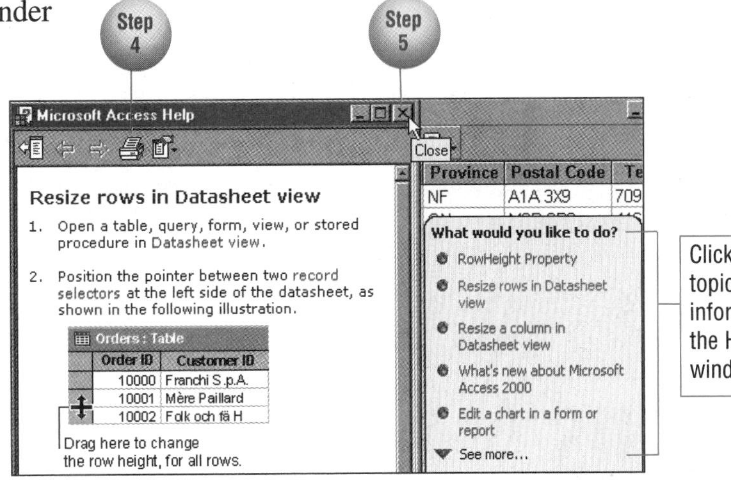

Click other topics to view information in the Help window.

5 Click the Close button on the Microsoft Access Help window Title bar.

6 Position the mouse pointer on the bottom row boundary for record 1 in the Canadian Distributors table until the pointer changes to a horizontal line with an up- and down-pointing arrow attached (as shown in the Help window).

7 Drag the pointer down until the row height is approximately doubled and then release the mouse button.

Step 7

Name	Street Address1
EastCoast Cinemas	62 Mountbatten Drive
Millennium Movies	4126 Yonge Street
MountainView Movies	5417 RoyalMount Avenue

8 Preview and then print the table.

9 Close the Canadian Distributors table. Click Yes when prompted to save the layout changes.

Take 2

Turning Off the Office Assistant

If you do not want the Office Assistant on all the time, you can turn it off. Click the Office Assistant and then click the Options button. Click the Use the Office Assistant check box to deselect the option and then click OK. To access online help when the Office Assistant is turned off, click Help and then Microsoft Access Help or press F1. This will open an expanded Microsoft Access Help window where you can search for information using one of three tabs: Contents, Answer Wizard, or Index. The Contents tab displays categories preceded by a book icon. Double-click a category to view additional categories. Use the Answer Wizard tab to key a question and search for topics in a manner similar to using the Office Assistant. Click the Index tab to enter a keyword and search through a list of topics related to the keyword.

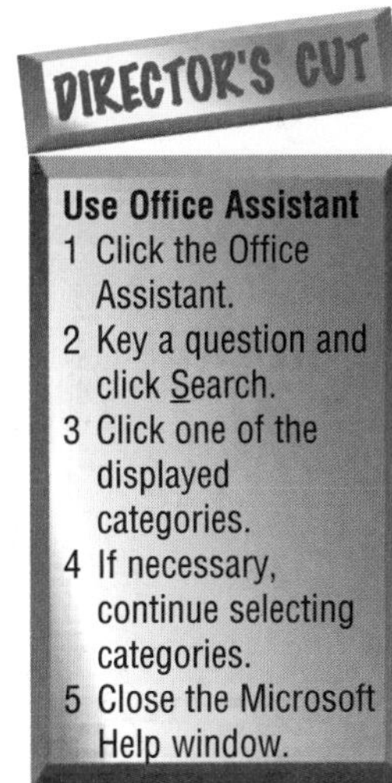

Compacting and Repairing a Database

Once you have been working with a database file for a period of time, the data can become fragmented because of records and objects that have been deleted. The disk space that the database uses may be larger than is necessary. Compacting the database defragments the file and reduces the required disk space. Compacting and repairing a database also ensures optimal performance while using the file.

PROJECT: You will run the compact and repair utility on the WE Distributors1 database.

steps

1. With the WE Distributors1 database open, minimize the Microsoft Access window.
2. Click Start, point to Programs, and then click *Windows Explorer*. If the Explorer window is not maximized, click the Maximize button on the Exploring Title bar.

Problem

If you are using Windows NT as your operating system, open Windows NT Explorer.

3. Click View and then Details.

   This displays the file names with the file size, date, and time.

4. Click the drive and/or folder where the WE Distributors1.mdb file is stored.

   If your data files are stored in a subfolder, click the plus sign to the left of the folder name in the Folders list to expand the display.

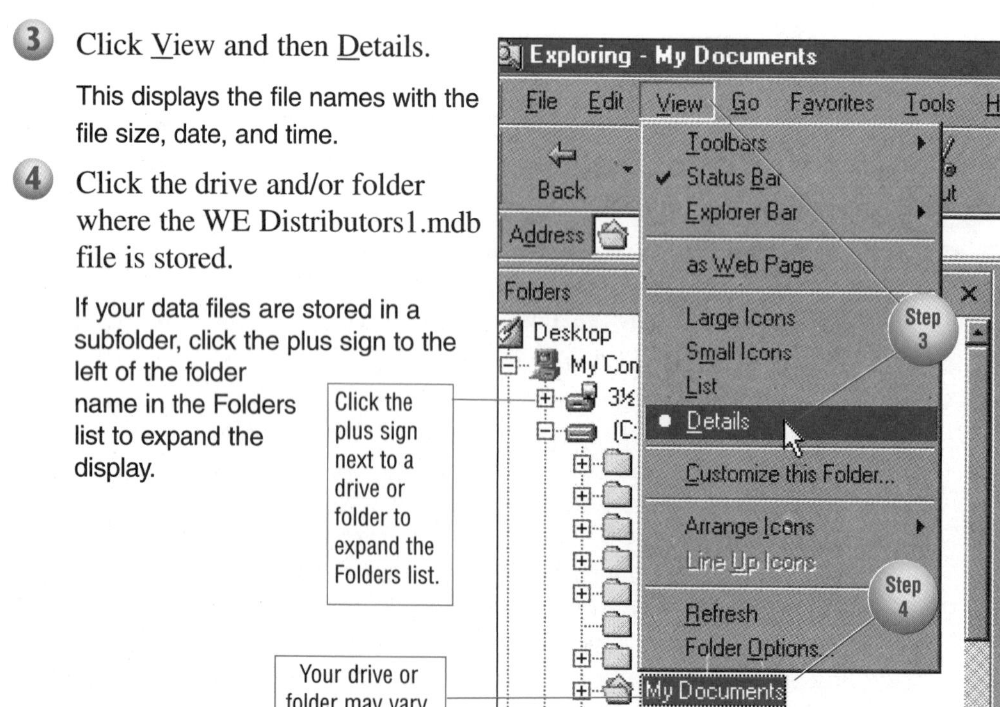

5. Locate the file WE Distributors1.mdb and write down the file size of the database.

   File size: ____________________

Two files may appear in the file list: WE Distributors1.ldb and WE Distributors1.mdb. The ldb file is used to lock records so that two users cannot request the same record at the same time.

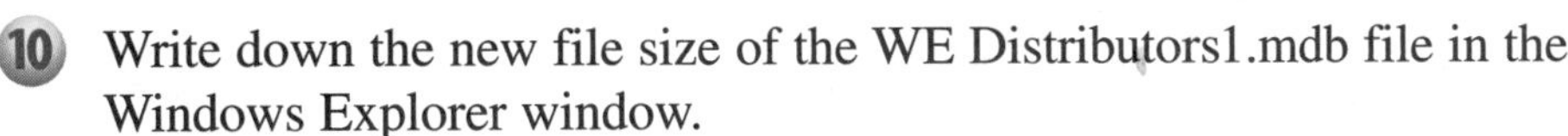

6. Click the button on the Taskbar representing Access.
7. Click Tools, point to Database Utilities, and then click Compact and Repair Database.

   A message will display on the Status bar indicating the progress of the compact and repair process. In a multi-user environment, no other user can have the database open while the compact and repair procedure is running.

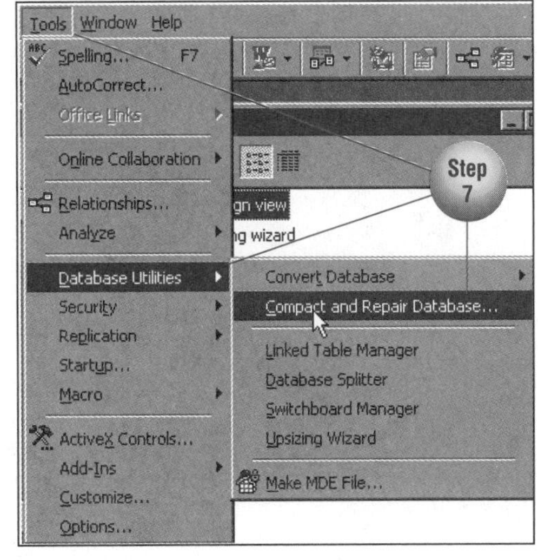

8. Click File and then Close to close the WE Distributors1.mdb database.
9. Click File and then Exit to exit Access.
10. Write down the new file size of the WE Distributors1.mdb file in the Windows Explorer window.

    File size: ____________________

11. Click File and then Close to exit Windows Explorer.

Automatic Compact and Repair

In the Options dialog box you can instruct Access to automatically compact a database every time you close it. To do this, open the database that you want Access to compact automatically. Click Tools and then Options. Select the General tab, click the Compact on Close check box, and then click OK.

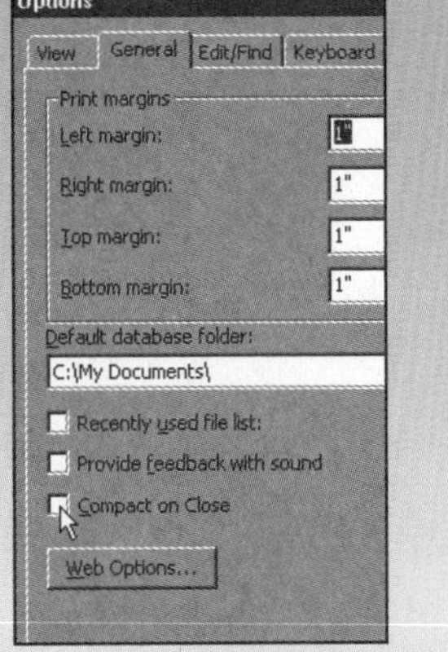

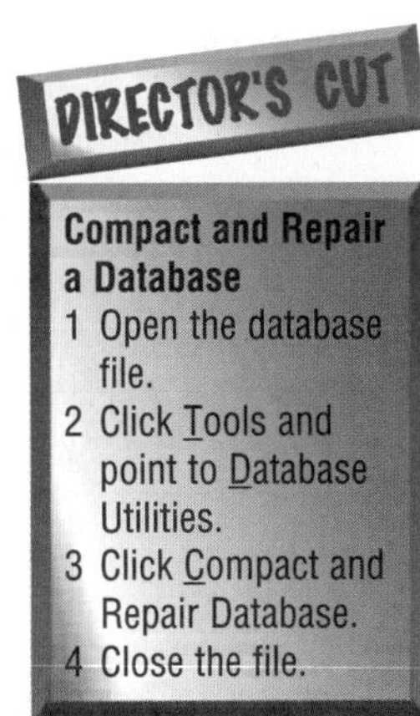

Compact and Repair a Database

1. Open the database file.
2. Click Tools and point to Database Utilities.
3. Click Compact and Repair Database.
4. Close the file.

Features Summary

Feature	Button	Menu	Keyboard
Add Records		Insert, New Record	
Clipboard toolbar		View, Toolbars, Clipboard	
Column Width		Format, Column Width	
Compact and Repair		Tools, Database Utilities, Compact and Repair Database	
Delete Records		Edit, Delete Record	
Find		Edit, Find	Ctrl + F
Help		Help, Microsoft Access Help	F1
Page Setup		File, Page Setup	
Print Preview		File, Print Preview	
Print		File, Print	Ctrl + P
Sort Ascending		Records, Sort, Sort Ascending	
Sort Descending		Records, Sort, Sort Descending	

Procedures Check

The Access screen on page 29 contains numbers pointing to elements of the datasheet window. Identify below the element that corresponds with the number in the screen.

Horizontal scroll box	Office Assistant	Maximize	Field
Record navigation bar	Close	Table Title bar	Field names
Active Record	Record selector bar	Scroll arrow	Minimize

1. ______________________________
2. ______________________________
3. ______________________________
4. ______________________________
5. ______________________________
6. ______________________________
7. ______________________________
8. ______________________________

1 Overseas Distributors : Table 2

3 8

	Name	Street Address	Street Address	City	Country	Postal Code	Telephone
▶	Aussie House	99 Honybun Co		Donvale	Australia	V1C 3988	61-3-555-6985
	Empire Movies	Unit 23 Chelmsl	Waterloo Avenu	London	England	B37 6QX	44-121-555-377
	Festival Cinema	Campos Eliseo	Col. Polante	Mexico City	Mexico	11499	52-5-555-413
	Gallery Movies	Strandvagen 66		Stockholm	Sweden	11847	46-8-55584-25
	Helsinki Cinema	Lonnrotinkatu 9		Helsinki	Finland	FIN-00122	358-9-555-966
	Kyatore Cinema	2-4-8 Hirakyoto		Tokyo	Japan	148	81-3-555-87
	New Wonder Ci	Gammel Konge		Copenhagen	Denmark	DK-1855	45-37-29-55-05
	Norstar Movie H	Ullveien 10		Oslo	Norway	N-0399	47-26-18-55-95
	Towerline Movie	Kewinterer Stra		Hamburg	Germany	54288	49-40-555-612
*							

4 6

5 Record: 1 of 9 7

Identify the following buttons:

9. ______________________________

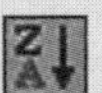 13. ______________________________

 10. ______________________________

 14. ______________________________

 11. ______________________________

 15. ______________________________

 12. ______________________________

Activity 1: Adjusting Column Widths; Finding and Editing Records

1 Start Access and open the WE Employees1 database.
2 Open the Employee Dates and Salaries table.
3 Maximize the table.
4 Adjust all columns to Best Fit.
5 Find the record for Carl Zakowski and then change the birth date from 5/9/67 to 9/5/67.
6 Find the record for Roman Deptulski and then change the salary from 67,850 to 71,320.
7 Find the record for Terry Yiu and then change the hire date from 4/12/99 to 5/15/99.
8 Close the Employee Dates and Salaries table. Click Yes when prompted to save changes to the layout.

Activity 2: Adding and Deleting Records

1 Open the Employee Dates and Salaries table.
2 Delete the record for Valerie Fistouris.
3 Delete the record for Edward Thurston.

4 Add the following employees to the table:

1085	**1090**	**1095**
Yousef J El-Sayed	**Maria D Aquino**	**Patrick J Kilarney**
12/22/68	**04/16/73**	**02/27/71**
03/14/01	**11/12/01**	**12/12/01**
European Distribution	**Overseas Distribution**	**North American Distribution**
$38,467	**$38,467**	**$38,467**

5 Close the Employee Dates and Salaries table.

Activity 3: Sorting Records

1 Open the Employee Dates and Salaries table.
2 Sort the table in ascending order by *Last Name*.
3 Sort the table in descending order by *Annual Salary*.
4 Sort the table in ascending order first by *Department* and then by *Last Name*.
5 Sort the table in ascending order first by *Annual Salary* and then by *Last Name*.
6 Close the Employee Dates and Salaries table without saving the changes to the design.

Activity 4: Using Print Preview, Page Orientation, and Print

1 Open the Employee Dates and Salaries table.
2 Preview the table.
3 Change the page orientation to landscape.
4 Print the table.
5 Close the Employee Dates and Salaries table.
6 Close the WE Employees1 database.

Performance Plus

Activity 1: Adjusting Column Widths; Finding and Editing Records; Using Preview and Print

1 Jai Prasad, instructor in the Theatre Arts Division of Niagara Peninsula College, has been called out of town to attend a family matter. The grades for SPE266 have to be entered into the database by the end today. Jai has provided you with the following grades:

Student Number	Final Grade	Student Number	Final Grade
138-456-749	A	255-158-498	C
111-785-156	C	221-689-478	B
378-159-746	B	314-745-856	B
348-876-486	A+	325-841-469	A
274-658-986	B	321-487-659	D
349-874-658	C		

2 Open the NPC Grades1 database.
3 Open the SPE266 Grades table.

4 Adjust column widths so that all data is entirely visible.
5 Enter the grades provided in step 1 in the related records.
6 Preview and then print the table.
7 Close the SPE266 Grades table. Click Yes if prompted to save changes.
8 Close the NPC Grades1 database.

Activity 2: Finding, Adding, and Deleting Records

1 Dana Hirsch, manager of The Waterfront Bistro, has ordered three new inventory items and decided to discontinue three others. Dana has asked you to update the inventory database.
2 Open the WB Inventory1 database.
3 Open the Inventory List table.
4 Locate and then delete the inventory items Pita Wraps; Tuna; and Lake Erie Perch.
5 Add the following new records to the Inventory List table:
- Item 051, Atlantic Scallops, case, Supplier Code 9
- Item 052, Lake Trout, case, Supplier Code 9
- Item 053, Panini Rolls, flat, Supplier Code 1

6 Adjust column widths so that all data is entirely visible.
7 Preview and then print the table.
8 Close the Inventory List table. Click Yes if prompted to save changes.
9 Close the WB Inventory1 database.

Activity 3: Sorting and Deleting Records

1 You are the assistant to Bobbie Sinclair, business manager of Performance Threads. You have just been informed that several costumes in the rental inventory have been destroyed in a fire at a site location. These costumes will have to be written off since the insurance policy does not cover them when they are out on rental. After updating the costume inventory, you will print two reports.
2 Open the PT Costume Inventory1 database.
3 Open the Costume Inventory table.
4 Delete the following costumes that were destroyed in a fire at a Shakespearean festival:
- Macbeth
- Hamlet
- King Lear
- Lady Macbeth
- Othello
- Richard III

5 Sort the table in ascending order by *Character*.
6 Preview and then print the table.
7 Sort the table in ascending order first by *Date Out,* then by *Date In,* and then by *Character*.
8 Save the changes to the design of the table.
9 Preview and then print the table.
10 Close the Costume Inventory table.
11 Close the PT Costume Inventory1 database.

Activity 4: Using Compact and Repair

1. You have been investigating buying larger hard drives for the computers in the Theatre Arts Division since the new software the college is using requires more disk space. Cal Rubine, chair of the Theatre Arts Division of Niagara Peninsula College, has advised you that the equipment budget for the current year is used up. You will have to try to find ways to use disk space more efficiently.
2. Open Windows Explorer.
3. Navigate to the folder where the student data files are stored.
4. Write down the disk space the NPC Grades1 database is currently using.
   File size: ____________________
5. Minimize the Windows Explorer window.
6. Open the NPC Grades1 database.
7. Compact the database.
8. Close the NPC Grades1 database.
9. Switch to the Windows Explorer window.
10. Write down the disk space the NPC Grades1 compacted database is using.
    File size: ____________________
11. Exit Windows Explorer.

Activity 5: Finding Information on Designing a Database

1. Use the online help to find information on the steps involved in designing a database. *(Hint: Use the keyword "create" in your question.)*
2. The help information lists eight steps in designing a database. Read the information presented in steps 1–4.
3. Use Microsoft Word to create a memo to your instructor as follows:
   - use one of the memo templates.
   - include an opening paragraph describing the body of the memo.
   - list the eight steps to designing a database in a bulleted list.
   - briefly describe the first four steps.
4. Save the memo in Word and name it Access S1-P1 Memo.
5. Print and close Access S1-P1 Memo and then exit Word.

Activity 6: Creating a Job Search Company Database

1. You are starting to plan ahead for your job search after graduation. You have decided to start maintaining a database of company information in Access.
2. Search the Internet for company names, addresses, telephone numbers, and fax numbers for at least 10 companies in your field of study. Include at least 5 companies that are out of state or out of province.
3. Open the Job Search1 database.
4. Open the Company Information table.
5. Enter at least 10 records for the companies you researched on the Internet.
6. Adjust column widths as necessary.
7. Preview and then print the table.
8. Close the Company Information table.
9. Close the Job Search1 database.

Access Creating Tables and Relationships

Tables in a database file are the basis upon which all other objects are built. A table can be created in three ways: using Design view, using the Table Wizard, or by entering data into a blank datasheet. When a common field exists in two or more tables, the tables can be joined to create a relationship. A relationship allows the user to extract data from multiple tables as if they were one. In this section you will learn the skills and complete the projects listed below.

Skills

- Create a table in Design view
- Set the primary key for a table
- Confine data to a list of values using the Lookup Wizard
- Set a pattern for data using the Input Mask Wizard
- Verify data entry using a Validation Rule
- Limit the number of characters allowed in a field
- Enter a default value to display in a field
- Create a table using the Table Wizard
- Create a table by adding records
- Create a relationship between two tables
- Enforce referential integrity
- Print database relationships
- Create a database using the Database Wizard

Projects

Create tables to store employee benefit information, employee addresses, employee expense reports, and employee development activities. Modify field properties in the four tables and create relationships between the tables. Create a new database to store contact information.

Create a table to store student grades for a course in the Theatre Arts Division.

Modify and correct field properties in the Costume Inventory table to improve the design.

Create a Suppliers table in the Inventory database and create a relationship between the Suppliers table and the Inventory List table.

Create a new database to track employee expense claims.

Creating a Table in Design View

Creating a new table in Design view involves the following steps: entering field names, assigning a data type to each field, entering field descriptions, modifying properties for the field, designating the primary key, and naming the table object. All of the preceding steps are part of a process referred to as "defining the table *structure.*" Fields comprise the structure of a table. Once the structure has been created, records can be entered into the table in Datasheet view.

PROJECT: Rhonda Trask, human resources manager of Worldwide Enterprises, has asked you to review the employee benefit plan files and enter the information in a new table in the WE Employees2 database.

steps

1. Open WE Employees2.
2. With *Tables* already selected in the Objects bar, double-click *Create table in Design view.*

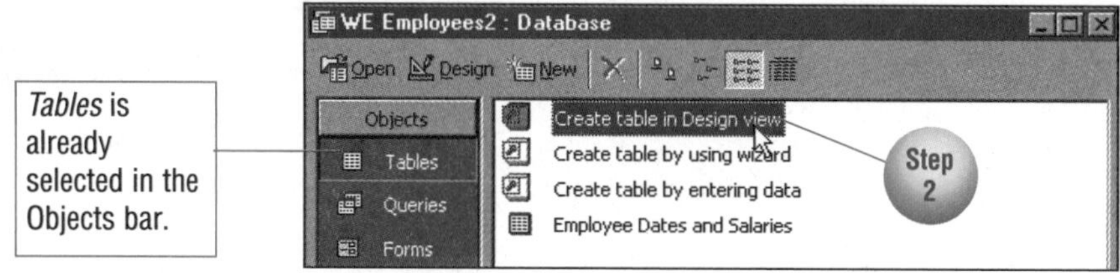

This opens the Table1 Table window, where the structure of the table is defined. Each row in the top section represents one field in the table.

3. With the insertion point already positioned in the *Field Name* column in the first row, key **Emp No** and then press Enter or Tab to move to the next column.

The message at the right side of the Field Properties section changes at each column to provide information on the current option (see Figure A2.1).

Do not key additional characters—field names can contain letters, numbers, and some symbols. Periods (.), commas (,), exclamation points (!), or square brackets ([]) are not accepted in a field name.

FIGURE A2.1 Field Properties Option Message

4. With *Text* already entered in the *Data Type* column, press Enter or Tab to move to the next column.

   Table A2.1 on page 37 provides a list and brief description of the available data types. The *Emp No* field will contain numbers; however, leave the data type defined as Text since no calculations will be performed with employee numbers.

5. Key **Enter the four digit employee number** in the *Description* column and then press Enter to move to the second row.

   Entering information in the *Description* column is optional. The *Description* text appears in the Status bar when the user is adding records in Datasheet view.

Table1 : Table

Field Name	Data Type	Description
Emp No	Text	Enter the four digit employee number

Step 3 Step 4 Step 5

6. Key **Pension Plan** in the *Field Name* column in the second field row and then press Enter.

7. Click the down-pointing triangle in the *Data Type* column, click *Yes/No* in the drop-down list, and then press Enter.

   See Table A2.1 for a description of the Yes/No data type.

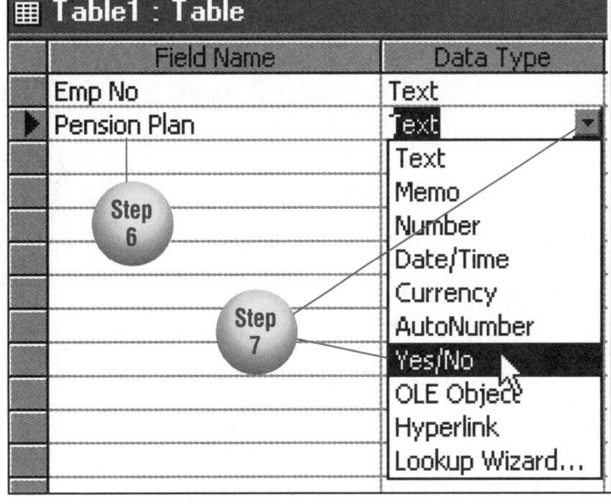

8. Key **Click or press the space bar for Yes; leave empty for No** and then press Enter.

9. Enter the remaining field names, data types, and descriptions as shown in Figure A2.2. Click the down-pointing triangle in the *Data Type* column to select data types other than Text.

FIGURE A2.2 Table Entries

Table1 : Table

Field Name	Data Type	Description
Emp No	Text	Enter the four digit employee number
Pension Plan	Yes/No	Click or press the space bar for Yes; leave empty for No
Dental Plan	Yes/No	Click or press the space bar for Yes; leave empty for No
Premium Health	Yes/No	Click or press the space bar for Yes; leave empty for No
Dependents	Number	Key the number of dependents
Life Insurance	Currency	Key the life insurance benefit

(continued)

10 Click the insertion point in any character in the *Emp No* field row.

This moves the field selector (right-pointing triangle) to the *Emp No* field. In the next step you will designate the *Emp No* field as the primary key for the table.

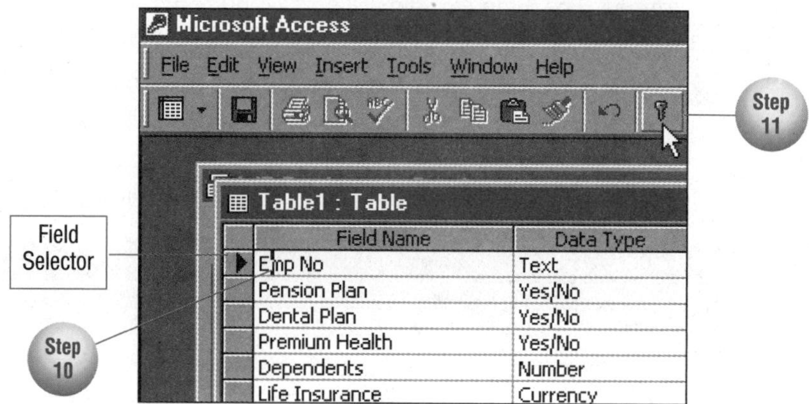

11 Click the Primary Key button on the Table Design toolbar.

A key icon will appear in the field selector bar to the left of *Emp No*, indicating the field is the primary key for the table. The primary key is the field that will contain unique data for each record in the table. In addition, Access automatically sorts the table data by the primary key field when the table is opened.

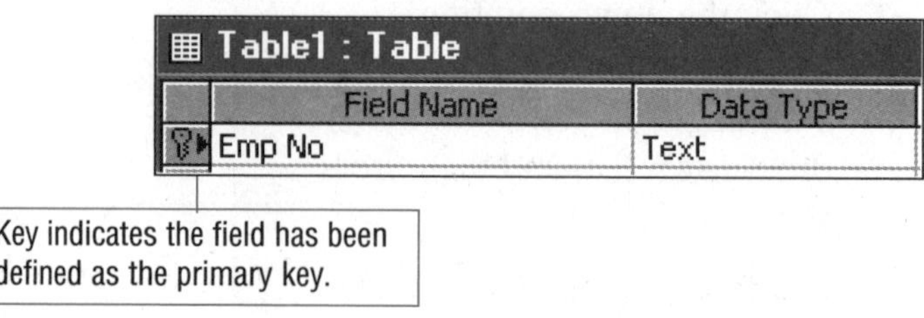

12 Click the Save button on the Table Design toolbar.

The Save As dialog box opens.

13 Key **Employee Benefits** in the Table Name text box and then press Enter or click OK.

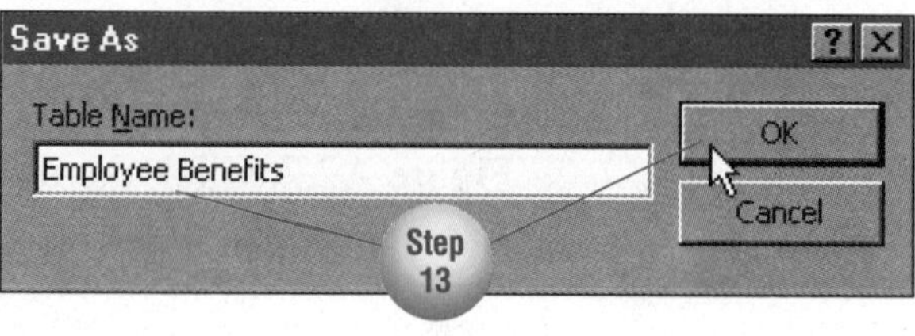

Once the table is saved, the table name appears in the Title bar.

14 Click the View button on the Table Design toolbar.

The View button switches to Datasheet view, where you can enter records into the new table. The insertion point is automatically positioned in the first field for the first record. Notice the description *Enter the four digit employee number* displays in the Status bar.

15 Key **1001** and then press Enter.

16 Press the spacebar or click the box in the *Pension Plan* column and then press Enter.

A check mark in the box indicates Yes, True, or On in a Yes/No data field.

17. Press Enter to leave the *Dental Plan* box empty and move to the next column.

    An empty box indicates No, False, or Off in a Yes/No data field.

18. Press the spacebar or click the box in the *Premium Health* column and then press Enter.

19. Key **2** in the *Dependents* column and then press Enter.

20. Key **150000** in the *Life Insurance* column and then press Enter.

    The dollar symbol, comma in the thousands, decimal point, and two zeros are automatically inserted in the field since the data type was defined as Currency.

Employee Benefits : Table

Emp No	Pension Plan	Dental Plan	Premium Heal	Dependents	Life Insurance
1001	☑	☐	☑	2	$150,000.00
	☐	☐	☐	0	$0.00

Step 15 · Step 16 · Step 17 · Step 18 · Step 19 · Step 20

21. Key the following two records in the datasheet:

Emp No	**1005**	*Emp No*	**1010**
Pension Plan	**Yes**	*Pension Plan*	**Yes**
Dental Plan	**Yes**	*Dental Plan*	**No**
Premium Health	**Yes**	*Premium Health*	**No**
Dependents	**3**	*Dependents*	**0**
Life Insurance	**175000**	*Life Insurance*	**100000**

22. Close the Employee Benefits table.

TABLE A2.1 Data Types

Data Type	Description
Text	Alphanumeric data up to 255 characters in length, such as a name or address. Fields that will contain numbers that will not be used in calculations, such as a student number or telephone number, should be defined as Text.
Memo	Alphanumeric data up to 64,000 characters in length.
Number	Positive and/or negative values that can be used in mathematical operations. Do not use for values that will calculate monetary amounts (see Currency).
Date/Time	Stores dates and times. Use this format to ensure dates and times are sorted properly. Access displays an error message if an invalid date is entered in a Date/Time data field.
Currency	Values that involve money. Access will not round off during calculations.
AutoNumber	Access will automatically number each record sequentially (incrementing by 1) when you begin keying a new record. If you do not define a primary key and you respond Yes for Access to define one for you when you save the table, Access creates an AutoNumber data field.
Yes/No	Data in the field will be either be Yes or No, True or False, On or Off.
OLE Object	Used to embed or link objects created in other Office applications (such as Microsoft Word or Microsoft Excel) to an Access table.
Hyperlink	Field that will store a hyperlink such as a URL.
Lookup Wizard	Starts the Lookup Wizard, which creates a data type based on the values selected during the wizard steps. The Lookup Wizard can be used to enter data in the field from another existing table or display a list of values in a drop-down list for the user to choose from.

Using the Lookup Wizard

Create a *Lookup* field when you want to restrict the data entered into the field to a list of values from an existing table, or a list of values that you enter in the wizard dialog box. The Lookup tab in the Field Properties section in Table Design view contains the options used to create a lookup field. Access includes the Lookup Wizard, which facilitates entering the option settings.

PROJECT: You will use the Lookup Wizard to create a new field in the Employee Benefits table that will display a drop-down list of vacation entitlements in Datasheet view.

steps

1. With WE Employees2 open, *right*-click the Employee Benefits table name in the WE Employees2 Database window and then click Design View on the shortcut menu.

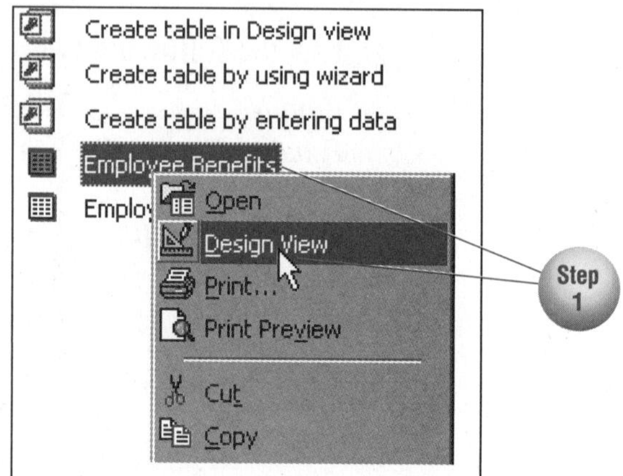

2. Click in the *Field Name* column in the blank row below Life Insurance, key **Vacation** and then press Enter.
3. Click the down-pointing triangle in the *Data Type* column and then click *Lookup Wizard* from the drop-down list.
4. Click *I will type in the values that I want* and then click Next.

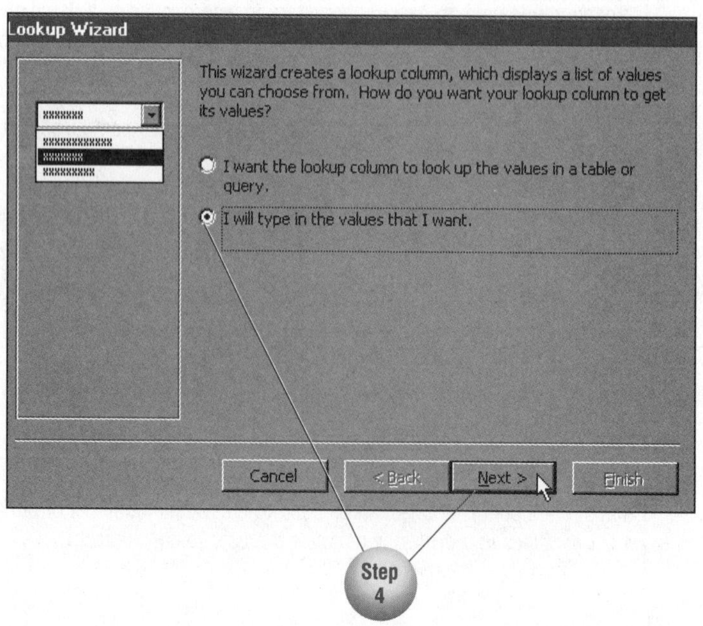

5 Click in the blank row below *Col1*, key **1 week** and then press Tab.

If you pressed Enter by mistake and find yourself at the next step in the Lookup Wizard, click Back to return to the previous dialog box.

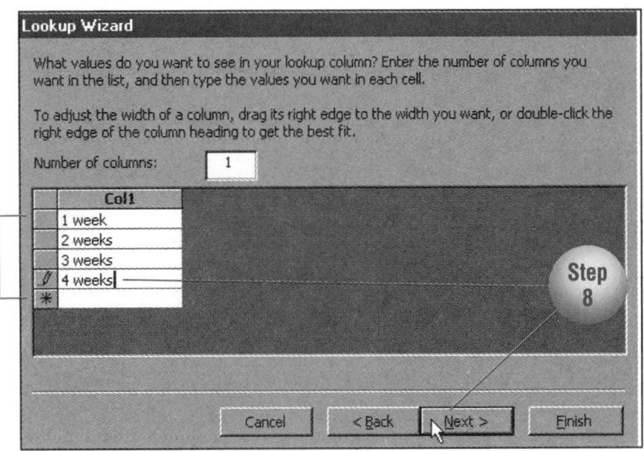

6 Key **2 weeks** and then press Tab.

7 Key **3 weeks** and then press Tab.

8 Key **4 weeks** and then click Next.

9 Click Finish in the last Lookup Wizard dialog box to accept the default label *Vacation*.

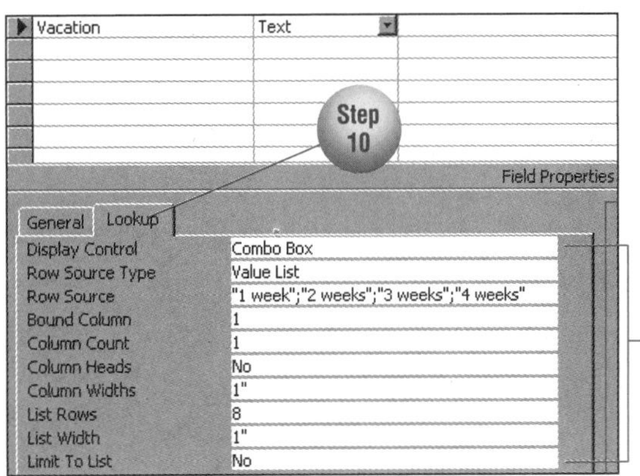

10 Click the Lookup tab in the Field Properties section and view the entries made to each setting by the Lookup Wizard.

Changes made to lookup options through Lookup Wizard.

11 Click Save.

12 Click View to switch to Datasheet view.

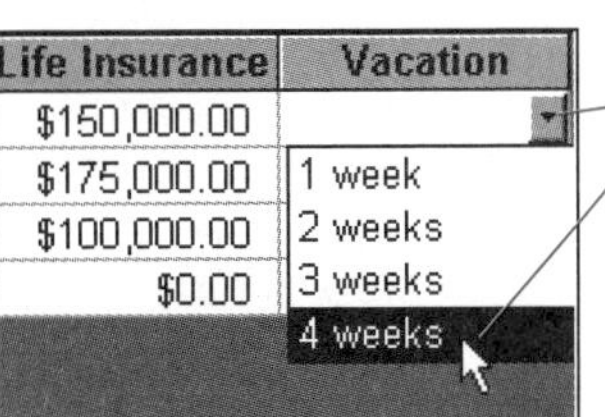

13 Click in the *Vacation* column in the first row in the datasheet, click the down-pointing triangle that appears, and then click *4 weeks* from the drop-down list.

14 Press the down arrow key to move to the *Vacation* column in the second row.

15 Click the down-pointing triangle and then click *3 weeks*.

16 Press the down arrow key, click the down-pointing triangle, and then click *3 weeks*.

17 Close the Employee Benefits table.

Create a Lookup Field Using Lookup Wizard

1 Open the table in Design view.
2 Key field name and press Enter.
3 Click down-pointing triangle in *Data Type* column.
4 Click Lookup Wizard.
5 Click *I will type in the values that I want* and click Next.
6 Key field values in *Col1* column and click Next.
7 Click Finish in the last wizard dialog box.
8 Click Save.

Using the Input Mask Wizard

An *input mask* displays a pattern specifying how data is to be entered into a field. For example, an input mask could be defined in a telephone number field to display (___)___-____. This input mask indicates to the user that the three-digit area code is required for all telephone numbers. Input masks ensure that data is entered consistently in tables. The Input Mask Wizard is used to help create the entry in the Input Mask property in the Field Properties section for the field.

PROJECT: You will create a new field in the Employee Benefits table for Pension Plan eligibility dates, and include an input mask in the field indicating that dates should be entered in the format *dd-mmm-yy*.

steps

1. With WE Employees2 open, open the Employee Benefits table in Design view.
2. Click in the *Field Name* column in the blank row below Vacation, key **RPP Eligibility Date** and then press Enter.
3. Change the *Data Type* to Date/Time and then press Enter.
4. Key **Enter date as dd-mmm-yy (example: 12-Dec-00)**.
5. Click Save.

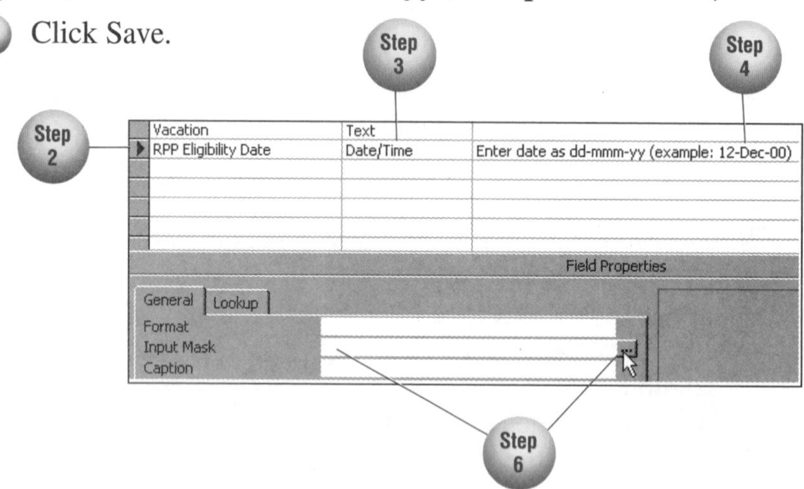

6. If necessary, click the General tab. Click in the Input Mask property in the Field Properties section and then click the Build button.

If the Input Mask Wizard has not been installed, a message will appear asking if you want to install it now. Check with your instructor.

7. Click *Medium Date* in the first Input Mask Wizard dialog box and then click Next.

   The available input masks that display in the list box are dependent on the data type for the field for which you are creating an input mask.

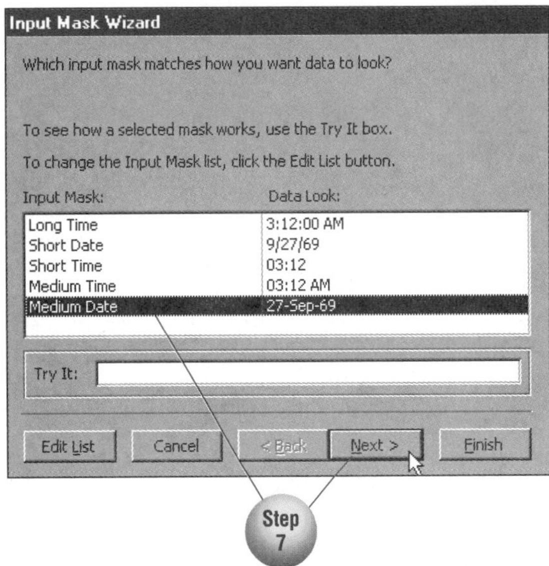

8. Click Next in the second Input Mask Wizard dialog box.

   This dialog box displays the input mask code in the Input Mask text box and sets the Placeholder character that will display in the field. The default Placeholder is the underscore character. Other available Placeholder characters are #, @, and !.

9. Click Finish at the last Input Mask Wizard dialog box.

   The input mask *99\->L<LL\-00;0;_* is entered in the Input Mask property for the *RPP Eligibility Date* field.

10. Click Save and then click View to switch to Datasheet view.

11. Maximize the Employee Benefits table if it is not already maximized.

12. Click in the *RPP Eligibility Date* column for the first row in the datasheet.

    The input mask __-___-__ appears in the field.

Input mask field property created by the Input Mask Wizard.

If the input mask does not appear right away, start to key the date in step 13. As soon as you key the first character in the field, the mask will appear.

(continued)

13 Key **22-Jan-98** and then press the down arrow key.

Access displays *1/22/98* in the field. By default, dates are displayed in the datasheet as *m/dd/yy*. In steps 14–17 you will format the field to display the date in the same format as the input mask.

14 Click the View button to switch to Design view.

The View button toggles between Datasheet view and Design view depending on which view is active.

15 With *RPP Eligibility Date* as the selected field, click in the Format field property, click the down-pointing arrow that appears, and then click *Medium Date* in the drop-down list.

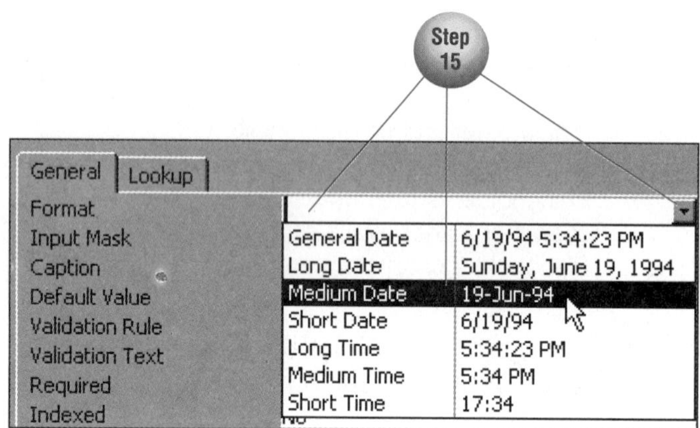

16 Click Save and then click View to switch to Datasheet view.

17 Click in the *RPP Eligibility Date* column in the second row in the datasheet and then key **15-Feb-99**.

In the next step you try to enter a date using the format *mm/dd/yy* to see how the input mask restricts this entry.

18 Click in the *RPP Eligibility Date* column in the third row in the datasheet and then key **07/09/99**.

A beep will sound when you key **/** and **09/**. The only part of the entry that will be accepted is 07. The insertion point remains in the month section of the date.

19 Press Backspace twice to delete 07, key **30-Jul-99** and then press Enter.

The difference between the input mask and the format property is that the input mask *restricts* the data that is entered into the field, while the format property controls the *display* of the data that is accepted into the field.

20 Close the Employee Benefits table.

FIGURE A2.3 Input Mask Wizard Dialog Box

Input Mask Wizard

Which input mask matches how you want data to look?

To see how a selected mask works, use the Try It box.

To change the Input Mask list, click the Edit List button.

Input Mask:	Data Look:
Phone Number	(206) 555-1212
Social Security Number	531-86-7180
Zip Code	98052-6399
Extension	63215
Password	********
Long Time	3:12:00 AM

Try It:

Edit List | Cancel | < Back | Next > | Finish

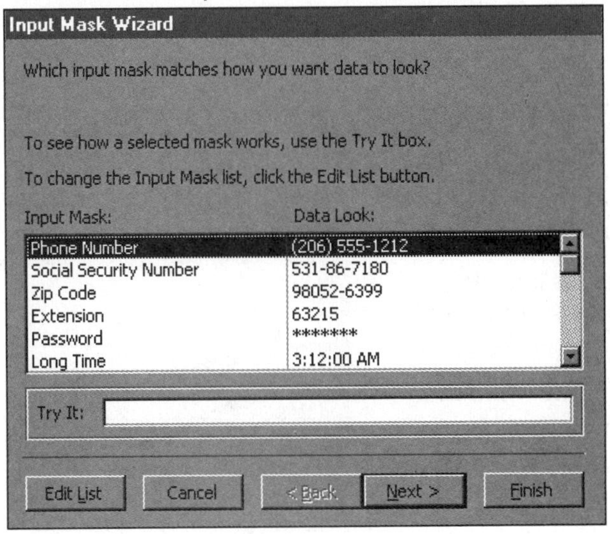

Take 2

Editing Input Masks

The Input Mask Wizard dialog box shown in Figure A2.3 displays the available input masks for a data field that is defined as Text. The Input Mask Wizard only works with Text or Date/Time data field types. Click in the Input Mask property and insert or delete characters as needed to edit an input mask created by the wizard. For example, the social security input mask does not accommodate social insurance number formats for countries other than the United States. To create an input mask for Canadian social insurance numbers, use the wizard to create the social security input mask. After the entry has been created, click in the Input Mask property and modify the entry as shown below. Other input masks such as a telephone number can be edited to include an extension number.

Input Mask created for Social Security Number:	000\-00\-0000;;_
Edited entry for Canadian Social Insurance Number:	000\-000\-000;;_

DIRECTOR'S CUT

Create an Input Mask for a Field

1 Open the table in Design view.
2 Key field name, assign data type, and key description.
3 Click Save.
4 Click in the Input Mask property.
5 Click the Build button.
6 Click the input mask you want to create.
7 Click Next.
8 Select Placeholder character.
9 Click Next.
10 Click Next to store data without symbols.
11 Click Finish.
12 Click Save.

Validating Field Entries

The *Validation Rule* property can be used to enter a conditional statement that is checked when data is entered into a field. Access displays an error message to the user if the data being entered does not meet the conditional test. For example, a validation rule for a customer number field could be that the customer number must be within a certain range of values. The *Validation Text* property is used to enter the content of the error message that you want the user to see. The Validation Rule and Validation Text properties are important data entry error checking tools.

PROJECT: Worldwide Enterprises offers life insurance benefits up to a maximum of $199,999. You will add a validation rule and enter an error message in the validation text for the *Life Insurance* field in the Employee Benefits table to ensure that no benefit exceeds this maximum.

steps

1. With WE Employees2 open, open the Employee Benefits table in Design view.
2. Click in the *Life Insurance* field row.

   This selects the *Life Insurance* field and displays the field properties.
3. Click in the Validation Rule property, key **<200000** and then press Enter.

   Pressing Enter after keying the validation rule moves the insertion point to the Validation Text property.
4. Key **Enter a value that is less than $200,000**.
5. Click Save.

   Since a validation rule has been created *after* data has been entered into the table, Access displays a warning message.
6. Click Yes to instruct Access to test the data with the new rules.

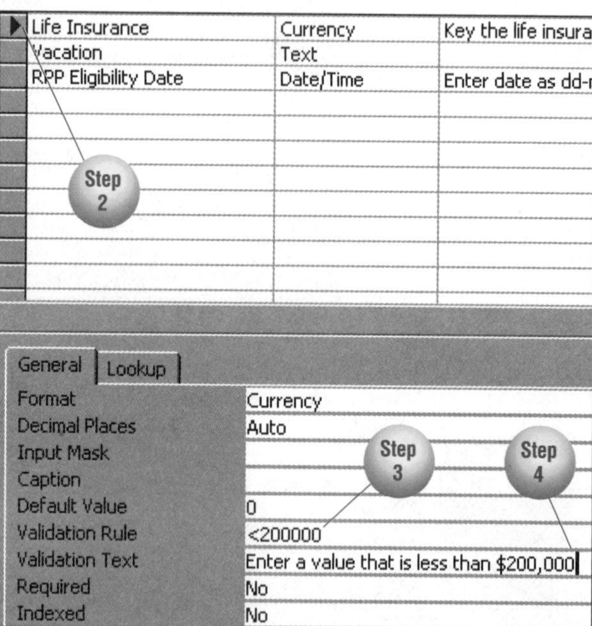

7. Click View to switch to Datasheet view.
8. Add the following record to the table:

Emp No	**1015**
Pension Plan	**Yes**
Dental Plan	**Yes**
Premium Health	**Yes**
Dependents	**2**
Life Insurance	**210000**

When you enter 210000 into the *Life Insurance* field and press Enter or Tab, Access will display an error message. The text in the error message is the text you entered in the Validation Text property.

Step 9

9. Click OK at the Microsoft Access error message.
10. Backspace to delete 210000, key **199999** and then press Enter.
11. Enter the following data in the two remaining fields:

Vacation	**4 weeks**
RPP Eligibility Date	**17-Nov-98**

Emp No	Pension Plan	Dental Plan	Premium Heal	Dependents	Life Insurance	Vacation	RPP Eligibility
1001	☑	☐	☑	2	$150,000.00	4 weeks	22-Jan-9
1005	☑	☑	☑	3	$175,000.00	3 weeks	15-Feb-9
1010	☑	☐	☐	0	$100,000.00	3 weeks	30-Jul-9
1015	☑	☑	☑	2	$199,999.00	4 weeks	17-Nov-9

Step 8 Step 10 Step 11

12. Close the Employee Benefits table.

Take 2

Other Validation Rule Examples

Validation rules should be created whenever possible to avoid data entry errors. The examples below illustrate various ways to use the validation rule to verify data.

Field Name	Validation Rule	Data Check
Customer No	>1000 And <1100	Limits customer numbers to 1001 through 1099
Credit Limit	<=5000	Restricts credit limits to values of 5000 or less
State	"CA"	Only the state of California is accepted
Order Qty	>=25	Quantity ordered must be a minimum of 25

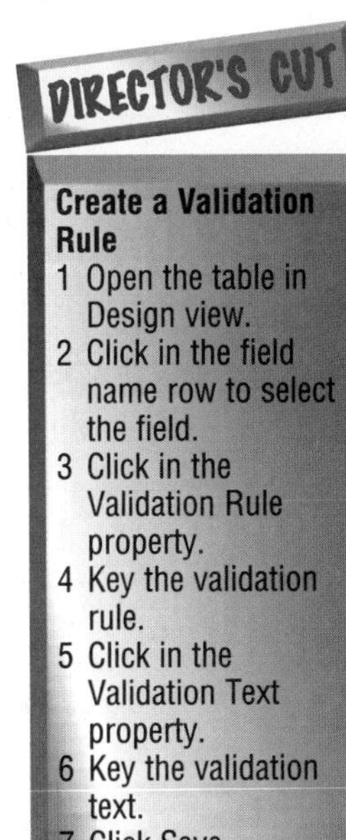

Modifying Field Size and Default Value

The *Field Size* property can be used to limit the number of characters that are allowed in a field entry. For example, a field size of 6 for a customer number field would prevent customer numbers greater than 6 digits from being stored in a record. The *Default Value* property is useful if most records will contain the same value. The value will appear in the field automatically when a new record is added to the table. The user will have the option of accepting the default value by pressing Enter or Tab at the field, or of overwriting the default by keying a different value.

PROJECT: Worldwide Enterprises uses a 4-digit employee number. You will modify the Field Size property for the *Emp No* field to set the maximum number of characters to 4. Since most employees opt into the pension plan, you will set the default value for the *Pension Plan* field to Yes.

steps

1. With WE Employees2 open, open the Employee Benefits table in Design view.
2. With the *Emp No* field already selected, drag the pointer over the value *50* that appears in the Field Size property.

   Alternatively, click in the Field Size property to activate the insertion point and then delete 50.

General	Lookup
Field Size	50
Format	
Input Mask	
Caption	
Default Value	
Validation Rule	
Validation Text	
Required	No
Allow Zero Length	No
Indexed	Yes (No Duplicates)
Unicode Compression	Yes

Step 2

3. Key **4**.
4. Click in the *Pension Plan* field row to display the *Pension Plan* field properties.
5. Click in the *Default Value* field property.
6. Key **Yes**.
7. Click Save.

   Since the field size for a field was changed *after* data had been entered into the table, Access displays a warning message that some data may be lost.

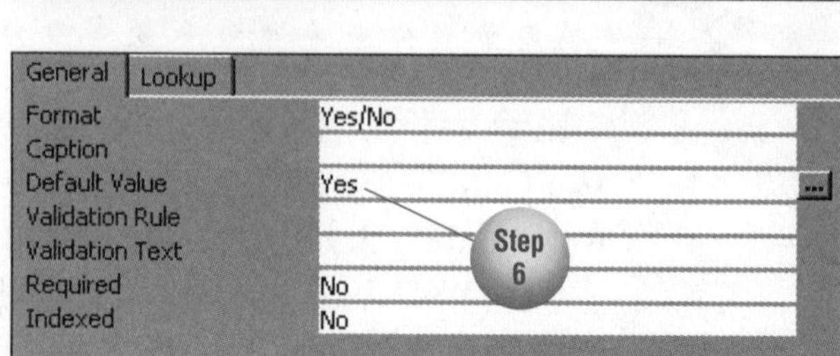

8. Click Yes to instruct Access to continue.

   If a large amount of data was entered into a table before the field size was changed, always make a backup of the file before continuing. To check for errors, compare the old data in the field with the new data after Access saves the table.

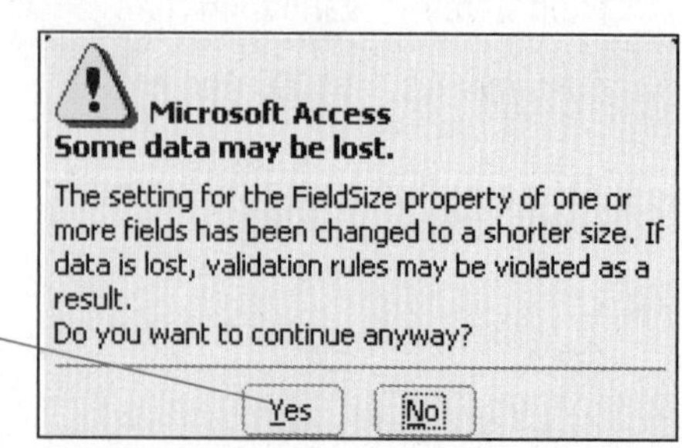

Step 8

9. Click View to switch to Datasheet view.

   Notice the *Pension Plan* column in the blank row at the bottom of the datasheet contains a check mark, since the default value is now Yes.

10. Key **10201** in the *Emp No* field in the blank row at the bottom of the datasheet and then press Enter.

    A beep will sound when you key **1** at the end of the field. Access did not accept any characters after the fourth character that was typed.

11. Press Enter at the *Pension Plan* field to accept the default value of Yes.

12. Enter the following data in the remaining fields:

Dental Plan	**No**
Premium Health	**No**
Dependents	**0**
Life Insurance	**100000**
Vacation	**4 weeks**
RPP Eligibility Date	**03-Feb-99**

Emp No	Pension Plan	Dental Plan	Premium Heal	Dependents	Life Insurance	Vacation	RPP Eligibility
1001	☑	☐	☑	2	$150,000.00	4 weeks	22-Jan-98
1005	☑	☑	☑	3	$175,000.00	3 weeks	15-Feb-99
1010	☑	☐	☐	0	$100,000.00	3 weeks	30-Jul-99
1015	☑	☑	☑	2	$199,999.00	4 weeks	17-Nov-98
1020	☑	☐	☐	0	$100,000.00	4 weeks	03-Feb-99

Step 10   Step 11   Step 12

13. Best Fit all columns in the datasheet, change the page orientation to landscape, and then print the Employee Benefits table.

14. Close the Employee Benefits table. Click Yes to save layout changes.

Take 2

Default Field Size

The default field size property will vary depending on the data type. The default value for a text field is 50. If the data type is Numeric, the default field size is *Long Integer*. Long Integer will store *whole numbers* from -2,147,483,648 to 2,147,483,648 (negative to positive). Press F1 while the insertion point is positioned in the Field Size property to display in the Help window the various field size settings for a numeric field.

DIRECTOR'S CUT

Set the Field Size
1. Open the table in Design view.
2. Click in the field name row to select the field.
3. Click in the Field Size property.
4. Key the maximum number of characters for the field.
5. Click Save.

Set the Default Value
1. Open the table in Design view.
2. Click in the field name row to select the field.
3. Click in the Default Value property.
4. Key the default value to appear in the field.
5. Click Save.

Creating a Table Using the Table Wizard

Creating a table using the Table Wizard involves choosing the type of table from a list of sample tables and then selecting fields from the sample field list. Access creates the field names and assigns data types based on the samples. Once created, the fields in the table can be edited in Design view.

PROJECT: You will use the Table Wizard to create a new table that will store employee addresses.

steps

1. With WE Employees2 open, double-click *Create table by using wizard.*

2. Click *Employees* in the Sample Tables list box.

3. Click *EmployeeNumber* in the Sample Fields list box and then click the AddField button > to the right of the Sample Fields list box.

   This inserts the *EmployeeNumber* field in the Fields in my new table list box and moves the selected field in the Sample Fields list box to the next field after *EmployeeNumber,* which is *NationalEmplNumber.*

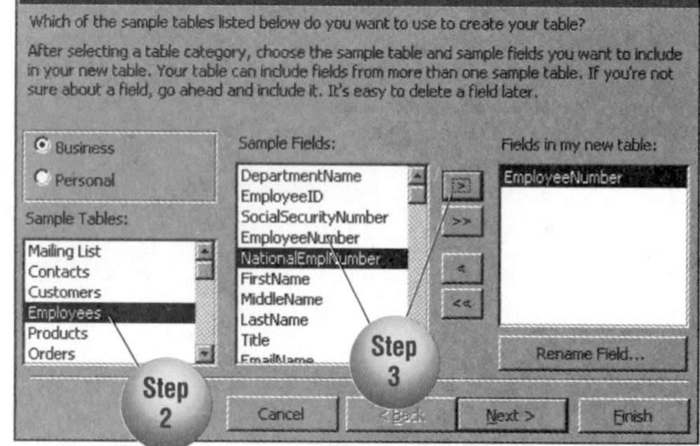

4. Double-click *FirstName* in the Sample Fields list box.

   Double-clicking a field name in the Sample Fields list box is another method of adding the field in the Fields in my new table list box.

5. Double-click the following field names in the Sample Fields list box:

   MiddleName
   LastName
   Address
   City
   StateOrProvince
   PostalCode

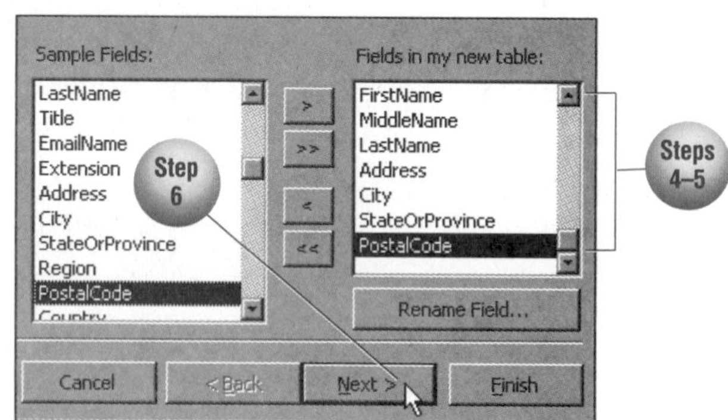

Can't locate some of the field names? You will need to scroll down the Sample Fields list box.

6 Click Next.

7 Click Next at the second Table Wizard dialog box to accept the table name *Employees* and *Yes, set a primary key for me*.

8 Click Next at the third Table Wizard dialog box, since the new table is not related to the existing tables in the database.

9 Click *Modify the table design* at the fourth Table Wizard dialog box, and then click Finish.

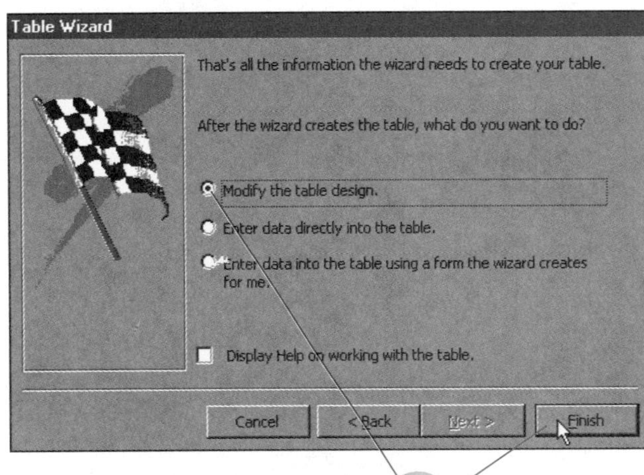

The new Employees table appears in the Design view window. When you elected to let Access set the primary key field, Access added the field *EmployeesID* to the table with the data type of AutoNumber. In steps 10–13 you will modify the primary key by deleting the *EmployeesID* field and modifying *EmployeeNumber*.

10 Click in the field selector bar next to *EmployeesID* and then click the Delete Rows button 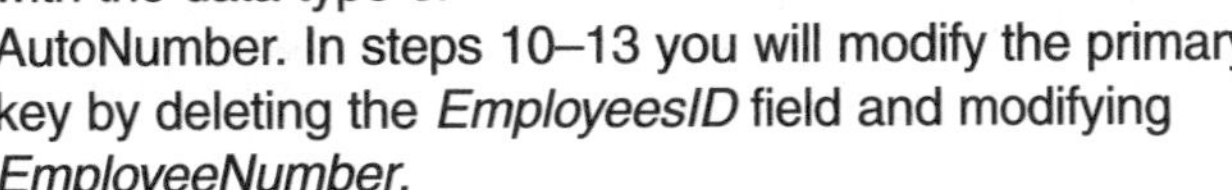 on the Table Design toolbar.

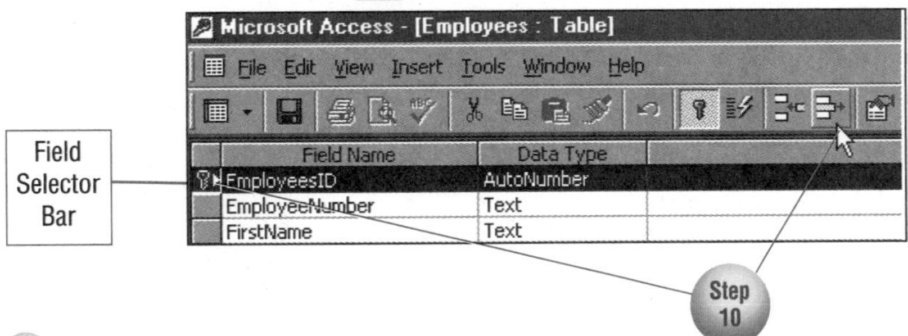

11 Click Yes to confirm the deletion.

12 Make the following changes to the *EmployeeNumber* field:

Field Name **Emp No**
Field Size **4**

13 Make *Emp No* the primary key field.

14 Click Save.

15 Close the Employees table.

DIRECTOR'S CUT

Create a Table Using Wizard

1 Open database file.
2 Double-click *Create table by using wizard.*
3 Click type of table in Sample Tables list box.
4 Add fields from Sample Fields list box to Fields in my new table list box.
5 Click Next.
6 Choose table name and primary key and click Next.
7 Choose to enter data directly in the table or edit the table in Design view.
8 Click Finish.

Creating a Table by Adding Records

A new table can be created by entering data directly into a blank datasheet. When you save the datasheet, Access assigns data types and formats for each field based on the data you entered in each column. Columns are initially named *Field1, Field2,* and so on. Double-click the column name, key a new name, and then press Enter to assign the field names in the new table. Once the table has been created, it can be edited by opening the table in Design view.

PROJECT: You will create a new table to store employee expense reports by entering expense report data in a new datasheet.

steps

1. With WE Employees2 open, double-click *Create table by entering data.*
2. Double-click *Field1*, key **Emp No** and then press Enter.
3. Double-click *Field2*, key **Date** and then press Enter.

4. Change the following column headings as shown:

   Field3 **Amount**
   Field4 **Type**
   Field5 **Description**

5. *Right*-click the column heading for *Field6* and then click Delete Column on the shortcut menu.

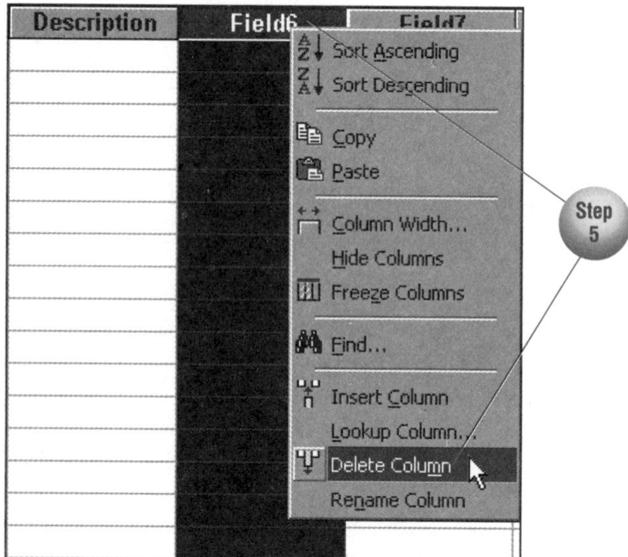

6. Click Yes to confirm the column deletion.
7. Delete the *Field7–Field10* columns.

8. Click in the first blank row below *Emp No,* key **1001** and then press Enter.
9. Key **03/15/02** in the *Date* column and then press Enter.
10. Key **$1,543.10** in the *Amount* column and then press Enter.
11. Key **Sales** in the *Type* column and then press Enter.
12. Key **NorthWest Sales Meeting** in the *Description* column and then press Enter.

Emp No	Date	Amount	Type	Description
1001	03/15/02	$1,543.10	Sales	NorthWest Sale

Step 8 Step 9 Step 10 Step 11 Step 12

13. Expand the column width for the *Description* column.
14. Click Save.
15. Key **Employee Expenses** in the Save As dialog box and then click OK.
16. Click No at the message asking if you want to create the primary key.
17. Click View to switch to Design view.
18. Make the following changes to the *Emp No* field:

    Data Type **Text**
    Field Size **4**

19. Make *Emp No* the primary key field.

Field Name	Data Type
Emp No	Text
Date	Date/Time
Amount	Currency
Type	Text
Description	Text

General Lookup
Field Size 4

Step 19
Step 18

Access assigns data types based on the values that were keyed in the columns in the datasheet.

20. Click Save.
21. Close the Employee Expenses table.

DIRECTOR'S CUT

Create a Table by Entering Data
1 Open database file.
2 Double-click *Create table by entering data.*
3 Double-click column headings, key new field names, and then press Enter.
4 Key data in datasheet.
5 Click Save.
6 Key a name for the table in the Save As dialog box.
7 Choose Yes to create a primary key or No to create one later.
8 Close the datasheet or switch to Design view to edit the table.

Creating and Printing Relationships

Access is sometimes referred to as a relational database management system. A relational database is one in which relationships exist between tables, allowing two or more tables to be treated as if they were one when generating reports or looking up data. Joining one table to another using a field common to both tables creates a relationship.

PROJECT: You will create a one-to-one relationship between the Employee Dates and Salaries table and the Employee Benefits table.

steps

1. With WE Employees2 open, click the Relationships button on the Database toolbar.
2. With *Employee Benefits* already selected in the Show Table dialog box with the Table tab selected, click Add.

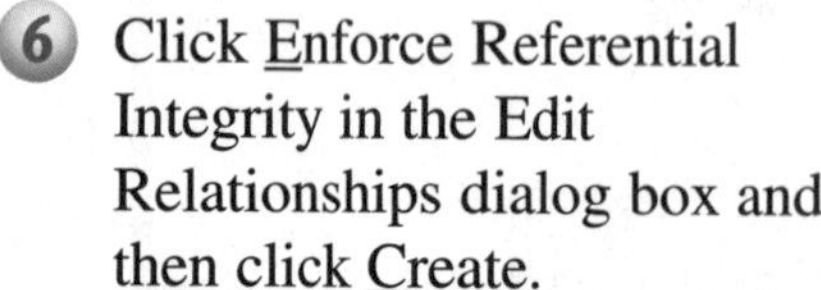

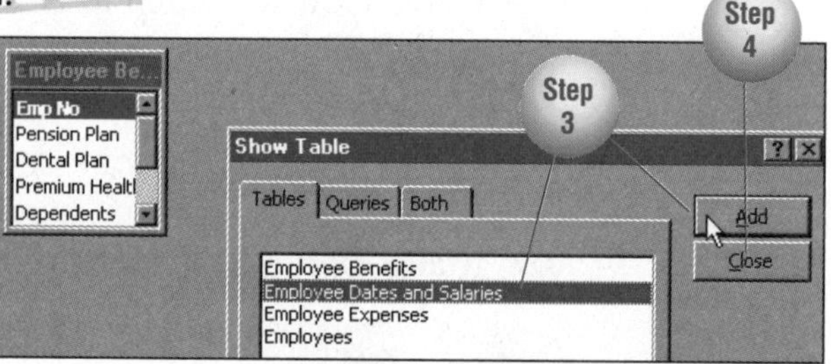

3. Click *Employee Dates and Salaries* and then click Add.
4. Click Close to close the Show Table dialog box.

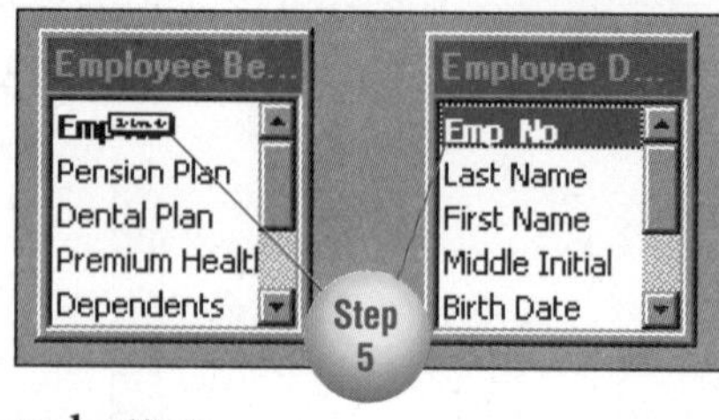

5. Position the mouse pointer over the *Emp No* field name in the Employee Dates and Salaries list box (list box on the right), hold down the left mouse button, drag the pointer left to the *Emp No* field name in the Employee Benefits list box, and then release the mouse button.
6. Click Enforce Referential Integrity in the Edit Relationships dialog box and then click Create.

   Referential integrity means that Access will ensure that a record with the same employee number already exists in the primary table (Employee Dates and Salaries) when a new record is being added to the related table (Employee Benefits).

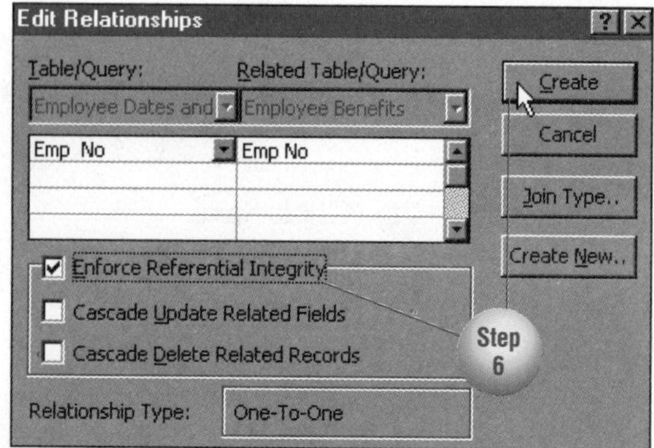

7 Click Save.

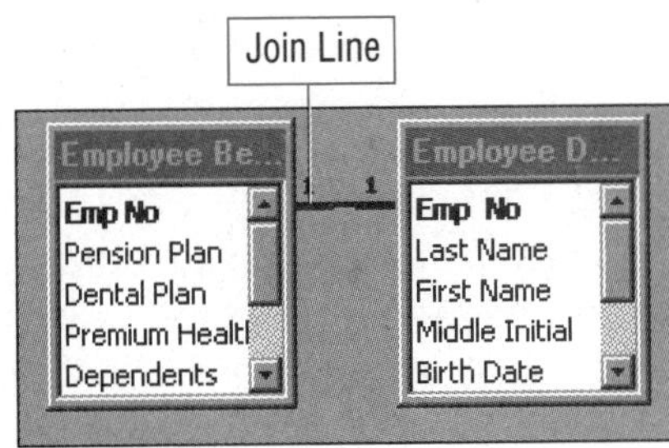

A black line (referred to as a *join line*) joins the two tables in the Relationships window. A 1 appears at each end of the join line indicating a *one-to-one* relationship. In a one-to-one relationship, one record exists in the primary table for every one record that exists in the related table.

8 Click File and then click Print Relationships.

9 Click the Print button on the Print Preview toolbar.

10 Click File and Close to close the Relationships report window. Click No to save changes.

11 Close the Relationships window.

12 Open the Employee Benefits table in Datasheet view.

In steps 13–15 you will test the referential integrity by attempting to add a record for an employee that does not exist in the primary table.

13 Click the New Record button on the Table Datasheet toolbar.

14 Key **1200** and then press Enter.

15 Press Enter through the remaining fields until you reach the end of the record.

Access displays an error message indicating you cannot add a record because a related record is required in the Employee Dates and Salaries table.

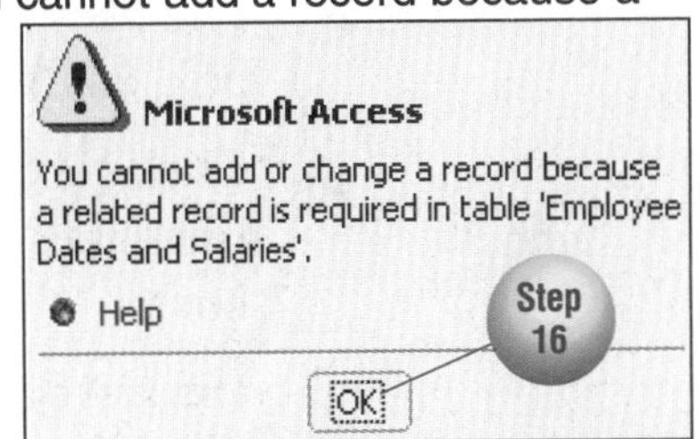

16 Click OK to close the message window.

17 Close the Employee Benefits table. Click OK at the error message that appears for the second time. Click Yes to close the object and confirm that the data changes will be lost.

18 Close the WE Employees2 database.

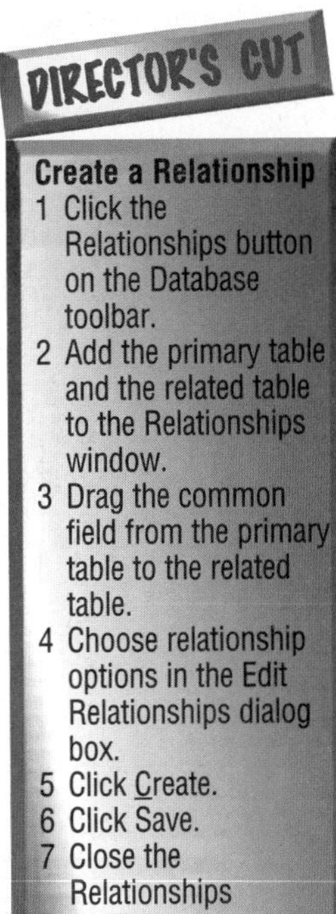

DIRECTOR'S CUT

Create a Relationship

1 Click the Relationships button on the Database toolbar.
2 Add the primary table and the related table to the Relationships window.
3 Drag the common field from the primary table to the related table.
4 Choose relationship options in the Edit Relationships dialog box.
5 Click Create.
6 Click Save.
7 Close the Relationships window.

Take 2

One-to-Many Relationship

A one-to-many relationship exists when the primary table will contain only one record for the common field, while the related table could contain several records for the common field on which the tables were joined. For example, the Employees table would contain only one record for each employee. The Employee Expenses table could, however, contain several records for the same employee, since an employee could submit several expense claims. If the tables were joined on the common *Emp No* field, a one-to-many relationship would be created.

Creating a New Database Using a Wizard

Access provides database wizards that can be used to create new database files. The wizards include a series of dialog boxes that guide you through the steps of creating the database by selecting from predefined tables, fields, screen layouts, and report layouts. When the database is created, a Main Switchboard window displays in the Access screen in place of the Database window. The Main Switchboard is a special type of form that contains options used to access the various objects generated by Access. The Main Switchboard form is automatically displayed each time the database is opened.

PROJECT: You will create a new database to store contact information for Worldwide Enterprises using the Contact Management Wizard.

steps

1. Click the New button on the Database toolbar.
2. Click the Databases tab in the New dialog box.
3. Double-click *Contact Management* in the Databases list box.
4. Key **WE Contacts** in the File name text box in the File New Database dialog box, and then click Create.
5. Click Next at the first Database Wizard dialog box.

   This first dialog box contains information about the type of data the database will store.
6. Click Next at the second Database Wizard dialog box to accept the default fields in the tables.

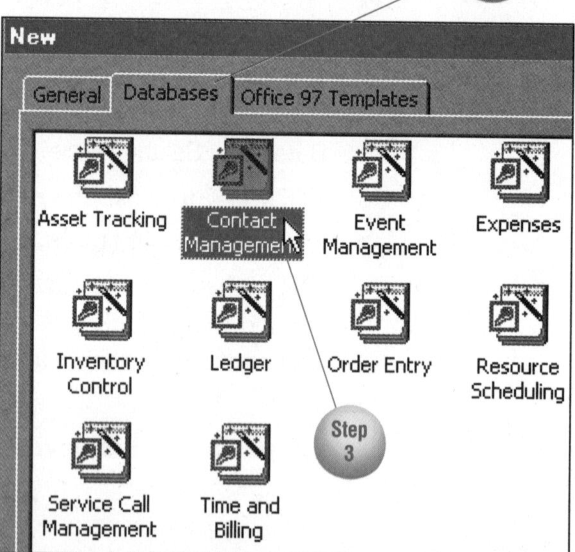

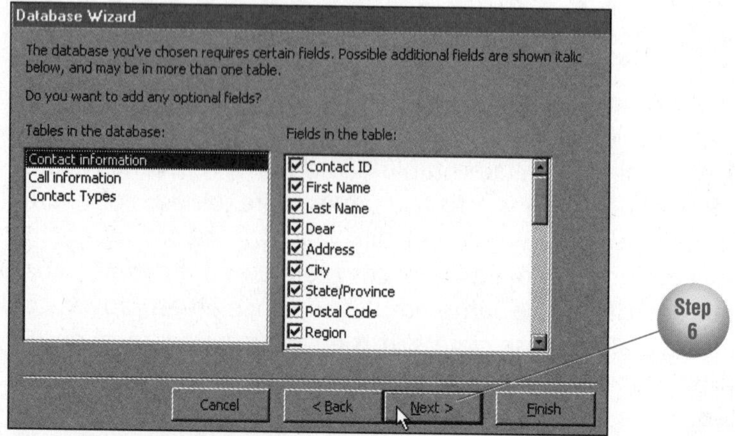

7 Click *International* as the screen display style in the third Database Wizard dialog box, and then click Next.

The Preview box at the left of the Database Wizard dialog box changes to display the selected screen display style.

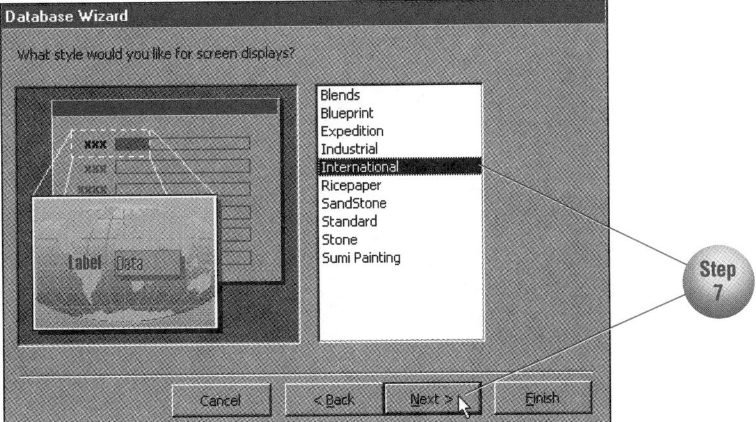

8 If necessary, click *Bold* for the report style in the fourth Database Wizard dialog box, and then click Next.

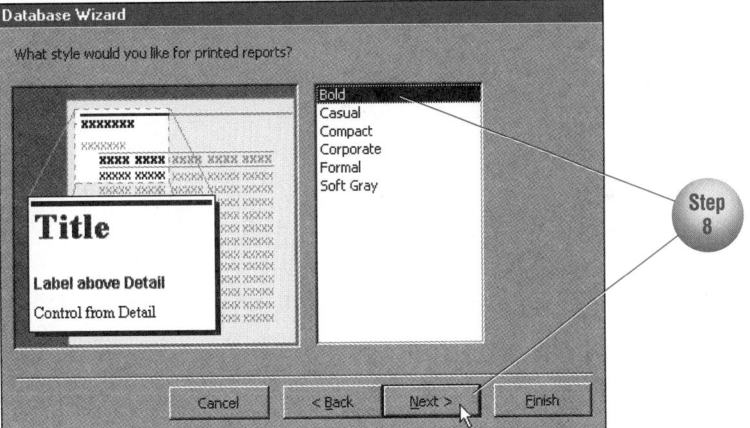

9 Click Finish at the last Database Wizard dialog box to accept the default title of *Contact Management* for the database.

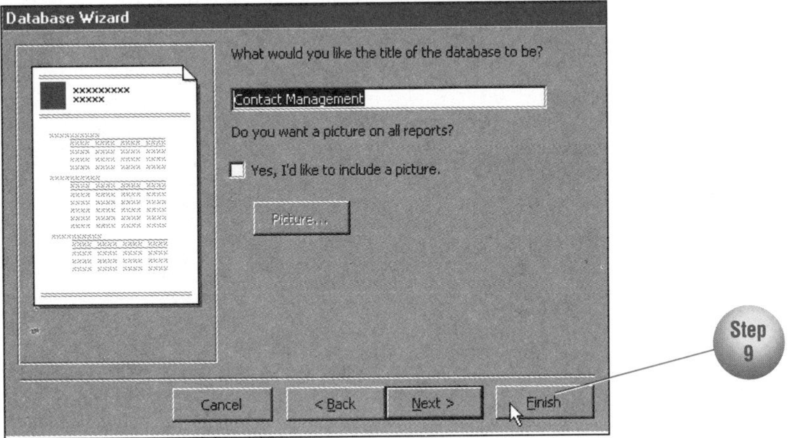

(continued)

The Database Wizard will take a moment or two to create the tables, forms, and reports for the new database. A progress box will display indicating the tasks Access is completing. When the database is complete, Access will display the Main Switchboard window that is used to access the various components of the new database.

10 Click Enter/View Contacts in the Main Switchboard window.

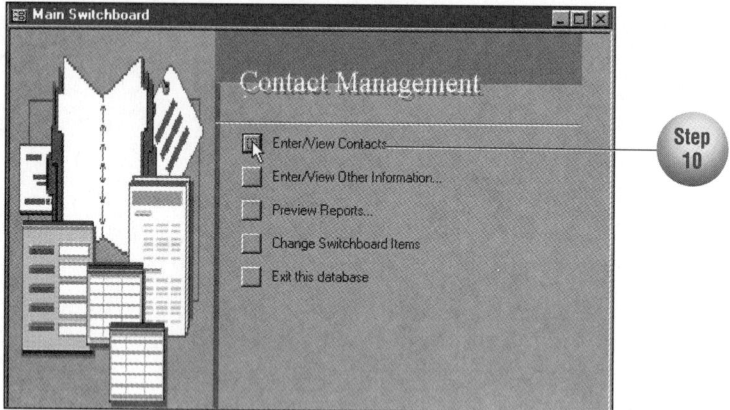

11 Key the data in the first record as shown in Figure A2.4.

FIGURE A2.4 Data for First Record

Contacts

First Name	Shannon	Contact ID	1
Last Name	Grey	Title	President
Company	Marquee Productions	Work Phone	(612) 555-2005
Dear	Shannon	Work Extension	
Address	955 South Alameda Street	Mobile Phone	
		Fax Number	(612) 555-2009
City	Los Angeles		
State/Province	CA		
Postal Code	90037-		
Country	USA		

Calls... Dial... Page: 1 2

Record: 1 of 1

Step 12

12 Click the button for Page 2 at the bottom of the record.

13 Key **sgrey@emcp.marquee.com** in the *Email Name* field.

14 Close the Contacts form.

15. Click Preview Reports in the Main Switchboard window.
16. Click Preview the Alphabetical Contact Listing Report.
17. Click the Print button on the Print Preview toolbar.
18. Click Close on the Print Preview toolbar.
19. Click Return to Main Switchboard in the Reports Switchboard window.
20. Click Exit this database in the Main Switchboard window.

FIGURE A2.5 Forms List

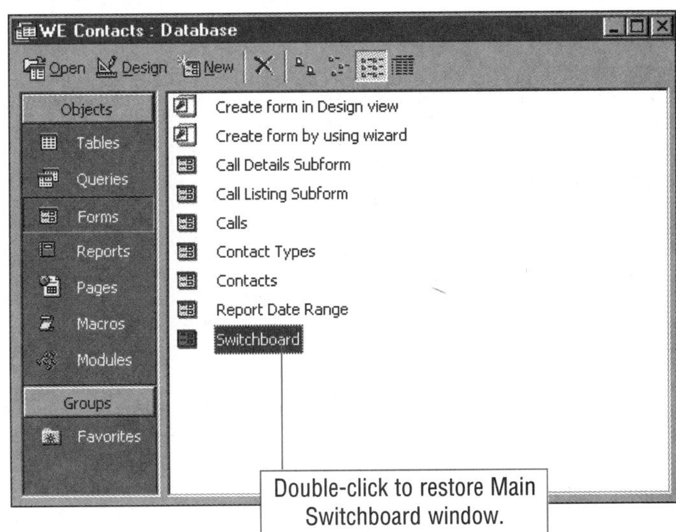

Closing the Main Switchboard

The Main Switchboard window can be closed if you prefer to work with the objects in the database in the Database window. Click the Close button on the Main Switchboard title bar. A minimized title bar with the name of the database will be positioned just above the Status bar. Click the Maximize or Restore button on the Database Title bar to restore the Database window. Tables or other objects can be customized by opening them in Design view and making the required changes. To return to the Main Switchboard after closing it, double-click *Switchboard* in the Forms list as shown in Figure A2.5.

Create a New Database Using a Wizard

1. Click New.
2. Click Databases tab in New dialog box.
3. Double-click desired database wizard.
4. Key database file name and click Create.
5. Click Next.
6. Select tables and fields to include and click Next.
7. Select screen layout and click Next.
8. Select report style and click Next.
9. Key title for database and click Next.
10. Click Finish.

Features Summary

Feature	Button	Menu	Keyboard
Database Wizard		File, New	Ctrl + N
Datasheet view		View, Datasheet View	
Delete Rows		Edit, Delete Rows	
Design view		View, Design View	
Lookup Wizard		Insert, Lookup Field	
Primary Key		Edit, Primary Key	
Relationships		Tools, Relationships	
Save table		File, Save	Ctrl + S
Table Wizard		Insert, Table, Table Wizard	

Procedures Check

In the space provided at the right, indicate the correct term or command.

1. A new table can be created in a database using the Table Wizard, by entering data directly into a blank datasheet, or using this view. __________
2. Assign a field this data type if the field will contain dollar values that you do not want rounded off in calculations. __________
3. This is the term for the field in a table that must contain unique information for each record. __________
4. This is the name of the wizard used to create a drop-down list of entries that will appear when the user clicks in the field. __________
5. This is the name of the wizard that is used to create a pattern in a field that indicates the format in which the data is to be entered. __________
6. Enter a conditional statement in this field property to prevent data that does not meet the criteria from being entered into the field. __________

7. This is the default field size for a Text data field. _______________

8. Enter a value in this field property if you want the value to appear automatically in the field whenever a new record is created. _______________

9. One table in a relationship is referred to as the primary table. The other table is referred to as this. _______________

10. Click this button on the Database toolbar to select a Database Wizard. _______________

Activity 1: Creating a Table in Design View

1 Open the WE Employees2 database.
2 Create a table in Design view using the following field names and data types. You determine an appropriate description.

Field Name	**Data Type**
Emp No	Text
Supervisor	Text
Performance Review Date	Date/Time
Salary Increment Date	Date/Time
PD Days	Number

3 Define the *Emp No* field as the primary key.
4 Save the table and name it Employee Development.
5 Switch to Datasheet view and then enter the following two records:

Emp No	**1015**	*Emp No*	**1030**
Supervisor	**Sam Vestering**	*Supervisor*	**Roman Deptulski**
Perf. Review Date	**5/17/02**	*Perf. Review Date*	**1/22/02**
Salary Increment Date	**7/01/02**	*Salary Increment Date*	**3/01/02**
PD Days	**5**	*PD Days*	**10**

6 Best Fit the column widths.
7 Close the Employee Development table. Click Yes if prompted to save changes.

Activity 2: Modifying Field Properties

1 Open the Employee Development table in Design view.
2 Change the field size for the *Emp No* field to 4.
3 Create a validation rule for the *PD Days* field to ensure that no number greater than 10 is entered into the field. Enter an appropriate validation text error message.
4 Save the table.

5 Use the Input Mask Wizard in the two date fields to set the pattern for entering dates to Medium Date.
6 Change the format property for the two date fields to display the date in the Medium Date format.
7 Save the table.
8 Switch to Datasheet view and add the following two records:

Emp No	**1035**	*Emp No*	**1040**
Supervisor	**Hanh Postma**	*Supervisor*	**Roman Deptulski**
Perf. Review Date	**15-Mar-02**	*Perf. Review Date*	**10-Mar-02**
Salary Increment Date	**01-May-02**	*Salary Increment Date*	**01-May-02**
PD Days	**8**	*PD Days*	**6**

9 Preview and then print the Employee Development table.
10 Close the Employee Development table.

Activity 3: Creating Relationships

1 Open the Employees table in Datasheet view.
2 Add the following record to the table:

Emp No	**1001**
First Name	**Sam**
Middle Name	**Lawrence**
Last Name	**Vestering**
Address	**287-1501 Broadway**
City	**New York**
State/Province	**NY**
Postal Code	**10110**

3 Best Fit the column widths.
4 Change the page orientation to landscape.
5 Print and then close the Employees table.
6 Open the Employee Expenses table in Design view.
7 With the *Emp No* field selected, click the Primary Key button to remove the *Emp No* field as a primary key.
8 Click Save and then close the Employee Expenses table.
9 Display the Relationships window.
10 Click the Show Table button on the Relationship toolbar.
11 Add the Employees and the Employee Expenses tables to the Relationships window and then close the Show Table dialog box.
12 Create a relationship by dragging the *Emp No* field name in the Employees list box to the *Emp No* field name in the Employee Expenses list box.
13 Enforce Referential Integrity and create the relationship.
14 Print the relationship.
15 Close the Relationships window. Click Yes if prompted to save changes.

Activity 4: Creating a Table by Entering Data

1 Create a new table by entering the following data into a blank datasheet:

Emp No	Pension Deduction	Dental Plan Deduction	Premium Health Deduction
1001	$225.15	$00.00	$67.33
1005	$225.15	$63.10	$87.41
1010	$225.15	$00.00	$00.00
1015	$186.54	$44.56	$67.33
1020	$189.72	$00.00	$00.00

2 Save the table and name it Employee Deductions. Click No to define a primary key.
3 Display the Employee Deductions table in Design view.
4 Make the following changes to the *Emp No* field:
  Data Type Text
  Field Size 4
5 Save the table and then switch to Datasheet view.
6 Best fit the column widths.
7 Preview, print, and then close the Employee Deductions table.
8 Close the WE Employees2 database.

Performance Plus

Activity 1: Creating a Table in Design View; Creating a Lookup Field

1 Gina Simmons, instructor in the Theatre Arts Division of Niagara Peninsula College, has asked you to create a new table to store the grades for the MKP245 course she teaches. Gina would like to be able to select the student grade from a drop-down list rather than key it in.
2 Open the NPC Grades2 database.
3 Create a new table in Design view using the following field names: *Student No*; *Last Name*; *First Name*; *Grade*. You determine the appropriate data type and descriptions for each field with the exception of the *Grade* field.
4 Use the Lookup Wizard in the *Grade* field to create a drop-down list with the following grades: A+, A, B, C, D, F.
5 Define the *Student No* field as the primary key.
6 Save the table and name it MKP245.
7 Enter the following four records in Datasheet view:

Student No	**111-785-156**	*Student No*	**118-487-578**
Last Name	**Bastow**	*Last Name*	**Andre**
First Name	**Maren**	*First Name*	**Ian**
Grade	**A+**	*Grade*	**C**

Student No	**137-845-746**	*Student No*	**138-456-749**
Last Name	**Knowlton**	*Last Name*	**Yiu**
First Name	**Sherri**	*First Name*	**Terry**
Grade	**B**	*Grade*	**D**

8 Best Fit the column widths.
9 Preview, print, and then close the MKP245 table.
10 Close the NPC Grades2 database.

Activity 2: Modifying Field Properties

1 Bobbie Sinclair, business manager of Performance Threads, has asked you to look at the design of the Costume Inventory table and try to improve it with data restrictions and validation rules. While looking at the design you discover an error was made in assigning the Data Type for the *Date In* field.
2 Open the PT Costume Inventory2 database.
3 Open the Costume Inventory table in Design view.
4 Change the *Date In* field to a Date/Time data field.
5 Set the field size for the *Costume No* field to 5.
6 Performance Threads has a minimum daily rental fee of $80.00. Create a validation rule and validation text property that will ensure no one enters a value less than $80.00 in the *Daily Rental Fee* field.
7 To ensure no one mixes the order of the month and day when entering the *Date Out* and *Date In* fields, create an input mask for these two fields to require that the date be entered in the format *dd-mmm-yy* (for example, 12-Dec-02).
8 Since Performance Threads is open seven days a week, format the *Date Out* and *Date In* fields to display the dates in the Long Date format. This will add the day of the week to the entry and spell the month in full.
9 Save the table and then switch to Datasheet view.
10 Best Fit the columns.
11 Preview, print, and then close the Costume Inventory table.
12 Close the PT Costume Inventory2 database.

Activity 3: Creating a Table Using the Table Wizard; Establishing Relationships

1 Dana Hirsch, manager of The Waterfront Bistro, has asked you to create a new table in the Inventory database that will store supplier information. Since the Table Wizard provides a sample Suppliers table, you decide the wizard would be the most expedient method to use.
2 Open WB Inventory2.
3 Create a new table using the Table Wizard. Use the Suppliers sample table and add the following fields to the new table: *SupplierID*; *SupplierName*; *Address*; *City*; *StateOrProvince*; *PostalCode*; *PhoneNumber*; *FaxNumber*.
4 Choose the option to set the primary key yourself, select the *SupplierID* field as the primary key field, and set the type of data to *Numbers and/or letters I enter when I add new records*.
5 Accept all other default settings in the wizard dialog boxes.
6 Switch to Design view for the new table.
7 Change the field name for *SupplierID* to *Supplier Code*, change the field size to 50, and delete the entry in the Caption field property.

8 Enter the following record in the new table:

Supplier Code	**1**
SupplierName	**Danby's Bakery**
Address	**3168 Rivermist Drive**
City	**Buffalo**
StateOrProvince	**NY**
PostalCode	**14280**
PhoneNumber	**(716) 555-4987**
FaxNumber	**(716) 555-5101**

9 Best Fit the column widths.

10 Change the page orientation to landscape; print and then close the Suppliers table.

11 Display the Relationships window.

12 Create a one-to-many relationship using the *Supplier Code* field, with the Suppliers table as the primary table and the Inventory List table as the related table.

13 Save and print the relationships.

14 Close the WB Inventory2 database.

Activity 4: Creating a New Database

1 Alex Torres, manager of the Toronto office of First Choice Travel, has asked you to help the accounting staff by creating a database to track employee expense claims information. You recall that Access includes a Database Wizard that will create the database tables, forms, and reports. The Database Wizard also creates the Main Switchboard form, which you feel the accounting staff would find easier to use.

2 Create a new database file named FCT Expenses using the Expenses Database Wizard. Use all the default fields. Select a screen display and report style that the accounting staff would like. Accept all other default settings in the Database Wizard.

3 Enter the following record in the Expense Reports by Employee form:

Terry Blessing
3341 Ventura Boulevard
Los Angeles, CA 90102
President
Employee # LA-104
Social Security # 345-99-1234
Work Phone (213) 555-0962

4 Click the Expense Report Form button at the bottom of the record for Terry Blessing and then enter the following expense report data:

Exp Rpt Name	**Head Office**
Exp Rpt Descr	**Meeting in Toronto Office**
Dept Charged	**Executive Administration**
Advance	**675.00**
Paid	(click the check box)

5 Close the Expense Reports form.

6 With the Expense Reports by Employee form in the current window, click File and then Print. Click Selected Record(s) in the Print dialog box and then click OK.

7 Close the Expense Reports by Employee form.

8 Exit the database.

Activity 5: Finding Information on Deleting Relationships

1 Use the online help to find information on how to delete a relationship.
2 Print the help topic that you find.
3 Open the WE Employees2 database.
4 Display the Relationships window and then delete the one-to-one relationship between the Employee Benefits and the Employee Dates and Salaries tables.
5 Print the relationship.
6 Save and then close the Relationships window.
7 Close the WE Employees2 database.

Activity 6: Finding Information on Required Entries

1 Use the online help to find information on requiring that data be entered into a field. For example, you want to specify that a field cannot be left blank.
2 Print the help topic you find.
3 Open the WE Employees2 database.
4 Open the Employees table in Design view.
5 You want to make sure that all records in the table have an entry in the *PostalCode* field, since you will be using this table to print mailing labels. Using the information you learned in the online help, change the field property for the *PostalCode* field to ensure that the field will have data entered in it.
6 Save the table and switch to Datasheet view.
7 Add a new record to the table. Use your name and address as the *Employee* information. When you reach the *PostalCode* field, try to press Enter or Tab to move past the field without entering any data. When Access displays the error message, click OK. Enter your postal code in the *Postal Code* field.
8 Change the page orientation to landscape and then print the Employees table.
9 Close the Employees table and then close the WE Employees2 database.

Activity 7: Car Shopping on the Internet

1 After graduation, you plan to reward yourself by buying a new car. There are at least four different makes and models of cars that you like.
2 Search the Internet for the manufacturer's suggested retail price (MSRP) for the cars you would like to own, including whatever options you would order with the vehicle. *(Hint: Try searching by the manufacturers' names to locate their Web sites.)*
3 Create a new database in Access to store the information you find.
   - Click the New button on the Database toolbar, click the General tab in the New dialog box, and then double-click Database.
   - Key **New Cars** in the File name text box in the File New Database dialog box and then click Create.
4 Create a table named New Car Pricing using one of the three methods you learned in this chapter. Include the manufacturer's name, brand, model of the car, options, and MSRP. Include other fields that you might want to track, such as color choice.
5 Best Fit the column widths.
6 Preview and then print the New Car Pricing table.
7 Close the New Car Pricing table and then close the New Cars database.

Access Modifying Tables, Creating Forms, and Viewing Data

The structure of a table can be modified by moving, inserting, and deleting fields. Data in related tables can be viewed together using subdatasheets. Filtering records allows the user to view a portion of the table data that meets a specific criterion. Forms are used to view, enter, and edit data. Generally, only one record at a time is displayed in a form. Forms can be designed to resemble existing forms used by the business, making the transition to an electronic database easier for employees. In this section you will learn the skills and complete the projects listed below.

Skills

- Move a field in a table
- Insert and delete fields in a table
- Modify field properties
- Display records in a subdatasheet
- Apply and remove filters to a table
- Create a form using AutoForm
- Create a form using the Form Wizard
- Move and resize control objects
- Modify properties of controls
- Add objects using the Control Toolbox
- Use a form to enter, edit, and print data

Projects

Move, insert, and delete fields in tables and modify field properties. Display the subdatasheet for a related table. Filter records to display employees in only one department. Create and modify forms to facilitate data entry and viewing in the employees and distributor databases.

Modify the structure of the Inventory List table and display data from the Purchases table in the Inventory datasheet.

Filter records of students who achieved A+ in a course.

Create and modify a form for browsing the costume inventory.

Moving Fields

Display a table in Design view to move a field from its current location in the table to another position. For example, you may realize after entering a few records that the flow of data is more logical if the layout is changed. In a previous topic you learned how to move columns in the datasheet for sorting purposes. Although the column can be moved in the datasheet, the position of the field in the table structure will remain where it was originally created unless the field is modified in Design view.

PROJECT: After consultation with Rhonda Trask, human resources manager of Worldwide Enterprises, you have decided to move the *Annual Salary* field in the Employee Dates and Salaries table between the *Birth Date* and *Hire Date* fields, in order to coincide with existing forms used in the department.

steps

1. Open WE Employees3.
2. Open the Employee Dates and Salaries table in Design view. 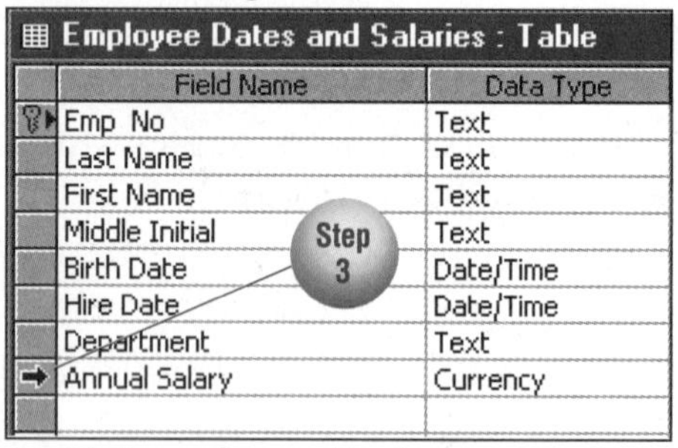
3. Move the mouse pointer in the field selector bar beside *Annual Salary* until the pointer changes to a right-pointing black arrow, and then click the left mouse button.

   This selects the *Annual Salary* field.

Employee Dates and Salaries : Table

Field Name	Data Type
Emp No	Text
Last Name	Text
First Name	Text
Middle Initial	Text
Birth Date	Date/Time
Hire Date	Date/Time
Department	Text
Annual Salary	Currency

Step 3

4. Move the mouse pointer in the field selector bar for the *Annual Salary* field until the pointer displays as a white arrow, hold down the left mouse button, drag the pointer up between the *Birth Date* and *Hire Date* fields, and then release the left mouse button.

   As you drag the mouse a black line appears between existing field names, indicating where the selected field will be repositioned when the mouse button is released.

Employee Dates and Salaries : Table

Field Name	Data Type
Emp No	Text
Last Name	Text
First Name	Text
Middle Initial	Text
Birth Date	Date/Time
Hire Date	Date/Time
Department	Text
Annual Salary	Currency

Step 4

Black line indicates new field location when mouse button is released.

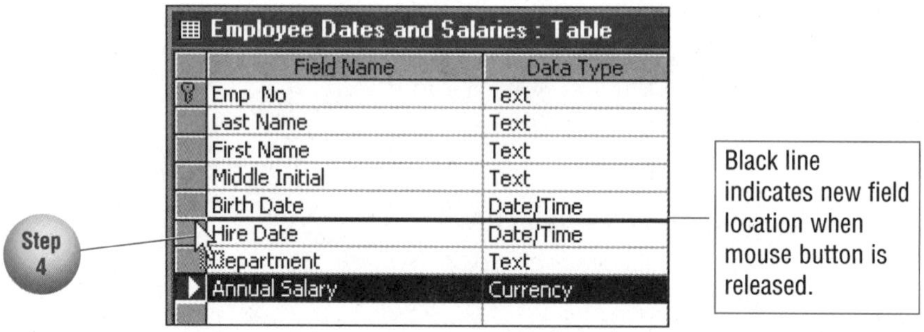

5. Click Save.
6. Move the mouse pointer in the field selector bar beside the *Department* field and then click the left mouse button to select the *Department* field.

7. Drag the *Department* field between the *Birth Date* and *Annual Salary* fields.
8. Click the Undo button on the Table Design toolbar.

   Undo restores the *Department* field to the end of the table.
9. Click Save.
10. Switch to Datasheet view and then view the records in the Employee Dates and Salaries table, as shown in Figure A3.1.

New location of Annual Salary field.

FIGURE A3.1 Employee Dates and Salaries Table

Employee Dates and Salaries : Table

Emp	Last Name	First Name	Middle Initial	Birth Date	Annual Salary	Hire Date	Department
1001	Vestering	Sam	L	2/18/57	$67,850.00	7/22/97	North American Distribution
1005	Deptulski	Roman	W	3/12/48	$67,850.00	8/15/98	Overseas Distribution
1010	Postma	Hanh	A	12/10/52	$67,850.00	1/30/98	European Distribution
1015	Besterd	Lyle	C	10/15/59	$44,651.00	5/17/97	North American Distribution
1020	Doxtator	Angela	B	5/22/63	$45,178.00	8/3/97	North American Distribution
1025	Biliski	Jorge	N	6/18/70	$43,152.00	12/1/97	North American Distribution
1030	Hicks	Thom	P	7/27/77	$41,624.00	1/22/98	Overseas Distribution
1035	Valerie	Fistouris	E	2/4/70	$43,664.00	3/15/98	European Distribution
1040	Lafreniere	Guy	F	9/14/72	$44,195.00	3/10/98	Overseas Distribution
1045	Yiu	Terry	M	6/18/61	$41,328.00	4/12/99	European Distribution
1050	Zakowski	Carl	W	5/9/67	$43,698.00	2/9/98	European Distribution
1055	Thurston	Edward	S	1/3/60	$41,498.00	6/22/99	Overseas Distribution
1060	McKnight	Donald	Z	1/6/64	$41,854.00	6/22/98	European Distribution
1065	Liszniewski	Norm	M	11/16/70	$42,659.00	2/6/99	North American Distribution
1070	Jhawar	Balfor	R	9/3/73	$43,661.00	11/22/99	Overseas Distribution
1075	Fitchett	Mike	L	4/18/66	$41,857.00	3/19/98	Overseas Distribution
1080	Couture	Leo	S	1/8/78	$42,185.00	1/17/99	European Distribution
					$0.00		

11. Close the Employee Dates and Salaries table.

Take 2

Using Undo in Access

The Undo button in Microsoft Access does not contain a down-pointing triangle to the right of the button, as does the Undo button in other Office applications that allow multiple preceding operations to be undone. Since Microsoft Access saves to the database as each record is entered or edited, Undo only works in limited situations.

DIRECTOR'S CUT

Move a Field

1. Open table in Design view.
2. Select field to be moved.
3. Drag field to the new location.
4. Save and close the table.

Inserting and Deleting Fields

Fields can be added to or deleted from the table after the table has been created. Exercise caution when making changes to the table structure after records have been entered. Data in deleted fields will be lost and existing records will have null values in new fields that have been added.

PROJECT: Rhonda Trask has suggested that the *Last Name, First Name,* and *Middle Initial* fields in the Employee Dates and Salaries table contain redundant information, since the table is related to the Employees table where this information already exists. You will delete these three fields and add a new field for the employee performance review date.

steps

1. With WE Employees3 open, open the Employee Dates and Salaries table in Design view.
2. Click the insertion point in any text in the *Last Name* row.
3. Click the Delete Rows button on the Table Design toolbar.

   You can also click Edit and then Delete Rows if you prefer to use the Menu bar.

4. Click Yes at the Microsoft Access message asking you to confirm that you want to permanently delete the selected field(s) and all the data in the field(s).

   Multiple fields can be deleted in one operation. In the next step you will select both the *First Name* and *Middle Initial* fields, and in step 6 you will delete both fields at the same time.

5. Position the mouse pointer to the left of the *First Name* field in the field selector bar until the pointer changes to a right-pointing black arrow, hold down the left mouse button, and then drag the pointer down until both the *First Name* and *Middle Initial* fields are selected.
6. Click the Delete Rows button on the Table Design toolbar.
7. Click Yes at the Microsoft Access message.

Step 3

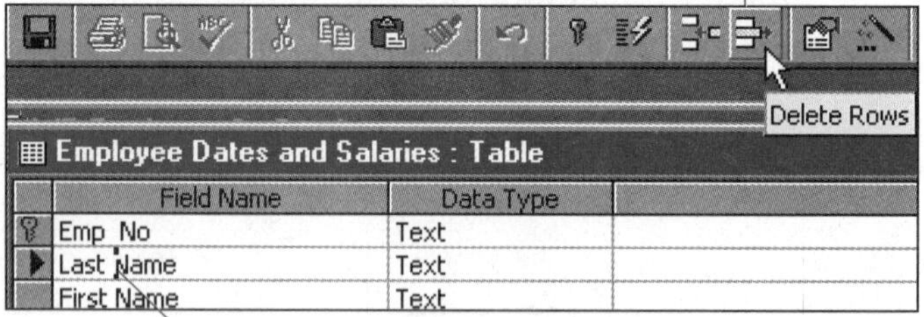

Delete Rows

Employee Dates and Salaries : Table

Field Name	Data Type
Emp No	Text
Last Name	Text
First Name	Text

Step 2

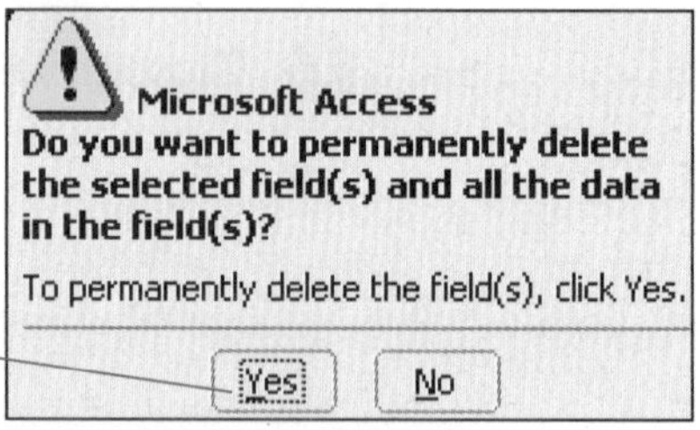

Microsoft Access

Do you want to permanently delete the selected field(s) and all the data in the field(s)?

To permanently delete the field(s), click Yes.

Yes No

Step 4

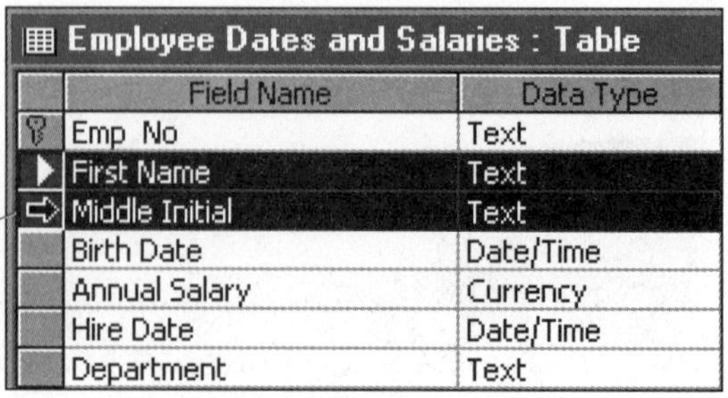

Employee Dates and Salaries : Table

Field Name	Data Type
Emp No	Text
First Name	Text
Middle Initial	Text
Birth Date	Date/Time
Annual Salary	Currency
Hire Date	Date/Time
Department	Text

Step 5

8. Click the insertion point in any text in the *Department* field row.

   New rows are inserted *above* the active field.

9. Click the Insert Rows button on the Table Design toolbar.

   You can also click Insert and then Rows if you prefer to use the Menu bar. The new row is positioned between the *Hire Date* and *Department* fields.

Employee Dates and Salaries : Table

	Field Name	Data Type
🔑	Emp No	Text
	Birth Date	
	Annual Salary	
	Hire Date	
▶		
	Department	Text

New row is inserted between the *Hire Date* and *Department* fields.

10. Key **Performance Review Date** in the *Field Name* column, and then change the data type to Date/Time.

11. Click Save.

12. Switch to Datasheet view and then view the records in the Employee Dates and Salaries table.

13. Best Fit the *Performance Review Date* column.

Employee Dates and Salaries : Table

Emp	Birth Date	Annual Salary	Hire Date	Performance Review Date	Department
1001	2/18/57	$67,850.00	7/22/97		North American Distribution
1005	3/12/48	$67,850.00	8/15/98		Overseas Distribution
1010	12/10/52	$67,850.00	1/30/98		European Distribution
1015	10/15/59	$44,651.00	5/17/97		North American Distribution
1020	5/22/63	$45,178.00	8/3/97		North American Distribution
1025	6/18/70	$43,152.00	12/1/97		North American Distribution
1030	7/27/77	$41,624.00	1/22/98		Overseas Distribution
1035	2/4/70	$43,664.00	3/15/98		European Distribution
1040	9/14/72	$44,195.00	3/10/98		Overseas Distribution
1045	6/18/61	$41,328.00	4/12/99		European Distribution
1050	5/9/67	$43,698.00	2/9/98		European Distribution
1055	1/3/60	$41,498.00	6/22/99		Overseas Distribution
1060	1/6/64	$41,854.00	6/22/98		European Distribution
1065	11/16/70	$42,659.00	2/6/99		North American Distribution
1070	9/3/73	$43,661.00	11/22/99		Overseas Distribution
1075	4/18/66	$41,857.00	3/19/98		Overseas Distribution
1080	1/8/78	$42,185.00	1/17/99		European Distribution
		$0.00			

Step 13

14. Save, print, and then close the Employee Dates and Salaries table. Click Yes when prompted to save changes to the layout of the table.

Take 2

Adding Data in a New Field

Consider the following tips for entering data in the datasheet for a new field that has been inserted into a table after several records have already been created:

- Click in the new column (e.g., *Performance Review Date)* in the first row of the table, key the data for the new field, and then press the down arrow key to remain in the same column for the next record.
- Press Ctrl + ' (apostrophe) if the data for the current record is the same field value as the data field immediately above the current record. Microsoft Access will automatically duplicate the entry that is above the active field.

DIRECTOR'S CUT

Delete a Field
1. Open table in Design view.
2. Select field to be deleted.
3. Click Delete Rows button on Table Design toolbar.
4. Click Yes.
5. Click Save.

Insert a Field
1. Open table in Design view.
2. Click in field row immediately below where new field is to be located.
3. Click Insert Rows button on Table Design toolbar.
4. Key field name and assign data type.
5. Click Save.

Modifying Field Properties

In the *Creating Tables and Relationships* section you learned how to add entries to field properties by creating an input mask, changing the date format, changing the field size, entering a default value, and creating Lookup field properties. To add or edit entries to a field property after the table has been created, open the table in Design view, add or edit the property as required, and then save the table.

PROJECT: You will add an entry to the Format field property for the *FirstName, MiddleName, LastName,* and *StateOrProvince* field rows in the Employees table to convert the existing data to uppercase letters.

steps

1. With WE Employees3 open, open the Employees table in Design view.
2. Click the insertion point in any text in the *FirstName* field row to select the field.
3. Click in the Format field property.
4. Key >.

   The *greater than* symbol in the Format field property for a Text field instructs Access to convert all data in the field to uppercase. New data will be converted to uppercase letters regardless of how it is keyed in the field when a new record is added to the table.

Employees : Table

Field Name	Data Type
Emp No	Text
FirstName	Text
MiddleName	Text
LastName	Text
Address	Text
City	Text
StateOrProvince	Text
PostalCode	Text

General | Lookup

Field Size	50
Format	>
Input Mask	

Step 2

Step 4

The *greater than* symbol (>) is located in the uppercase position on the period key in the alphabetic section of the keyboard. Hold down the Shift key and type period (.).

5. Click the insertion point in any text in the *MiddleName* field row.
6. Click in the Format field property and then key >.
7. Repeat steps similar to those in 5 and 6 to add the uppercase symbol to the Format field property for the *LastName* and *StateOrProvince* fields.
8. Click Save.

9 Switch to Datasheet view and then view the records in the Employees table.

The existing data in the *First Name, Middle Name, Last Name,* and *State/Province* columns has been converted to uppercase, as shown in Figure A3.2.

FIGURE A3.2 Data Converted to Uppercase

Emp No	First Name	Middle Name	Last Name	Address	City	State/Province	Postal Code
1001	SAM	LAWRENCE	VESTERING	287-1501 Broadway	New York	NY	10110-
1005	ROMAN	WILLIAM	DEPTULSKI	112-657 E 39th St.	New York	NY	10111-
1010	HANH	ASTER	POSTMA	259 Lexington Avenu	New York	NY	10110-
1015	LYLE	CAMERON	BESTERD	1258 Park Avenue	New York	NY	10110-
1020	ANGELA	BONNIE	DOXTATOR	201-654 W 50th St.	New York	NY	10110-
1025	JORGE	NAIRN	BILISKI	439 7th Avenue	New York	NY	10111-
1030	THOM	PETER	HICKS	329-5673 W 63rd St.	New York	NY	10111-
1035	VALERIE	ELIZABETH	FISTOURIS	210 York Avenue	New York	NY	10111-
1040	GUY	FALLON	LAFRENIERE	329-8745 E 41st St.	New York	NY	10110-
1045	TERRY	MICHAEL	YIU	398-90 Little Brazil S	New York	NY	10110-
1050	CARL	WAYLON	ZAKOWSKI	65 Dyer Avenue	New York	NY	10110-
1055	EDWARD	SAMUEL	THURSTON	900-321 10th Avenue	New York	NY	10110-
1060	DONALD	ZAVIER	MCKNIGHT	43-874 Beekman Pla	New York	NY	10111-
1065	NORM	MATTHEW	LISZNIEWSKI	78-824 Madison Ave	New York	NY	10111-
1070	BALFOR	RICHARD	JHAWAR	54-908 WcHandys P	New York	NY	10111-
1075	MIKE	LYLE	FITCHETT	329-1009 W 23rd St.	New York	NY	10111-
1080	LEO	SAUNDERS	COUTURE	908-1200 W 46th St.	New York	NY	10110-

10 Add the following new record to the table. Key the data exactly as shown below. Access will automatically convert the name and state data to uppercase.

Emp No.	**1085**
First Name	**Cassandra**
Middle Name	**Rose**
Last Name	**Gauthier**
Address	**18-3142 Center Drive**
City	**New York**
State/Province	**ny**
Postal Code	**10111**

Emp No	First Name	Middle Name	Last Name
1001	SAM	LAWRENCE	VESTERING
1005	ROMAN	WILLIAM	DEPTULSKI
1010	HANH	ASTER	POSTMA
1015	LYLE	CAMERON	BESTERD
1020	ANGELA	BONNIE	DOXTATOR
1025	JORGE	NAIRN	BILISKI
1030	THOM	PETER	HICKS
1035	VALERIE	ELIZABETH	FISTOURIS
1040	GUY	FALLON	LAFRENIERE
1045	TERRY	MICHAEL	YIU
1050	CARL	WAYLON	ZAKOWSKI
1055	EDWARD	SAMUEL	THURSTON
1060	DONALD	ZAVIER	MCKNIGHT
1065	NORM	MATTHEW	LISZNIEWSKI
1070	BALFOR	RICHARD	JHAWAR
1075	MIKE	LYLE	FITCHETT
1080	LEO	SAUNDERS	COUTURE
1085	CASSANDRA	ROSE	Gauthier

When you press Enter or Tab to move to the next field, Access converts the data to uppercase.

11 Best Fit the *Address* column.

12 Change the page orientation to landscape and then print the table.

13 Save and then close the Employees table.

Take 2

Caption Field Property

An entry in the Caption field property becomes the column heading for the field in the table in Datasheet view. If no entry exists in the Caption property, the field name is used as the column heading. The Caption property can contain up to 2,048 characters. Use the Caption property to enter a user-friendly label for a field if the field name has been abbreviated, does not include spaces between words, or is otherwise unsuitable as a column heading.

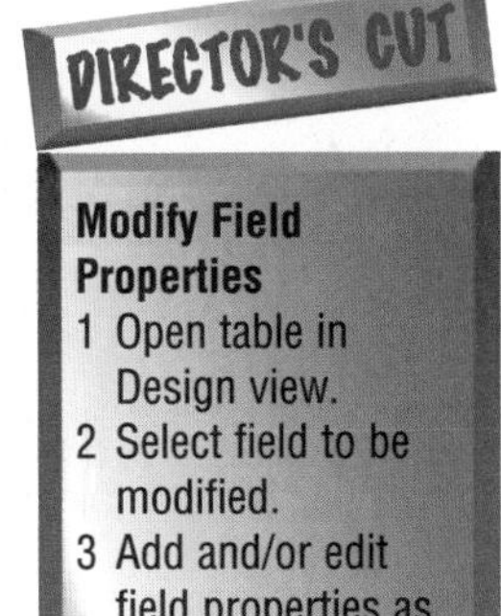

Use the Caption property to enter a label for the field that is different from the field name.

DIRECTOR'S CUT

Modify Field Properties

1. Open table in Design view.
2. Select field to be modified.
3. Add and/or edit field properties as required.
4. Click Save.

Displaying Records in a Subdatasheet

When two tables are joined by establishing a relationship, you can view the two tables at the same time by displaying the subdatasheet. To do this, open the primary table in Datasheet view. A column between the record selector bar and the first field in each row displays a plus symbol (+). Click the plus symbol (referred to as the *expand indicator*) next to the record for which you want to view the data in the related table. A subdatasheet will appear within the primary datasheet. To remove the subdatasheet, click the minus symbol (-) to collapse it (the plus symbol changes to a minus symbol after the record has been expanded).

PROJECT: The Employees table is joined to the Employee Expenses table in a one-to-many relationship. You will open the Employees table in Datasheet view, expand records to display expenses for an employee, print the table, display the subdatasheets for several other employees, and then close the subdatasheets.

steps

1. With WE Employees3 open, open the Employees table in Datasheet view.
2. Click the plus symbol (expand indicator) between the record selector bar and 1001 in the first row in the datasheet.

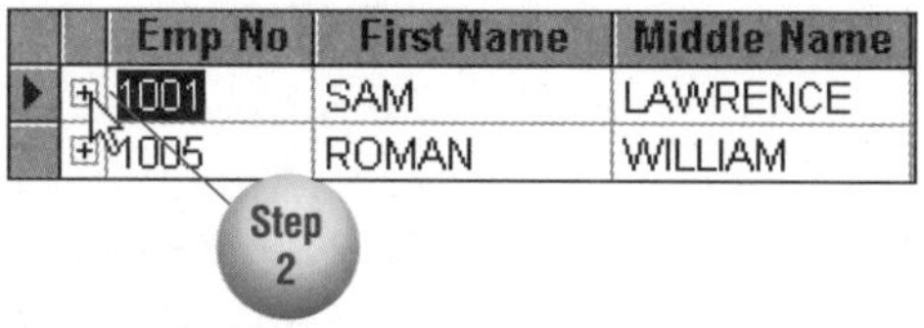

Emp No	First Name	Middle Name
1001	SAM	LAWRENCE
1005	ROMAN	WILLIAM

Step 2

The subdatasheet (see Figure A3.3) opens to display the records for the same employee (Sam Vestering) in the related table (Employee Expenses).

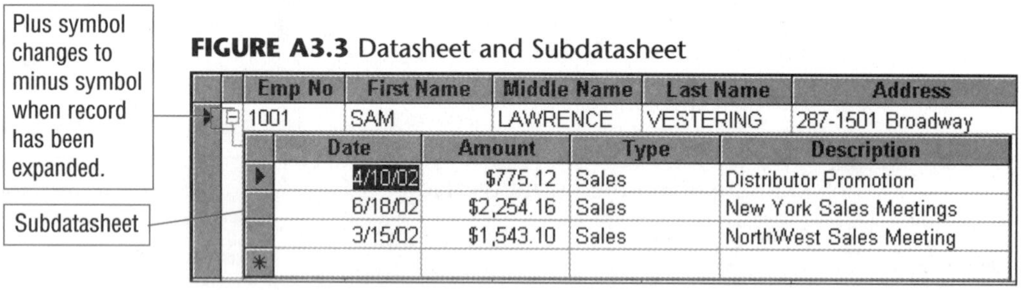

FIGURE A3.3 Datasheet and Subdatasheet

Plus symbol changes to minus symbol when record has been expanded.

Subdatasheet

Emp No	First Name	Middle Name	Last Name	Address
1001	SAM	LAWRENCE	VESTERING	287-1501 Broadway

Date	Amount	Type	Description
4/10/02	$775.12	Sales	Distributor Promotion
6/18/02	$2,254.16	Sales	New York Sales Meetings
3/15/02	$1,543.10	Sales	NorthWest Sales Meeting

3. Click in the blank row at the bottom of the subdatasheet and then key the following record:

Date **6/27/02**
Amount **955.67**
Type **Professional Development**
Description **E-Commerce Conference**

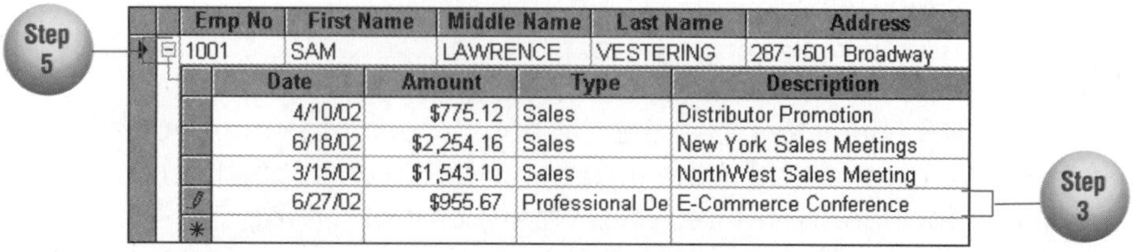

Step 5

Emp No	First Name	Middle Name	Last Name	Address
1001	SAM	LAWRENCE	VESTERING	287-1501 Broadway

Date	Amount	Type	Description
4/10/02	$775.12	Sales	Distributor Promotion
6/18/02	$2,254.16	Sales	New York Sales Meetings
3/15/02	$1,543.10	Sales	NorthWest Sales Meeting
6/27/02	$955.67	Professional De	E-Commerce Conference

Step 3

4. Change the page orientation to landscape and then print the datasheet.

   Both the datasheet and the subdatasheet will print.

5. Click the minus symbol (collapse indicator) between the record selector bar and 1001 in the first row in the datasheet.

   The subdatasheet closes.

6. Display the subdatasheet for employee number 1005.
7. Display the subdatasheet for employee number 1010.
8. Display the subdatasheet for employee number 1015.
9. Click Format, point to Subdatasheet, and then click Collapse All at the Subdatasheet menu.

   All open subdatasheets close. The Subdatasheet menu also contains an option to display all subdatasheets (Expand All).

10. Close the Employees table.

Step 9

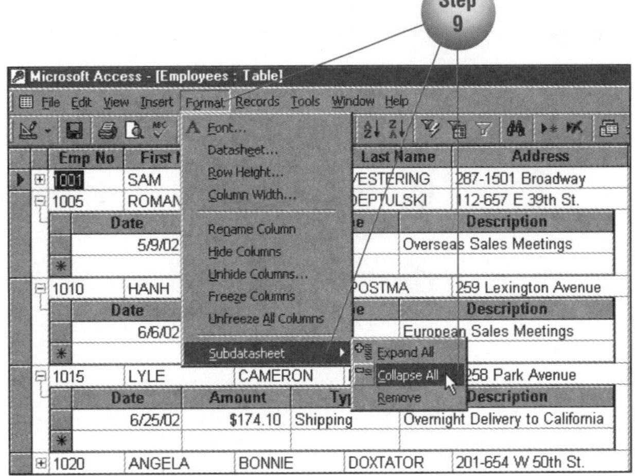

Printing a Selected Subdatasheet

To print only the active record and its related subdatasheet, click File and then Print. Click Selected Record(s) in the Print Range section of the Print dialog box and then click OK.

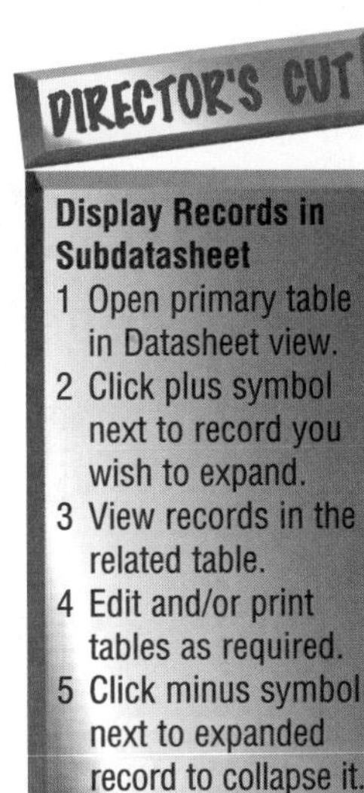
DIRECTOR'S CUT

Display Records in Subdatasheet

1. Open primary table in Datasheet view.
2. Click plus symbol next to record you wish to expand.
3. View records in the related table.
4. Edit and/or print tables as required.
5. Click minus symbol next to expanded record to collapse it.

Applying and Removing Filters

A *filter* is used to view only those records in a datasheet that meet specified criteria. For example, you might want to view only records of employees who work in a specific department. Once the filter has been applied, you can view, edit, and print the filtered records. The records that do not meet the criteria are temporarily removed from the datasheet. Click the Remove Filter button on the Table Datasheet toolbar to redisplay all records in the table. Records can be filtered using two methods—Filter By Selection and Filter By Form.

PROJECT: You will use the Filter By Selection method in the Employee Dates and Salaries table to display and print records of employees who work in the European Distribution department. In the Employee Benefits table you will use the Filter By Form method to print a list of employees who receive four weeks of vacation.

steps

1. With WE Employees3 open, open the Employee Dates and Salaries table in Datasheet view.
2. Select the text *European Distribution* in the *Department* column in the third row of the datasheet.
3. Click the Filter By Selection button on the Table Datasheet toolbar.

   Only records of employees in the European Distribution department are displayed, as shown in Figure A3.4.

Department
North American Distribution
Overseas Distribution
European Distribution
North American Distribution
North American Distribution
North American Distribution

Step 2

If the Table Datasheet toolbar is not visible, click View, point to Toolbars, and then click Table Datasheet.

FIGURE A3.4 Filtered Datasheet

Emp	Birth Date	Annual Salary	Hire Date	Performance Review Date	Department
1035	2/4/70	$43,664.00	3/15/98		European Distribution
1010	12/10/52	$67,850.00	1/30/98		European Distribution
1045	6/18/61	$41,328.00	4/12/99		European Distribution
1050	5/9/67	$43,698.00	2/9/98		European Distribution
1060	1/6/64	$41,854.00	6/22/98		European Distribution
1080	1/8/78	$42,185.00	1/17/99		European Distribution
		$0.00			

4. Change the page orientation to landscape and then print the table.
5. Click the Remove Filter button on the Table Datasheet toolbar.

   All records in the table are redisplayed.
6. Close the Employee Dates and Salaries table. Click No if prompted to save changes.

7. Open the Employee Benefits table in Datasheet view.
8. Click the Filter By Form button on the Table Datasheet toolbar.

   All records are temporarily removed from the datasheet and a blank row appears. Specify the field and the field value you want to filter by using the fields in the blank row.
9. Click in the *Vacation* column, click the down-pointing triangle that appears, and then click *4 weeks* in the drop-down list.

Step 9

Blank row displays when you click Filter By Form.

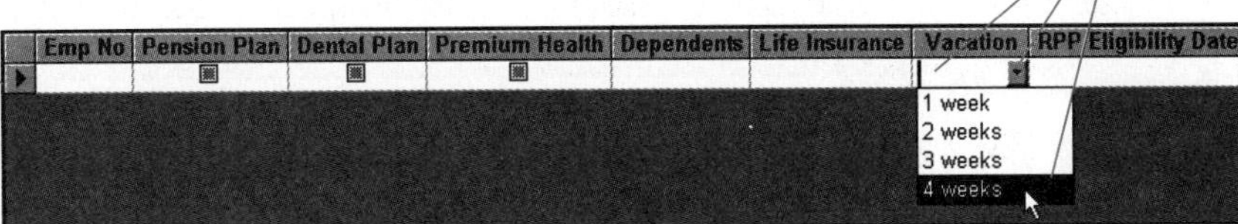

10. Click the Apply Filter button on the Table Datasheet toolbar.

    The Apply Filter button changes to the Remove Filter button once a filter has been applied to a table.
11. Change the page orientation to landscape and then print the table.
12. Click the Remove Filter button on the Table Datasheet toolbar.
13. Close the Employee Benefits table. Click No if prompted to save changes.

Take 2

Filtering By Two Criteria

Use this tab to filter by more than one criterion.

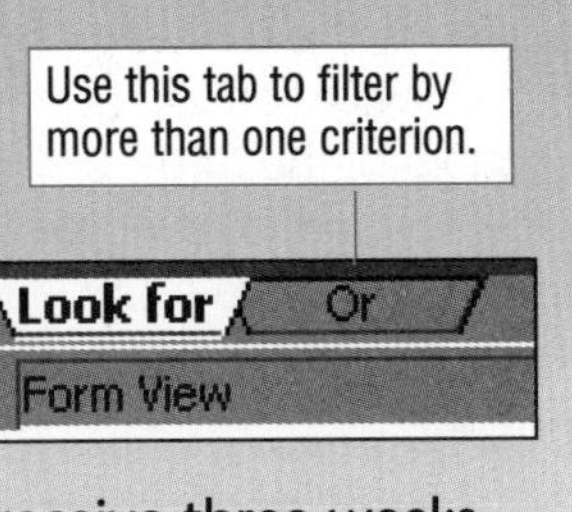

The Filter By Form window contains a tab labeled *Or* at the bottom of the window, just above the Status bar. Use this tab to filter by more than one criterion. For example, you could display records of employees who receive three weeks or four weeks of vacation. To do this, click the Filter By Form button and select *3 weeks* in the *Vacation* field, then click the Or tab and select *4 weeks* in the *Vacation* field in the second form. Click the Apply Filter button. Records that meet either the 3 weeks or 4 weeks criterion will be displayed.

DIRECTOR'S CUT

Filter By Selection
1. Open table in Datasheet view.
2. Select field value in the field you want to filter by.
3. Click Filter By Selection.
4. View, print, and/or edit data as required.
5. Click Remove Filter.

Filter By Form
1. Open table in Datasheet view.
2. Click Filter By Form.
3. Click in field you want to filter by.
4. Click down-pointing triangle and click value you want to filter by.
5. Click Apply Filter.
6. View, print, and/or edit data as required.
7. Click Remove Filter.

Creating a Form Using AutoForm

A form provides a better alternative than a datasheet to view, enter, and edit records. With a form, only one record is displayed at a time. The fields can be arranged so that all fields are visible in one screen. If tables are related in the database, the related tables can be displayed in subforms in the primary form so that all the tables can be updated at the same time. This alleviates the need to open each table individually and enter records. A form created with AutoForm inserts all of the fields in the specified table in columnar, tabular, or datasheet format.

PROJECT: You will use AutoForm to create a columnar form for the Employees table.

steps

1. With WE Employees3 open, click *Forms* in the Objects bar.

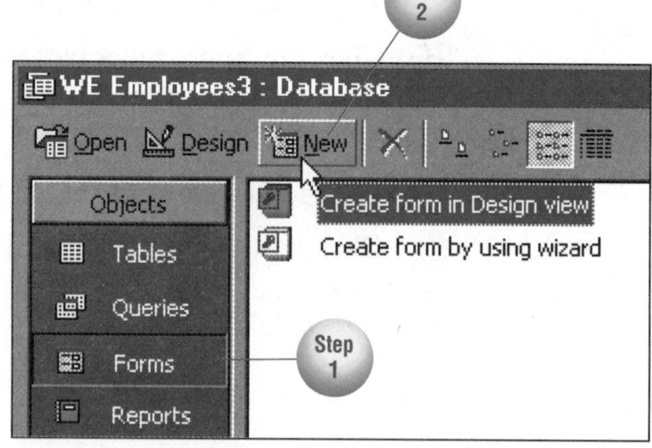

2. Click the New button on the Database window toolbar.
3. Click *AutoForm: Columnar* in the New Form list box.
4. Click the down-pointing triangle next to the Choose the table or query where the object's data comes from text box, click *Employees* in the drop-down list, and then click OK.

   In a few seconds the Employees form appears, with the data from the first record in the table displayed in the form. A Record Navigation bar at the bottom of the form window is used to navigate through the records in the table, as shown in Figure A3.5.

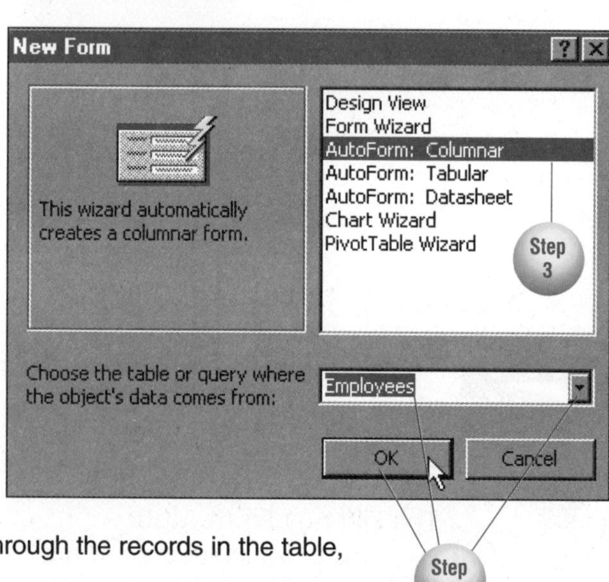

FIGURE A3.5 Columnar Employees Form

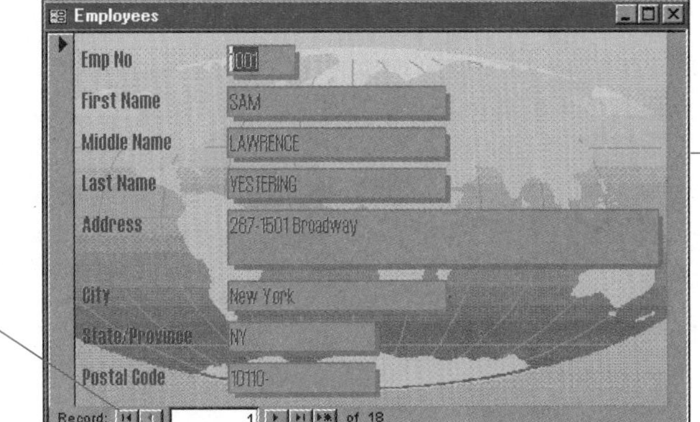

Your form background and/or colors may vary.

Record Navigation Bar

5. Click the Next Record button on the Record Navigation bar to display record 2 in the form.
6. Click the LastRecord button on the Record Navigation bar to display record 18 in the form.
7. Click the FirstRecord button on the Record Navigation bar to display record 1 in the form.
8. Print only the first record of the table. To do this, click File and then Print. Click Selected Record(s) in the Print Range section of the Print dialog box and then click OK.
9. Click the Close button at the right edge of the Employees form title bar.
10. Click Yes to save changes to the design of the form.
11. Click OK in the Save As dialog box to accept the default form name *Employees*.

FIGURE A3.6 Tabular Employees Form

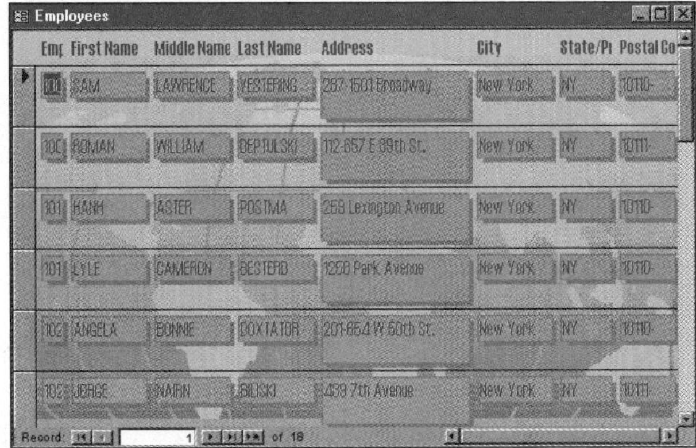

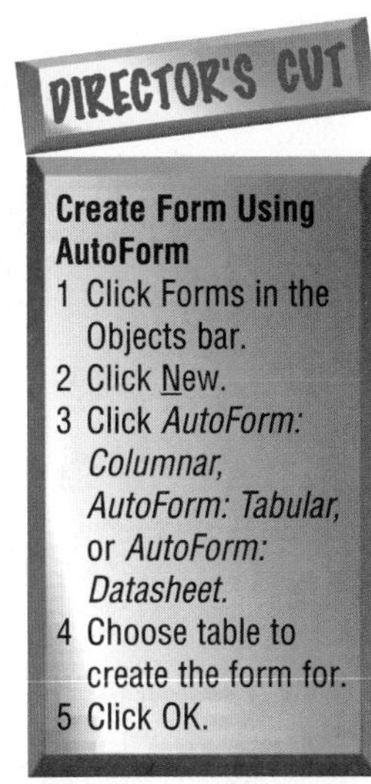

Take 2

Tabular AutoForm

A tabular form displays one record below the other in a manner similar to a datasheet. The form displayed in Figure A3.6 was created by selecting *AutoForm: Tabular* and *Employees* in the New Form dialog box.

Using the Form Wizard

The Form Wizard provides more choices for form design than AutoForm. In the Form Wizard the user is guided through a series of dialog boxes to generate the form, including selecting the table and fields that will be used to make up the form; choosing a layout for the fields; selecting the form style from various colors and backgrounds; and entering a title for the form.

PROJECT: You will create a form for the Employee Dates and Salaries table and another form for the Employee Benefits table using the Form Wizard.

steps

1. With WE Employees3 open and *Forms* still selected in the Objects bar, double-click *Create form by using wizard.*
2. Click the down-pointing triangle next to Tables/Queries in the first Form Wizard dialog box and then click *Table: Employee Dates and Salaries* in the drop-down list.

   The list of fields in the Available Fields list box changes to the field names for the Employee Dates and Salaries table. In the next step you will choose which fields to include in the form.

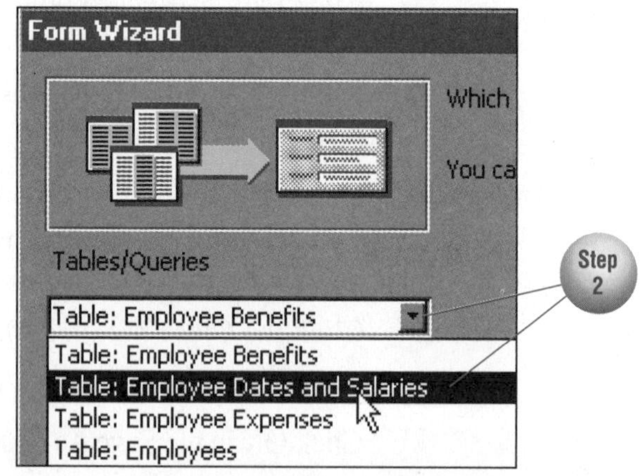

3. Click the Add All Fields button >> to move all of the fields in the Available Fields list box to the Selected Fields list box, and then click Next.

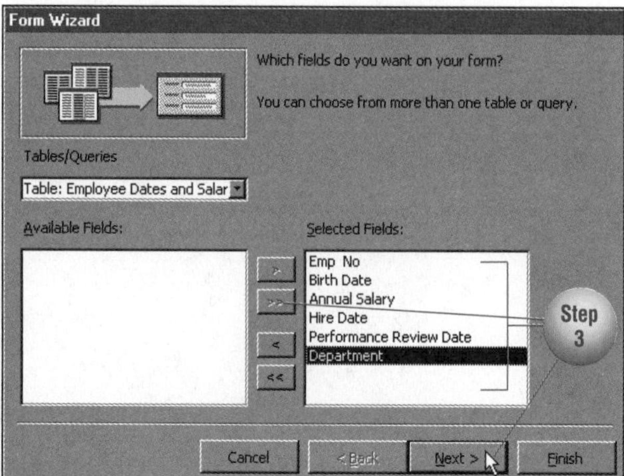

4. Click Tabular in the second Form Wizard dialog box to view the tabular layout in the preview window.
5. Click Datasheet to preview the datasheet layout.
6. Click Justified to preview the justified layout.

7 Click Columnar and then click Next.

8 Click each of the styles in the list box in the third Form Wizard dialog box to preview each style's colors and backgrounds in the preview window.

9 Click Blends and then click Next.

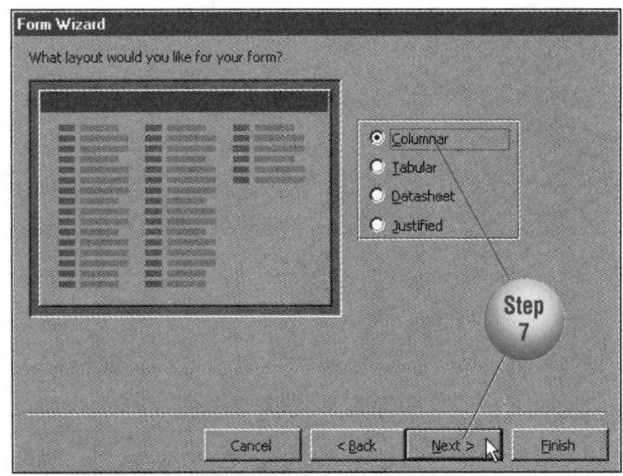

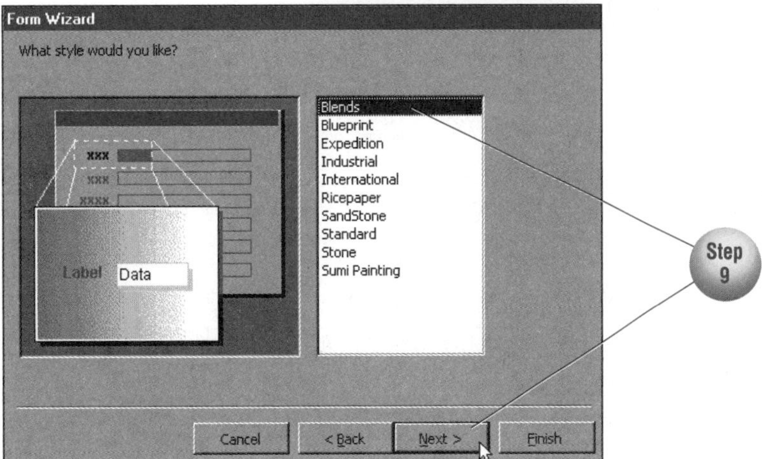

10 Click Finish at the last Form Wizard dialog box to accept the default title of *Employee Dates and Salaries* and the default choice to *Open the form to view or enter information.*

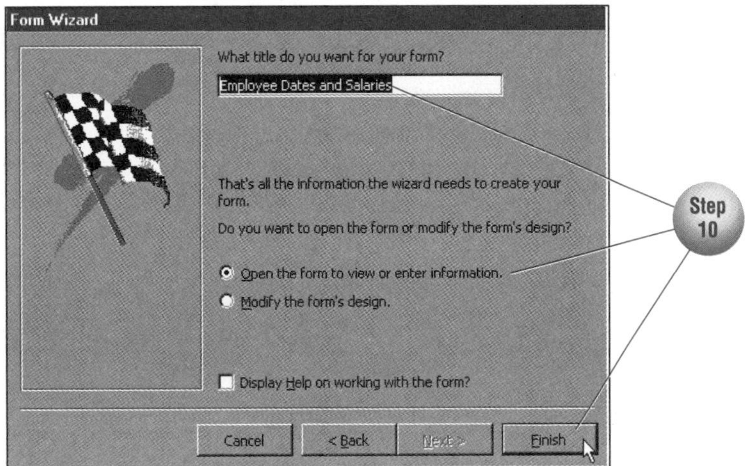

(continued)

In a few seconds the Employee Dates and Salaries form appears as shown in Figure A3.7.

FIGURE A3.7 Employee Dates and Salaries Form

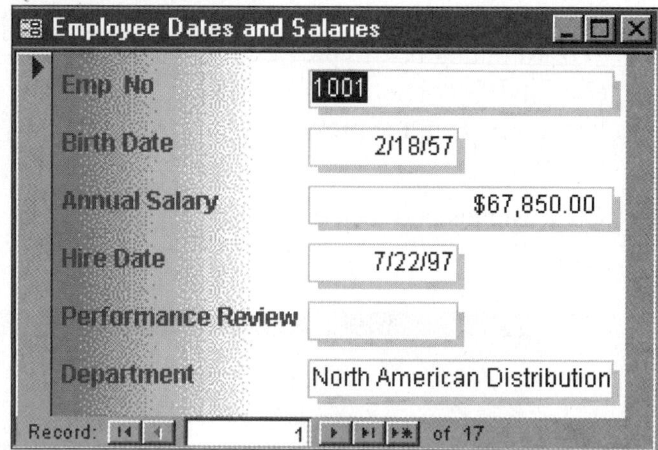

11 Click the Next Record button to display record 2 in the form.

12 Continue clicking the Next Record button until you have viewed all of the records in the form.

13 Close the Employee Dates and Salaries form.

14 Double-click *Create form by using wizard.*

15 Create a new form for the Employee Benefits table using the following specifications:

- Add all of the fields in the Employee Benefits table to the form.
- Choose the columnar layout.
- Choose the Sumi Painting style.
- Accept the default title and open the form to view information.

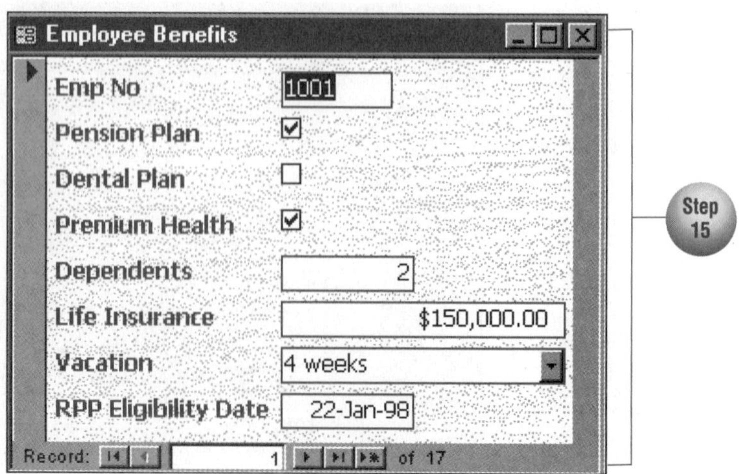

16 Scroll through all of the records in the Employee Benefits form.

17 Close the Employee Benefits form.

FIGURE A3.8 Form in Design View

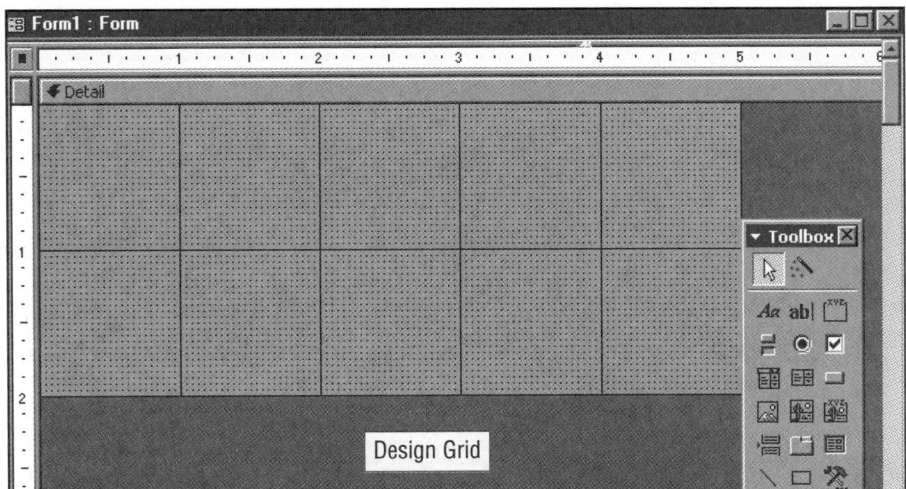

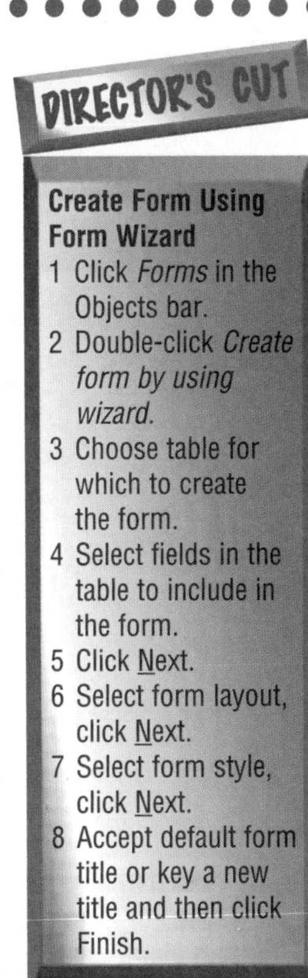

DIRECTOR'S CUT

Create Form Using Form Wizard

1 Click *Forms* in the Objects bar.
2 Double-click *Create form by using wizard.*
3 Choose table for which to create the form.
4 Select fields in the table to include in the form.
5 Click Next.
6 Select form layout, click Next.
7 Select form style, click Next.
8 Accept default form title or key a new title and then click Finish.

Take 2

Creating a Form in Design View

A third method that can be used to create a form is by using Design view. In Design view a form is created from scratch, using the buttons in the Toolbox to add control objects to the form, as shown in Figure A3.8. The form layout includes gridlines and horizontal and vertical rulers to assist with placement of the control objects. Refer to pages 82–87 for information on adding controls to and modifying controls in a form.

Modifying Controls in a Form

Once a form has been created using AutoForm or the Form Wizard, the form can be modified by opening it in Design view. A form is comprised of a series of objects referred to as *controls*. A form created with the Form Wizard contains a label control and a text box control for each field included from the specified table. The label control contains the field name and is used to describe the data that will be entered or viewed in the adjacent text box control. The text box control is the field placeholder where data is entered or edited. The controls can be moved, resized, or deleted from the form.

PROJECT: Some of the controls in the Employee Dates and Salaries form are wider than necessary for the data that will be entered or viewed. You will open the form in Design view, resize these controls, and modify the format properties.

steps

1. With WE Employees3 open and *Forms* still selected in the Objects bar, right-click Employee Dates and Salaries and then click Design View at the shortcut menu.

   A form contains three sections, as shown in Figure A3.9: Form Header, Detail, and Form Footer. The control objects for the fields in the table are displayed in the Detail section.

   FIGURE A3.9 Employee Dates and Salaries Form Design View

   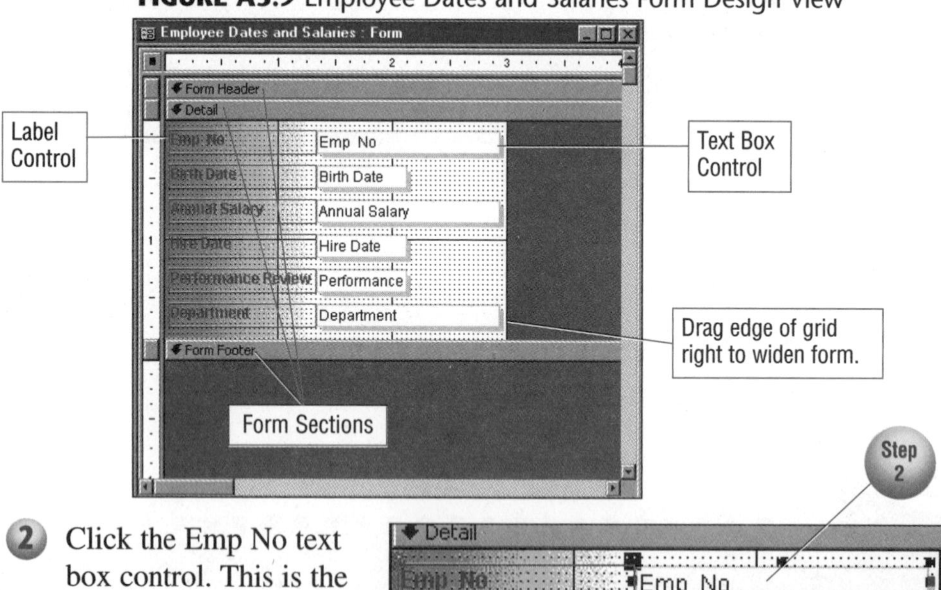

2. Click the Emp No text box control. This is the control object with the white background and yellow shadowed border, containing the text *Emp No*. Eight sizing handles display around the object.

   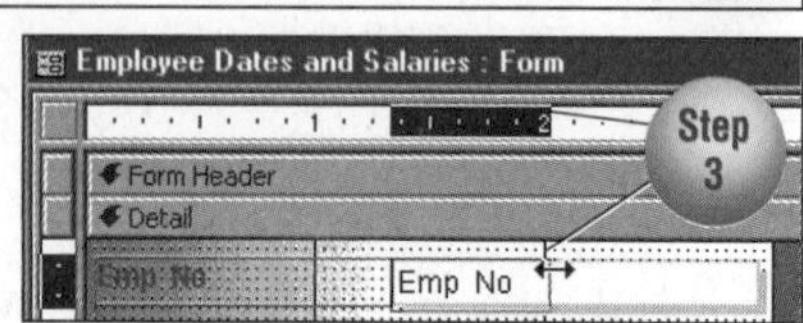

3. Position the mouse pointer on the middle sizing handle at the right edge of the control object until the pointer changes to a left- and right-pointing double arrow, hold down the left mouse button, drag left until the right border is at position 2 in the horizontal ruler, and then release the left mouse button.

4. Resize the Annual Salary text box control to position 2.5 in the horizontal ruler.
5. Click Edit and then Select All.

   All of the controls in the form are selected. You can also use the Shift key and click control objects to select multiple controls.
6. Click the Properties button on the Form Design toolbar.

   This opens the Multiple selection property sheet for the selected controls. Each control object in the form contains a property sheet that can be opened to change formats for the control, such as font, font size, color, and so on.
7. If necessary, click the Format tab in the Multiple selection property sheet.
8. Scroll down the property sheet, click in the Font Name property, click the down-pointing triangle that appears, scroll down the font list, and then click *Times New Roman* in the drop-down list.

Changes made to the property sheet will affect all selected objects.

9. Click in the Font Size property, click the down-pointing triangle that appears, and then click *10* in the drop-down list.
10. Close the Multiple selection property sheet.
11. Click Save.
12. Click the View button on the Form Design toolbar to switch to Form view.
13. Scroll through the records in the form.
14. Close the Employee Dates and Salaries form.

Take 2

Deleting and Moving Control Objects

A selected control object can be deleted from the form by pressing the Delete key. To move a selected object, position the mouse pointer on the border of the selected control object until the pointer changes to a hand. Hold down the left mouse button, drag the control to the desired location, and then release the mouse button. To move a text box control separately from its corresponding label control, drag the large black handle that appears in the top left corner of the control object.

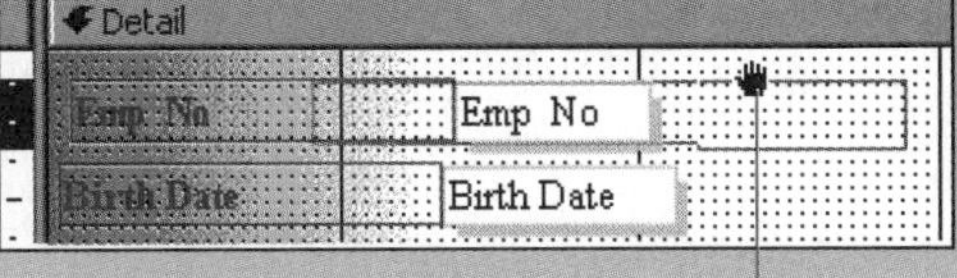

Move a control by dragging the border of the selected control. The label and text box control move simultaneously.

Adding Controls to a Form

The Toolbox that displays when the form is opened in Design view contains a palette of control object buttons that are used to add controls to a form. To add a control to a form, click the control object button in the Toolbox for the type of control you want to add, and then drag the outline of the object in the design grid the approximate height and width you want the control to be. Depending on the control object created, key the text or expression for the object and modify properties as required.

PROJECT: You will add label control objects that add descriptive text to the Employee Dates and Salaries form in the form header and form footer sections.

steps

1. With WE Employees3 open and *Forms* still selected in the Objects bar, open the Employee Dates and Salaries form in Design view.

2. Position the mouse pointer at the top of the gray Detail border line until the pointer changes to a black horizontal line with an up- and down-pointing arrow, hold down the left mouse button, drag the pointer down approximately 1 inch, and then release the mouse button.

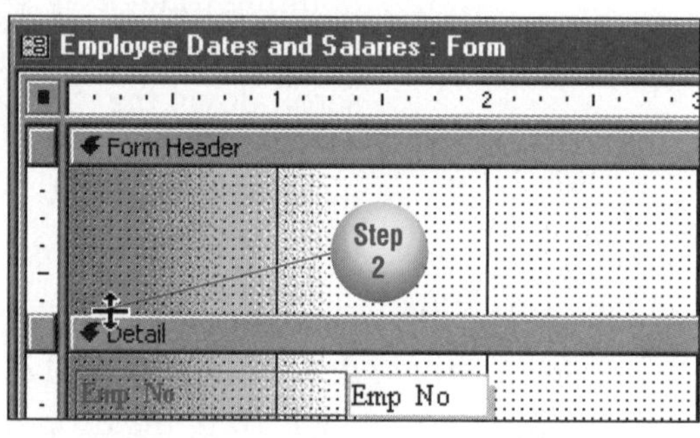

If the Form Header and Form Footer section headings do not display in the form, right-click the Employee Dates and Salaries Form Title bar and then click Form Header/Footer at the shortcut menu.

3. Click the Label object button in the Toolbox.

The Toolbox palette is not visible? Click the Toolbox button in the Form Design toolbar.

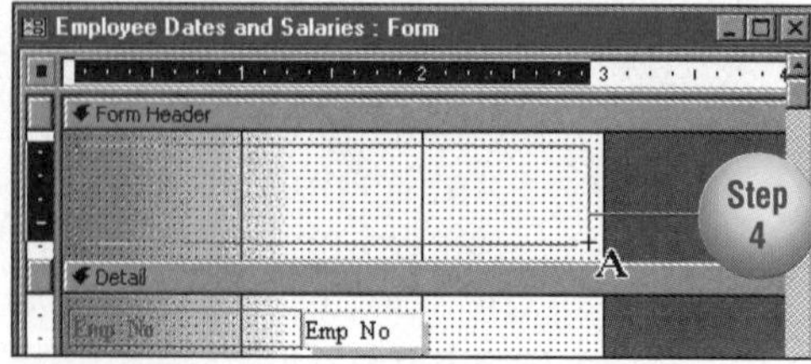

4. Position the crosshairs pointer with the label icon attached to it at the top left edge of the Form Header section, drag the mouse down to the approximate height and width shown at the right, and then release the mouse button.

   A label box will appear with the insertion point at the top left edge of the box.

5. Key **Employee Dates and Salaries Form** and then click outside the box.

6 Click the label control object in the Form Header section to select it.

7 Display the Formatting (Form/Report) toolbar if it is not currently visible and then click the Center button on the toolbar.

8 Click the Properties button on the Form Design toolbar to open the Label property sheet.

9 Click the Format tab, if necessary, and then change the font name to Times New Roman and the font size to 12.

10 Close the Label property sheet.

11 Maximize the Form window if it is not currently maximized.

12 Position the mouse pointer on the Form Footer bottom gray border line until the pointer changes to a black horizontal line with an up- and down-pointing arrow, drag the bottom of the form down until the Form Footer section is approximately 1 inch in height, and then release the mouse button.

13 Add a label control object to the Form Footer section as shown using the following specifications:

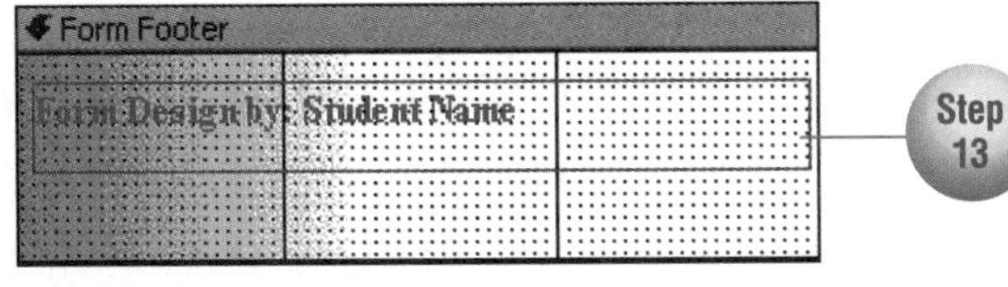

- Substitute your first and last name for *Student Name*.
- Change the font name to Times New Roman and the font size to 10 using the drop-down list buttons on the Formatting (Form/Report) toolbar.

14 Click Save.

15 Switch to Form view and then scroll through the records in the form.

16 Close the Employee Dates and Salaries form.

DIRECTOR'S CUT

Add Controls to a Form

1 Open form in Design view.
2 Click control object button in Toolbox.
3 Drag control in design grid the approximate height and width desired.
4 Key text or expression as required.
5 Click Save.
6 Close the form.

Adding a Calculated Control to a Form

A calculated control displays the results of a mathematical operation in a control object. The mathematical operation is performed on existing fields in the table. The results are displayed in the object in a similar manner as a field entry displays; however, the calculated results do not exist in the underlying table associated with the form. For example, if the table used to create the form is opened in Datasheet view, the calculated results will not appear in a column in the datasheet, since a calculated control is not stored as a field.

PROJECT: Worldwide Enterprises pays its employees 4% of their annual salary as vacation pay each year. You will add a calculated control object to the Employee Dates and Salaries form that will display the vacation pay entitlement for each employee.

steps

1. With WE Employees3 open and *Forms* still selected in the Objects bar, open the Employee Dates and Salaries form in Design view and then drag the top of the Form Footer gray border line down approximately 1 inch to create more space in the Detail section.
2. Click the Text Box object button ab| in the Toolbox.
3. Position the crosshairs pointer with the text box icon attached to it at the horizontal black gridline below the Department text box control, drag to create the object the approximate height and width shown at the right, and then release the mouse button.

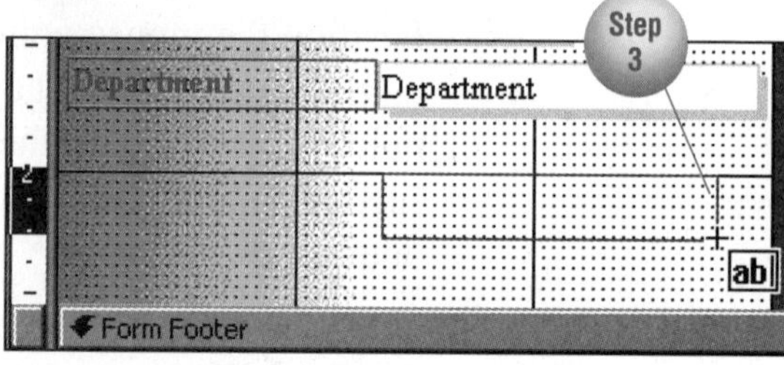

A text box label control object and an unbound control object box appear. An *unbound* control contains data that is not stored anywhere. A control that displays a field entry in a table is referred to as a *bound* control object, since the object contents are bound to the table.

4. Click the Properties button on the Form Design toolbar to display the Text Box property sheet.
5. Click the Data tab in the Text Box property sheet.
6. Click in the Control Source property and key **=[Annual Salary]*0.04**.

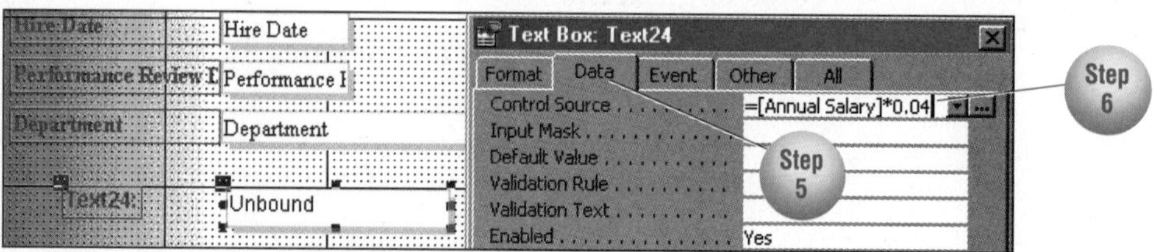

A mathematical expression begins with the equals sign (=); field names are encased in square brackets. Use +, -, *, and / as mathematical operators within the expression.

7 Click the Format tab in the Text Box property sheet.

8 Click in the Format property, click the down-pointing triangle that appears, and then select *Currency* from the drop-down list.

Format is the first property listed in the Format tab. Scroll up if it is not currently visible.

9 Change the font name to Times New Roman and the font size to 10.

10 Close the Text Box property sheet.

11 Click the label control object adjacent to the text box control (currently displays *Text14* [your number may vary]) to select it.

12 Click inside the selected label control object to display the insertion point, delete the current text, and then key **Vacation Pay** inside the control. The width of the box will increase as you key the text.

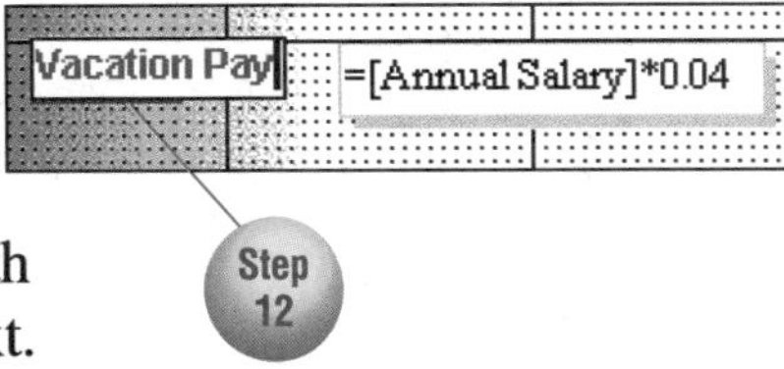

Step 12

13 Display the property sheet for the label control, change the font name to Times New Roman and the font size to 10, and then close the property sheet.

14 Position the mouse pointer on the large black handle at the top left of the label control object until the pointer changes to a black hand with the index finger pointing upward, hold down the left mouse button, drag left as shown, and then release the mouse button.

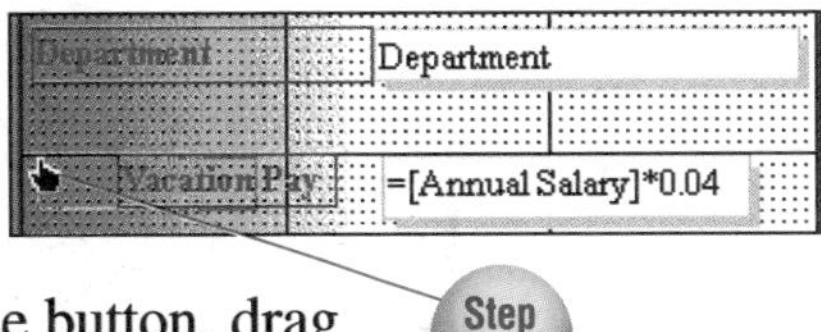

Step 14

Dragging the large black handle moves the label control object separately from the text box control.

15 Click Save.

16 Switch to Form view, scroll through the records to view the vacation pay for each employee, and then close the Employee Dates and Salaries form.

DIRECTOR'S CUT

Add a Calculated Control Object

1. Open form in Design view.
2. Click Text Box object button in Toolbox.
3. Drag control in the design grid the approximate height and width desired.
4. Key label you want to appear beside the result in text box label control.
5. Select text box control and display property sheet.
6. Key mathematical expression in Control Source property.
7. Close the property sheet.
8. Save and close the form.

The Expression Builder

Access includes the Expression Builder, which can be used to create a mathematical expression in a calculated control object. To display the Expression Builder dialog box, open the property sheet for the control object, click the Data tab, click in the Control Source property, and then click the Build button that appears [...]. The Expression Builder displays field names and mathematical symbols. Create an expression by clicking field names and symbol buttons, and/or keying text in the window.

Using Forms

Forms are used to enter, edit, view, and print data in tables. Entering records in a form is easier than using the datasheet since all of the fields in the table are presented in the current window. Other records in the table do not distract the user since only one record displays at a time.

PROJECT: You will add a new record using the Employee Dates and Salaries form, adjust the placement of controls in Design view, and then print the active record.

steps

1. With WE Employees3 open and *Forms* still selected in the Objects bar, double-click Employee Dates and Salaries to display the form in Form view.
2. Click the New Record button on the Form View toolbar or in the Record Navigation bar.
3. Enter the data in the new form shown in Figure A3.10.

FIGURE A3.10 New Employee Dates and Salaries Form

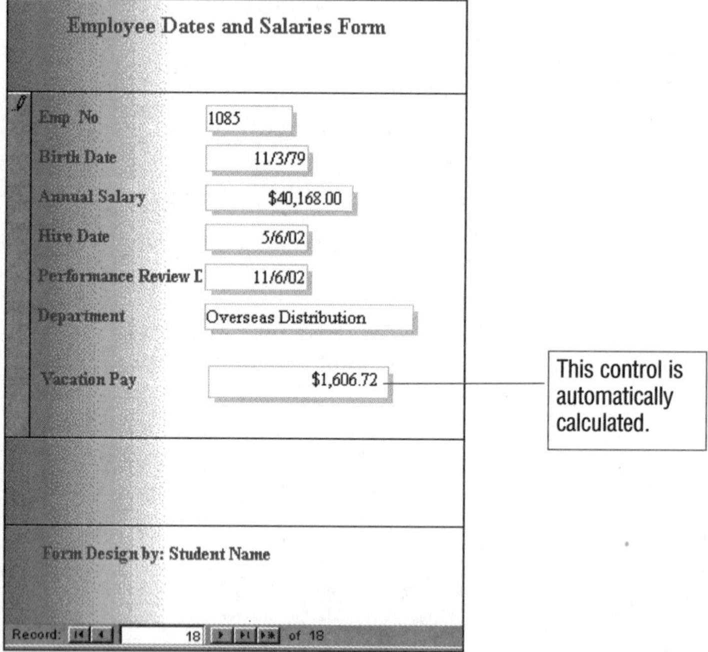

The Performance Review Date label control is overlapped by the text box control, the Department names need more space, and the Vacation Pay label and control object could be moved closer to the controls above it.

4. Click the View button on the Form Design toolbar to switch to Design view.

5 Position the mouse pointer on the right edge of the design grid until the pointer changes to a vertical black line with a left- and right-pointing arrow, hold down the left mouse button, and then drag the width of the form right approximately 1 inch.

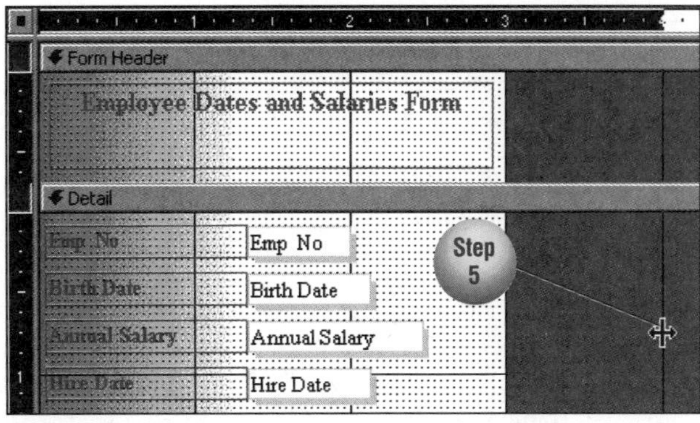

6 Click the Emp No text box control to select it. Drag the large black handle at the top left of the control object right until the left edge of the control is aligned at the black gridline at position 2 on the horizontal ruler.

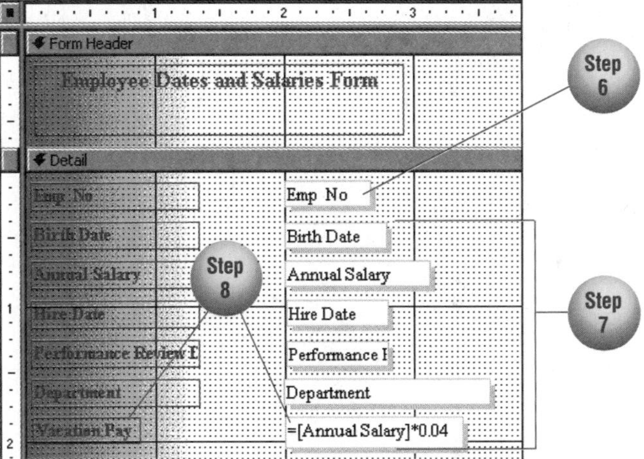

7 Align the remaining text box controls below Emp No to the same position in the form.

8 Move up the Vacation Pay label control and its corresponding calculated control as shown.

9 Click the Performance Review Date label control object to select it. Drag the right middle sizing handle to the right approximately 0.5 inch or until the entire label is visible.

10 Increase the width of the Department text box control object approximately 0.5 inch.

11 Click Save.

12 Switch to Form view and then view the revised layout.

13 Click the Print Preview button on the Form View toolbar.

Notice that each form will print, one below the other on the page.

14 Close the Print Preview window, click File and then Print. Click Selected Record(s) in the Print Range section of the Print dialog box and then click OK.

Only the active form will print.

15 Close the Employee Dates and Salaries form.

16 Close the WE Employees3 database.

Features Summary

Feature	Button	Menu	Keyboard
AutoForm		Insert, Form, AutoForm: Columnar	
Collapse all records		Format, Subdatasheet, Collapse All	
Properties Sheet		View, Properties	
Delete Rows		Edit, Delete Rows	
Design view		View, Design View	
Expand all records		Format, Subdatasheet, Expand All	
Filter By Form		Records, Filter, Filter By Form	
Filter By Selection		Records, Filter, Filter By Selection	
Form view		View, Form View	
Form Wizard		Insert, Form, Form Wizard	
Insert Rows		Insert, Rows	
Select all controls		Edit, Select All	Ctrl + A

Procedures Check

In the space provided at the right, indicate the correct term or command.

1. To move, insert, or delete a field in a table, open the table in this view. _______________
2. Key this symbol in the Format property for a Text field to convert all characters to uppercase. _______________
3. Click this symbol next to a record to view the subdatasheet for the related table. _______________
4. Click this button on the Datasheet toolbar to temporarily remove all records from the display, and then select a criterion from a drop-down list of field values in a field. _______________

5. Click this button in the Database window toolbar to display the New Form dialog box. _______________
6. Use this method of creating a form if you want to choose the layout and style of the form. _______________
7. The label object button is located in this palette. _______________
8. Click this button on the Form Design toolbar to change the font and font size of a selected control object. _______________
9. Display the form in this view to add new records. _______________
10. Click this option in the Print dialog box to print only the active form. _______________

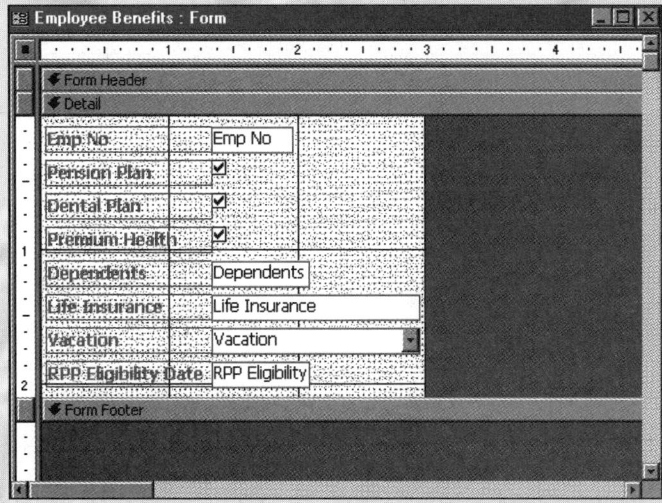

Use the Form Design window shown above to answer questions 11–14.

11. List the steps you would complete to increase the width of the form.

____

____

12. List the steps you would complete to move the Dental Plan label control and its corresponding text box control beside the Pension Plan label and text box control.

____

____

____

13. List the steps you would complete to change the font name and font size of all of the controls in the form to 12-point Times New Roman.

____

____

____

14. List the steps you would complete to add your name in a label control object in the Form Header section.

____

____

____

Identify the following buttons:

15. __________________________

16. __________________________

17. __________________________

18. __________________________

19. __________________________

20. __________________________

Activity 1: Moving and Deleting Fields; Modifying Field Properties

1 Open the WE Employees3 database.
2 Open the Employee Expenses table in Design view.
3 Move the *Amount* field between the *Emp No* and *Date* fields.
4 Delete the *Type* field.
5 Modify the *Description* field so that all text will be converted to uppercase letters.
6 Save the table.
7 Switch to Datasheet view.
8 Best Fit the *Description* column.
9 Print the datasheet.
10 Close the Employee Expenses table. Save the layout changes.

Activity 2: Displaying Subdatasheets

1 With WE Employees3 open, open the Employee Benefits table in Datasheet view.
2 Expand the first four records in the table.
3 Change the page orientation to landscape and then print the datasheet.
4 Collapse all of the subdatasheets. *(Hint: Make sure a record is not active inside a subdatasheet when you select Collapse All.)*
5 Close the Employee Benefits table.

Activity 3: Creating a Form Using the Form Wizard; Entering Records

1 With WE Employees3 open, create a new form for the Employee Expenses table using the following specifications:
- Add all of the fields in the Employee Expenses table to the form.
- Choose the Columnar layout.
- Choose the Industrial style.
- Accept the default title for the form.

2 Add the following records to the Employee Expenses table using the form created in step 1:

Emp No	**1045**	*Emp No*	**1085**
Amount	**1510.45**	*Amount*	**1123.41**
Date	**5/13/02**	*Date*	**6/18/02**
Description	**Spring Promotion**	*Description*	**Sales Conference**

3 Print all records using the form.
4 Close the Employee Expenses form.

Activity 4: Modifying a Form

1 With WE Employees3 open, open the Employee Expenses form in Design view.
2 Maximize the form window.
3 Expand the Form Header section and then insert the title *Employee Expenses Form* in a label object in the Form Header. Center the text in the label object and then change the font size to 12 point.
4 Expand the Form Footer section and insert the text *Form Design by: Student Name.* Substitute your first and last name for Student Name.
5 Decrease the width of the Amount text box control. You determine the width.
6 Increase the width of the Description text box control. You determine the width. *(Hint: Expand the width of the form before you complete this step.)*
7 Switch to Form view.
8 Print the first record only in the form.
9 Close the Employee Expenses form. Save the changes.
10 Close the WE Employees3 database.

Performance Plus

Activity 1: Modifying a Table; Displaying Subdatasheets

1. After reviewing the inventory list with Dana Hirsch, manager of The Waterfront Bistro, you realize some adjustments need to be made to the structure of the table.
2. Open WB Inventory3.
3. Open the Inventory List table in Design view.
4. Make the following changes to the table:
   - Move the *Unit* field between the *Item No* and *Item* fields.
   - Edit the properties of the *Unit* and *Item* fields so that all text is automatically converted to uppercase letters.
   - Move the *Supplier Code* field between the *Item No* and *Unit* fields.
5. Save the table and then switch to Datasheet view.
6. Expand the first three records to display the subdatasheets and Best Fit the *Description* Column.
7. Print the first three records only. *(Hint: Select the three records in the record selector bar before displaying the Print dialog box.)*
8. Collapse all the subdatasheets.
9. Close the Inventory List table. Click Yes if prompted to save layout changes.
10. Close the WB Inventory3 database.

Activity 2: Applying and Removing Filters

1. Niagara Peninsula College has received three grants from Performance Threads to be awarded to the top three students in the Theatre Arts Division. Cal Rubine, chair of the Theatre Arts Division of Niagara Peninsula College, has requested a list of students who achieved A+ in a course for review by the selection committee.
2. Open NPC Grades3.
3. Open the ACT104 Grades table.
4. Filter the table to display only those records with an A+ in the *Grade* field.
5. Print and then close the table. Click No to save changes.
6. Open the PRD112 Grades table.
7. Filter the table to display only those records with an A+ in the *Grade* field.
8. Print and then close the table. Click No to save changes.
9. Open the SPE266 Grades table.
10. Filter the table to display only those records with an A+ in the *Grade* field.
11. Print and then close the table. Click No to save changes.
12. Close NPC Grades3.

Activity 3: Creating and Modifying a Form; Adding a Calculated Control

1. Staff at Performance Threads have mentioned that looking up a costume in the Costume Inventory datasheet is difficult, since there are so many records in the table. You decide to create a form for the staff in which they see only one record in the screen at a time as they are browsing the inventory.
2. Open PT Costume Inventory3.
3. Create a new form using the Form Wizard for the Costume Inventory table. You determine the layout, style, and title of the form. Include all of the fields in the form.
4. Modify the form as follows:
   - Add the title *Costume Inventory* in the Form Header.
   - Add the text *Check for damage/repairs upon return* in the Form Footer.
   - Position the *Date Out* and *Date In* fields side-by-side in the form.
5. Performance Threads adds two taxes to each rental fee: 7% GST and 8% PST. Add two calculated controls to the form that will display the tax amounts. You determine where to position the controls, what to key in the label and text controls, and which formats to apply to the data.
6. Change the font and font size of all the control objects in the form.
7. Make any other modifications to the form as necessary, such as resizing or repositioning controls.
8. Display the form in Form view.
9. Print the first record only in the form.
10. Close the form.
11. Close PT Costume Inventory3.

Activity 4: Modifying a Form

1. Sam Vestering, manager of North American Distribution for Worldwide Enterprises, created three forms in the Distributors database. After working with the forms for a while, you decide they would look and perform better if the fields were presented in a layout similar to the way addresses are positioned on an envelope.
2. Open WE Distributors3.
3. Open the Canadian Distributors form in Design view.
4. Modify the layout of the form to conform to the following sample record:

   Millennium Movies
   4126 Yonge Street
   Suite 302
   Toronto ON M2P 2B8
   Telephone: 416-555-9355   Fax: 416-555-9338
   millennium@emcp.skynet.ca
5. Display the form in Form view.
6. Print the first record only and then close the form.
7. Make the same layout changes to the Overseas Distributors form.
8. Print the first record only and then close the Overseas Distributors form.
9. Make the same layout changes to the US Distributors form.
10. Print the first record only and then close the US Distributors form.
11. Close WE Distributors3.

Activity 5: Finding Information on Adding a Picture to a Form

1 Use the online help to find out how to insert a picture into an image control in a form. *(Hint: A picture would be considered an unbound object.)*
2 Print the help topic that you found.
3 Open WE Employees3.
4 Open the Employee Dates and Salaries form in Design view.
5 Add the company logo in the Form Header section. The logo file name is Worldwide.tif. If the logo is not completely visible within the control object, display the Property sheet and then change the Size Mode property to Zoom.
6 Print the first record only in the form.
7 Close the Employee Dates and Salaries form.
8 Close WE Employees3.

Activity 6: Researching Travel Destinations on the Internet

1 You are considering taking a one-week vacation at the end of the term. The destination is flexible and will depend on available flights, costs, and activities.
2 Search the Internet for flight information to at least four destinations to which you might like to travel. Determine departure times, arrival times, and air fares for the week following the end of the current term.
3 Search the Internet for additional travel costs that you might incur for the destinations you used in step 2. Include hotel accommodations, car rentals, and any tours or other activities that you might like to purchase.
4 Create a new database named *Travel Destinations* to store your travel data. Design and create a table within the database that will include all of the data you collected.
5 Design and create a form to be used to enter the data into the tables.
6 Enter data using the form created in step 5.
7 Print all the records in the form.
8 Close the form.
9 Close Travel Destinations.

Access

Creating Queries, Reports and Web Pages

The ability to extract specific information from a table that can contain hundreds or thousands of records is an important feature of Access. Data is extracted from a table by performing a *query*. Creating a query is analogous to asking Access a question, such as *How many distributors are located in New York?* Reports are created to print the information in tables or queries in a variety of formats or styles. Tables and queries can be converted to a Web page to post on the Internet or a company's intranet by saving data in a data access page. In this section you will learn the skills and complete the projects listed below.

Skills

- Create, run, and print a select query in Design view
- Add multiple tables to a query
- Create and run a query using the Simple Query Wizard
- Add criteria statements to a query
- Perform calculations in a query
- Create a report using the Report Wizard
- Resize controls in a report
- Modify properties of report controls
- Add objects to the report using the Control Toolbox
- Create a calculated control
- Save a table and a query as a Web page
- Add a hyperlink to a Web page

Projects

Create queries to extract fields from tables to print custom employee lists; add criteria; and calculate pension contributions and monthly salaries. Create and modify reports to produce custom printouts of employee and distributor data. Save a table and query as a Web page and insert hyperlinks.

Create and print a query that will extract the records of students who achieved A+ in all their courses.

Create a query, and create and print a report that lists all costumes rented in the month of August 2002.

Create a Web page for the Purchases table.

Creating a Query in Design View

A *query* is an Access object that is designed to extract specific data from a table. Queries can be created to serve a variety of purposes, from very simple field selection to complex conditional statements or calculations. When a table is viewed or printed in Datasheet view, all of the fields in the table are included. In its simplest form, a query selects only some of the fields from the table(s) to display or print. A criteria statement can be added to a query to display or print only certain records from the table(s). Queries can be saved for future use.

PROJECT: Rhonda Trask, human resources manager of Worldwide Enterprises, has asked for a list that includes employee number, employee name, date hired, department, and salary. This data is stored in two different tables. You will create a query to obtain the required fields from each table to generate the list.

steps

1. Open WE Employees4.
2. Click *Queries* in the Objects bar.
3. Double-click *Create query in Design view*.
4. Double-click *Employees* in the Show Table dialog box with the Tables tab selected.

   A field list box for the Employees table is added to the top of the Query1 : Select Query window.

5. Double-click *Employee Dates and Salaries* in the Show Table dialog box.

   The black join line between the Employees and the Employee Dates and Salaries tables appears, indicating the one-to-one relationship between the two tables.

6. Click Close to close the Show Table dialog box.
7. Double-click *Emp No* in the Employees field list box.

   Emp No is added to the Field row in the first column of the design grid. In steps 8 and 9 you will practice two other methods of adding fields to the design grid.

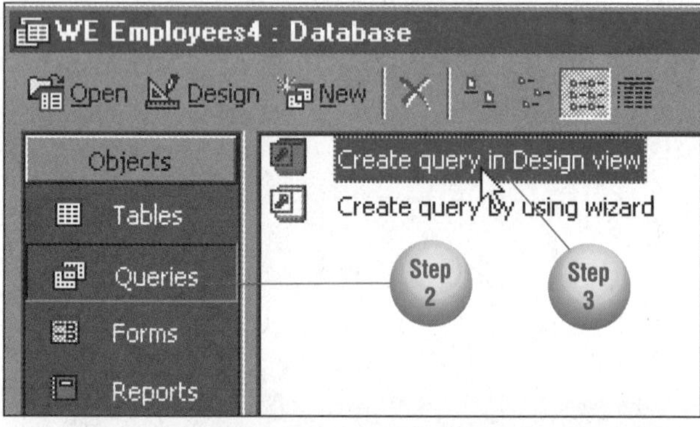

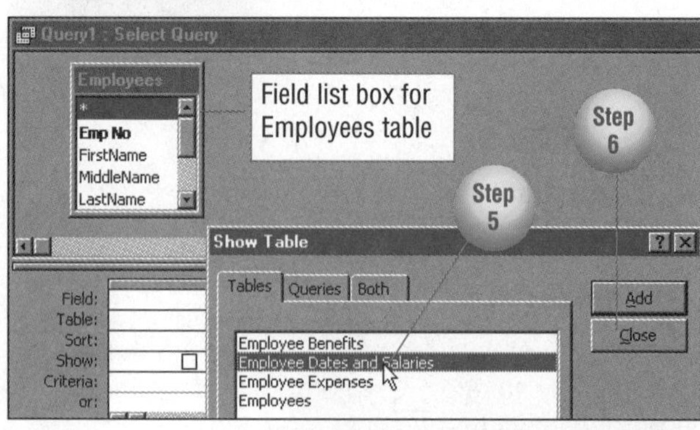

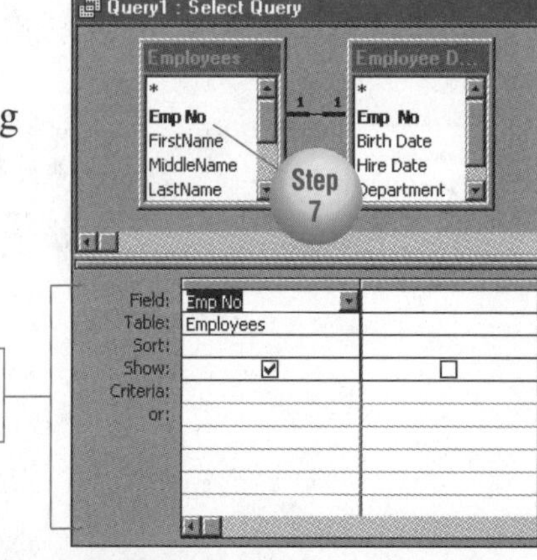

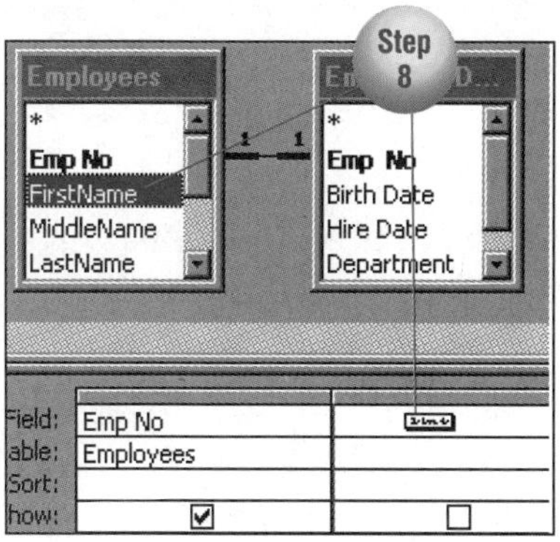

8 Position the mouse pointer on the *FirstName* field in the Employees field list box, hold down the left mouse button, drag the field to the Field row in the second column of the design grid, and then release the mouse button.

9 Click in the Field row in the third column of the design grid, click the down-pointing triangle that appears, and then click *Employees.LastName* in the drop-down list.

10 Add the fields *Hire Date, Department,* and *Annual Salary* from the Employee Dates and Salaries field list box to the design grid.

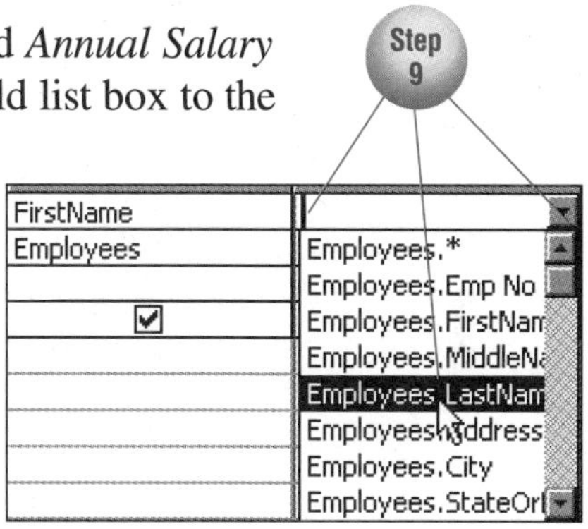

11 Click the Save button on the Query Design toolbar.

12 Key **Hire Date, Department, and Salaries** in the Query Name text box in the Save As dialog box, and then press Enter or click OK.

13 Click the Run button on the Query Design toolbar.

The query results are displayed in Datasheet view, as shown in Figure A4.1

FIGURE A4.1 Query Datasheet

Emp No	First Name	Last Name	Hire Date	Department	Annual Salary
1001	Sam	Vestering	7/22/97	North American Distribution	$67,850.00
1005	Roman	Deptulski	8/15/98	Overseas Distribution	$67,850.00
1010	Hanh	Postma	1/30/98	European Distribution	$67,850.00
1015	Lyle	Besterd	5/17/97	North American Distribution	$44,651.00
1020	Angela	Doxtator	8/3/97	North American Distribution	$45,178.00
1025	Jorge	Biliski	12/1/97	North American Distribution	$43,152.00
1030	Thom	Hicks	1/22/98	Overseas Distribution	$41,624.00
1035	Valerie	Fistouris	3/15/98	European Distribution	$43,664.00
1040	Guy	Lafreniere	3/10/98	Overseas Distribution	$44,195.00
1045	Terry	Yiu	4/12/99	European Distribution	$41,328.00
1050	Carl	Zakowski	2/9/98	European Distribution	$43,698.00
1055	Edward	Thurston	6/22/99	Overseas Distribution	$41,498.00
1060	Donald	McKnight	6/22/98	European Distribution	$41,854.00
1065	Norm	Liszniewski	2/6/99	North American Distribution	$42,659.00
1070	Balfor	Jhawar	11/22/99	Overseas Distribution	$43,661.00
1075	Mike	Fitchett	3/19/98	Overseas Distribution	$41,857.00
1080	Leo	Couture	1/17/99	European Distribution	$42,185.00

14 Click the Print button on the Query Datasheet toolbar.

15 Close the Hire Date, Department, and Salaries : Select Query window.

Using the Simple Query Wizard

Access includes the Simple Query Wizard to facilitate creating a query. At the first Simple Query Wizard dialog box, the table(s) and the fields within the table(s) are added to the query. Select a Detail or Summary query in the second dialog box. If you select Summary, click Summary Options to specify which field to group by and whether to calculate the sum, average, minimum, or maximum values in the group. Key the name for the query in the last dialog box.

PROJECT: Using the Simple Query Wizard, you will generate a printout that lists each employee's name, number of dependents, life insurance, vacation entitlement, and pension plan eligibility date.

steps

1. With WE Employees4 open and *Queries* selected in the Objects bar, double-click *Create query by using wizard.*
2. Click the down-pointing triangle next to the Tables/Queries text box and then click *Table: Employees* in the drop-down list.

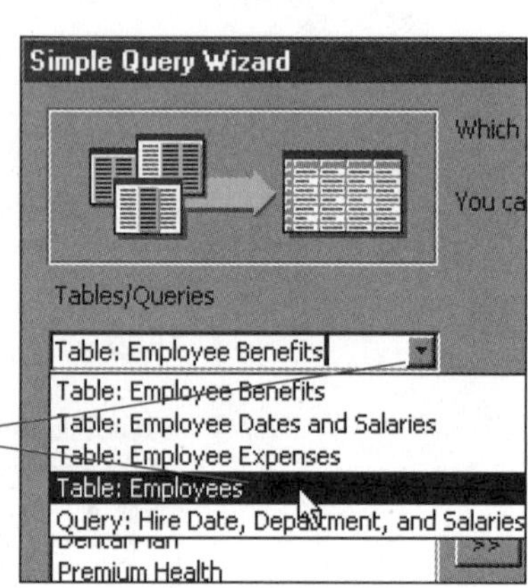

3. With *Emp No* selected in the Available Fields list box, click the Add Field button [>] to move *Emp No* to the Selected Fields list box.
4. Click [>] to move *FirstName* to the Selected Fields list box.
5. Click *LastName* in the Available Fields list box and then click [>].
6. Click the down-pointing triangle next to the Tables/Queries text box and then click *Table: Employee Benefits* in the drop-down list.
7. Double-click *Dependents* in the Available Fields list box.

   Double-clicking a field name is another way to move a field to the Selected Fields list box.

8. Move the following fields from the Available Fields list box to the Selected Fields list box:

   Life Insurance
   Vacation
   RPP Eligibility Date

9. Click Next.

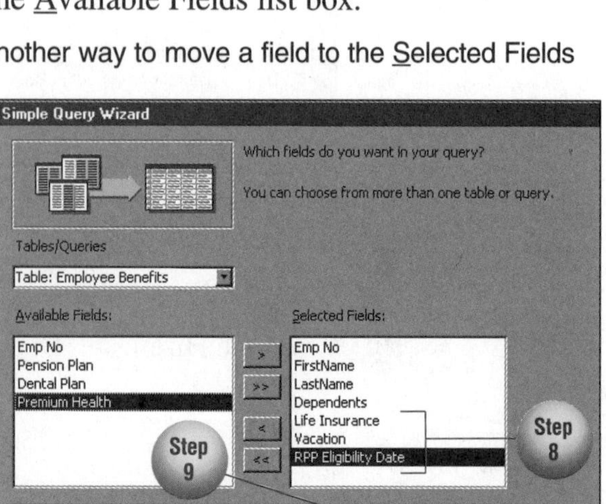

10. Click Next at the second Simple Query Wizard dialog box to accept the default Detail report.
11. Key **Dependents, Life Insurance, Vacation, and RPP** in the What title do you want for your query? text box, and then click Finish.

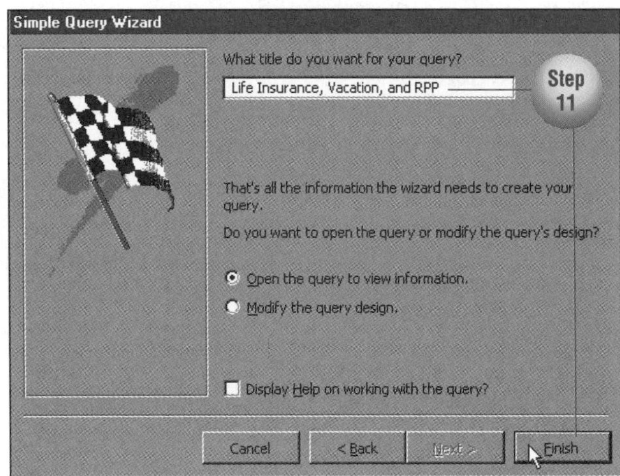

12. View the query results in the datasheet and then click the View button on the Query Datasheet toolbar to switch to Design view.

    In the next step you will modify the query design to sort the query results in ascending order by employee's last name.

13. Click in the Sort row in the *LastName* column in the design grid, click the down-pointing triangle that appears, and then click *Ascending* in the drop-down list.

Step 13

Field:	Emp No	FirstName	LastName
Table:	Employees	Employees	Employees
Sort:			Ascending / Descending / (not sorted)
Show:	☑	☑	
Criteria:			
or:			

14. Click Save on the Query Design toolbar and then click Run.
15. Change the page orientation to landscape and then print the query results.
16. Close the Dependents, Life Insurance, Vacation, and RPP : Select Query window.

Take 2

Action Queries

In the last topic and in this topic you have created *Select* queries that displayed specific fields from a table. An *action* query makes changes to records in one procedure. There are four types of action queries: delete, update, append, and make-table. A delete query will delete a group of records from one or more tables. An update query is used to make global changes to a group of records in one or more tables. An append query adds a group of records from one or more tables to the end of one or more other tables. A make-table query will create a new table from all or part of the data in existing tables.

DIRECTOR'S CUT

Create a Query Using the Simple Query Wizard

1. Double-click *Create query by using wizard.*
2. Choose table(s) and field(s) to include in the query.
3. Click Next.
4. Choose Detail or Summary query.
5. Click Next.
6. Key title for query.
7. Click Finish.

Extracting Records Using Criteria Statements

All of the records in the tables were displayed in the query results datasheet in the two queries you have done so far. Adding a criterion statement to the query design grid will cause Access to display only those records that meet the criterion. For example, you could generate a list of employees who are entitled to 4 weeks of vacation. Extracting specific records from the tables is where the true power in creating queries is found since you are able to separate out only those records that serve your purpose. Using criteria statements is similar to filtering the data with the added benefit of being able to save the criteria for future use.

PROJECT: Rhonda Trask has requested a list of employees who receive either 3 weeks or 4 weeks vacation. Since you already have the employee names and vacation fields in a query, you will modify the existing query to add the criteria statement.

steps

1. With WE Employees4 open and *Queries* selected in the Objects bar, right-click the Dependents, Life Insurance, Vacation, and RPP query and then click Design View at the shortcut menu.
2. Maximize the query window if it is not already maximized.
3. Click in the Criteria row in the *Vacation* column in the design grid.
4. Key **4 weeks** and then press Enter.

   The insertion point moves to the Criteria row in the next column and Access inserts quotation marks around *4 weeks* in the *Vacation* column. Since quotation marks are required in criteria statements for text fields, Access automatically inserts them if they are not keyed into the Criteria text box.

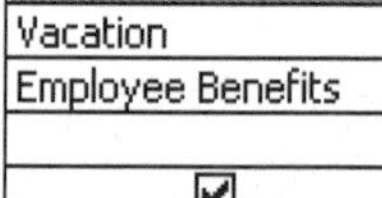

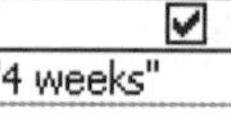

5. Click in the *or* row in the *Vacation* column in the design grid (blank row below 4 weeks), key **3 weeks** and then press Enter.

   Including a second criteria statement below the first one instructs Access to display records that meet either of the two criteria.

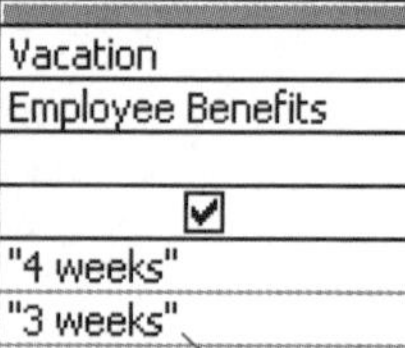

6. Click Save on the Query Design toolbar.
7. Click Run on the Query Design toolbar.

Problem ?

Is the datasheet blank? Check the criteria statement in Design view. A keying error, such as keying **4 weks** instead of **4 weeks,** can cause a blank datasheet to appear.

8. View the query results in the datasheet and then click the View button on the Query Datasheet toolbar to switch to Design view.

   Since Rhonda Trask is interested only in the employee names and vacation weeks, you will instruct Access not to display the other fields in the query results datasheet.

9. Click the check box in the Show row in the *Dependents* column to remove the check mark.

Dependents
Employee Benefits
☐

Deselecting the check box instructs Access to hide the column in the query results datasheet.

10. Deselect the Show check boxes in the *Life Insurance* and *RPP Eligibility Date* columns in the design grid.
11. Run the query.
12. Print the query results datasheet.
13. Close the Dependents, Life Insurance, Vacation, and RPP : Select Query window. Click No when prompted to save changes to the design of the query.

Examples of other criteria statements are listed in Table A4.1.

TABLE A4.1 Criteria Examples

Criteria Statement	Records That Would Be Extracted
"Finance Department"	Those with Finance Department in the field
Not "Finance Department"	All *except* those with Finance Department in the field
"Fan*"	Those that begin with Fan and end with any other characters in the field
>15000	Those with a value greater than 15,000 in the field
>=15000 And <=20000	Those with a value from 15,000 to 20,000 in the field
#05/01/02#	Those that contain the date May 1, 2002 in the field
>#05/01/02#	Those that contain dates after May 1, 2002 in the field

Take 2

More on Criteria Statements

A query can be created that extracts records based on meeting two or more criteria statements at the same time. In the query design grid shown below, Access will display the records of employees who work in the North American Distribution department *and* who earn over $40,000. The record will have to satisfy *both* criteria to be displayed in the query results datasheet.

Field:	FirstName	LastName	Department	Annual Salary
Table:	Employees	Employees	Employee Dates and Salaries	Employee Dates and
Sort:				
Show:	☑	☑	☑	☑
Criteria:			"North American Distribution"	>40000
or:				

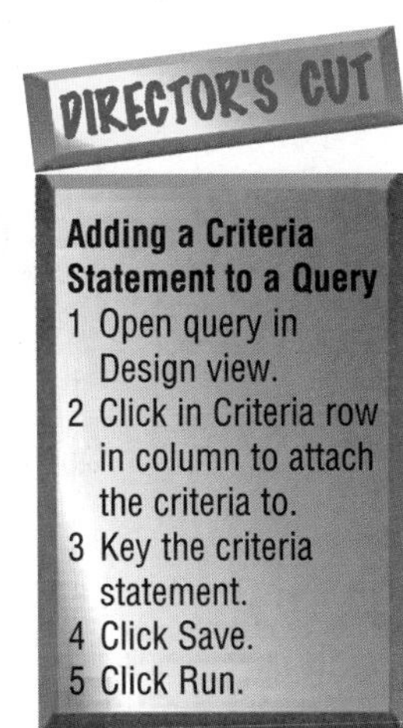

Performing Calculations in a Query

A calculated field can be included in the query design grid. To do this, key in a blank Field text box in the design grid a field name followed by a colon and then the mathematical expression for the calculated values. Field names included in the mathematical expression are encased in square brackets. For example, the entry *Total Salary:[Base Salary]+[Commission]* would add the value in the field named *Base Salary* to the value in the field named *Commission*. The result would be placed in a new column in the query datasheet with the column heading *Total Salary*. The values in the *Total Salary* column do not exist in the table used to create the query; they are dynamically calculated each time the query is run.

PROJECT: Worldwide Enterprises contributes 6% of each employee's annual salary to a registered pension plan. You will modify the Hire Date, Department, and Salaries query to include a calculation for the employer pension contribution.

steps

1. With WE Employees4 open and *Queries* selected in the Objects bar, open the Hire Date, Department, and Salaries query in Design view.
2. Click File and then Save As.
3. Key **Employer Pension Contributions** and then click OK in the Save As dialog box.

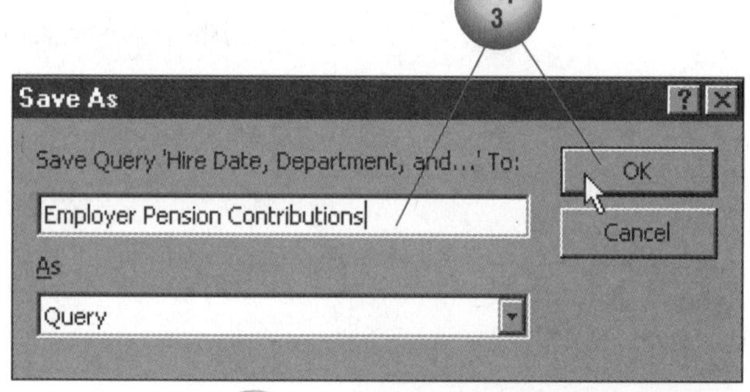

   In the next step you will delete the *Hire Date* and *Department* columns in the design grid, since they are not required in the new query.

4. Position the mouse pointer in the gray bar above the *Hire Date* field in the design grid until the pointer changes to a downward-pointing black arrow, hold down the left mouse button, drag right to select both the *Hire Date* and *Department* columns, and then release the mouse button.
5. Click Edit and then Cut.

   The selected columns are deleted from the design grid.

6. Click in the blank Field row next to the *Annual Salary* column in the design grid.
7. Key **Pension Contribution:[Annual Salary]*.06** and then press Enter.

If you receive a message stating that the expression contains invalid syntax, check that you have used the correct type of brackets and keyed a colon (uppercase value of the semicolon key).

8 Position the mouse pointer on the right vertical boundary line in the gray bar above the *Pension Contribution* column until the pointer changes to a black vertical line with a left- and right-pointing arrow, and then double-click the left mouse button.

Double-clicking the right field boundary line adjusts the width of the column to the length of the text in the field row.

9 Click Save and then click Run.

Does an Enter Parameter Value dialog box appear? A mistake in keying of *[Annual Salary]* in the calculated field will cause Access to display this dialog box, since it does not recognize the field name.

10 Best Fit the *Pension Contribution* column in the query datasheet.

The values in the calculated column need to be formatted to display a consistent number of decimal values.

11 Switch to Design view.

12 Click the insertion point anywhere within the Pension Contribution field row in the design grid and then click the Properties button on the Query Design toolbar.

13 Click in the Format property, click the down-pointing triangle that appears, and then select *Currency* in the drop-down list.

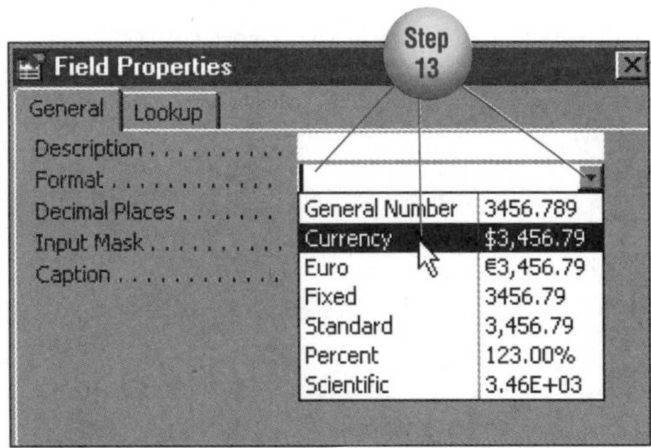

14 Close the Field Properties sheet.

15 Click Save and then click Run.

16 Print the query results datasheet.

17 Close the Employer Pension Contributions query.

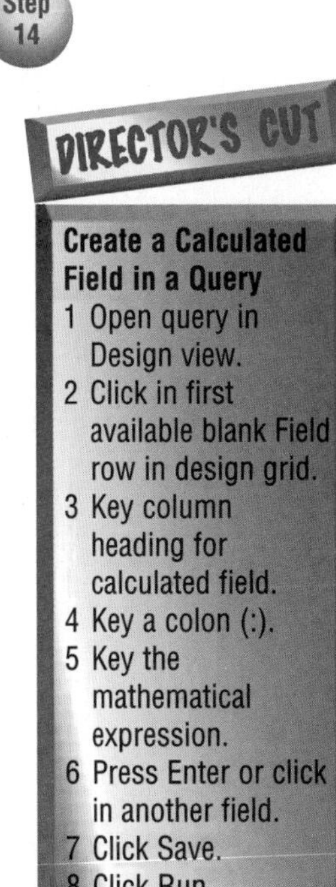

Creating and Previewing a Report

Information from the database can be printed while viewing tables in Datasheet view or while viewing a query datasheet by clicking the Print button on the toolbar. In these printouts all of the fields are printed in a tabular layout, with the fields displayed in rows. Create a report when you want to specify which fields to print and to have more control over the report layout and format. Access includes the Report Wizard, which generates the report based on selections made in a series of dialog boxes.

PROJECT: You will use the Report Wizard to create a report that will list the mailing addresses of the employees in a columnar format.

steps

1. With WE Employees4 open, click *Reports* in the Objects bar.
2. Double-click *Create report by using wizard.*
3. Click the down-pointing triangle next to the Tables/Queries text box and then click *Table: Employees* in the drop-down list.
4. Click the Add All Fields button >> to move all the fields in the Employees table from the Available Fields list box to the Selected Fields list box.
5. Click *Emp No* in the Selected Fields list box and then click the Remove Field button < to move *Emp No* back to the Available Fields list box.
6. Click *MiddleName* in the Selected Fields list box and then click < to move *Middle Name* back to the Available Fields list box.
7. Click Next.

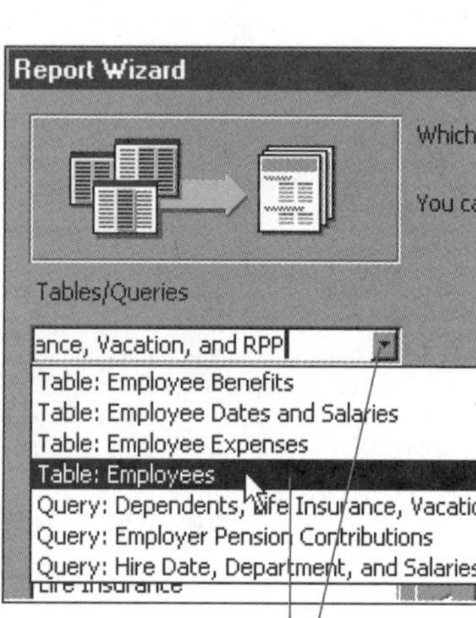

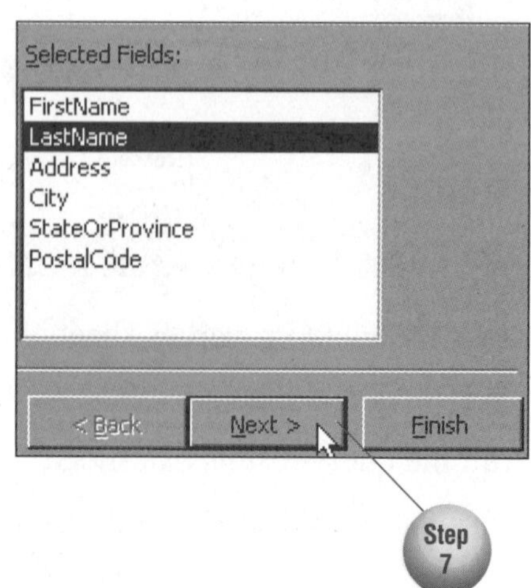

8 Click Next at the second Report Wizard dialog box to indicate that there is no grouping in the report.

A grouping level in a report allows you to print records by sections within a table. For example, in an employee report you could print the employees grouped by department. In this example, you would double-click the department field to define the grouping level. The buttons with the up- and down-pointing arrows are used to modify the position of a field in the grouping level in order to increase or decrease its priority level.

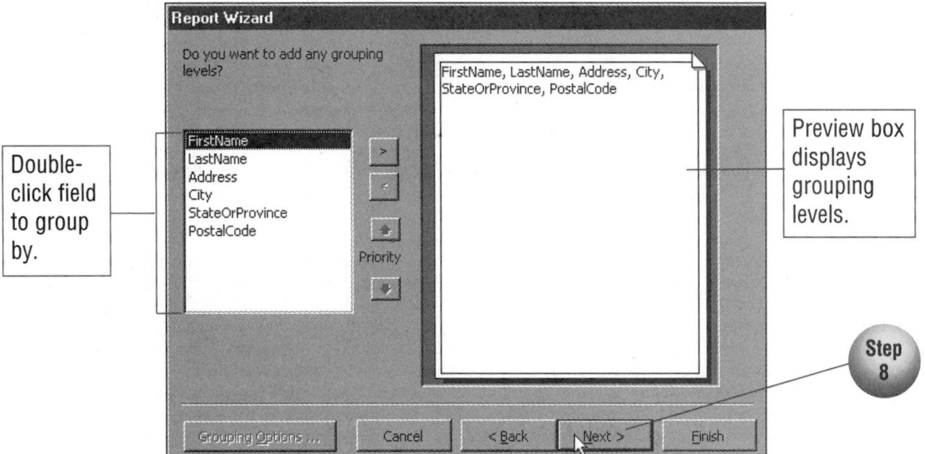

9 Click the down-pointing triangle next to the first text box in the third Report Wizard dialog box and then click *LastName* in the drop-down list.

You can sort a report by up to four fields in the table.

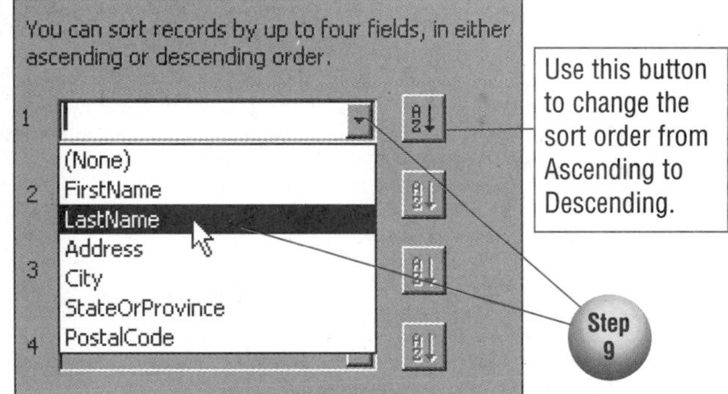

10 Click Next.

11 Click Columnar in the Layout section in the fourth Report Wizard dialog box and then click Next.

Use the Preview box to view the selected layout before clicking the Next button.

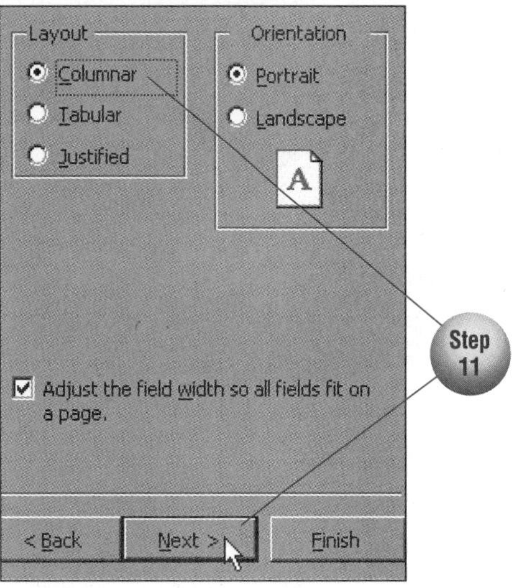

(continued)

12 Click *Corporate* in the style list box in the fifth Report Wizard dialog box and then click Next.

13 Key **Employee Mailing Addresses** in the title text box in the sixth Report Wizard dialog box and then click Finish.

In a few seconds the report will appear in the Print Preview window.

14 Move the pointer (displays as a magnifying glass) to the middle of the report and then click the left mouse button.

The zoom changes to *Fit* and the entire page is displayed in the Print Preview window, as shown in Figure A4.2.

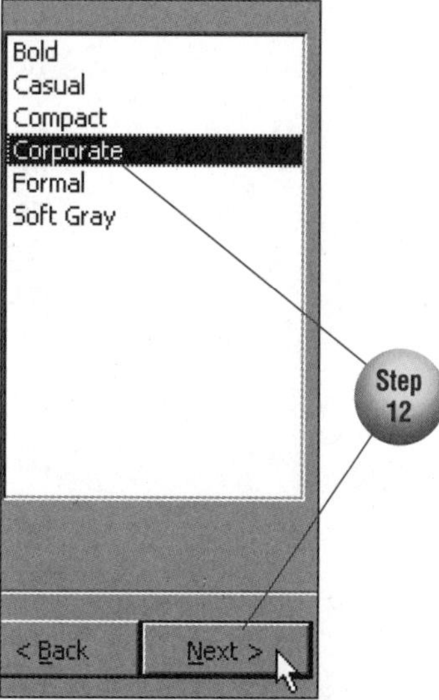

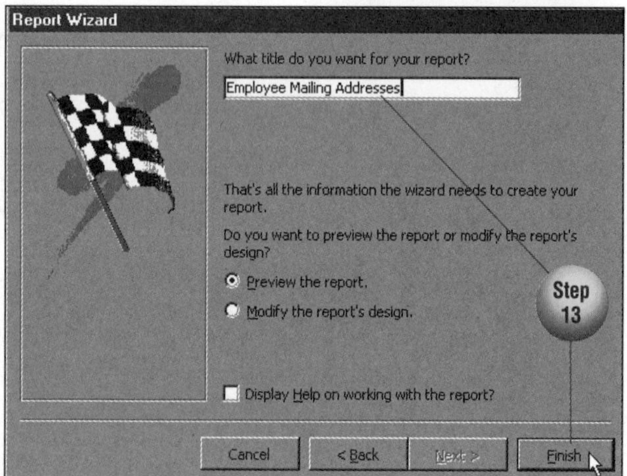

FIGURE A4.2 Report Page in Print Preview

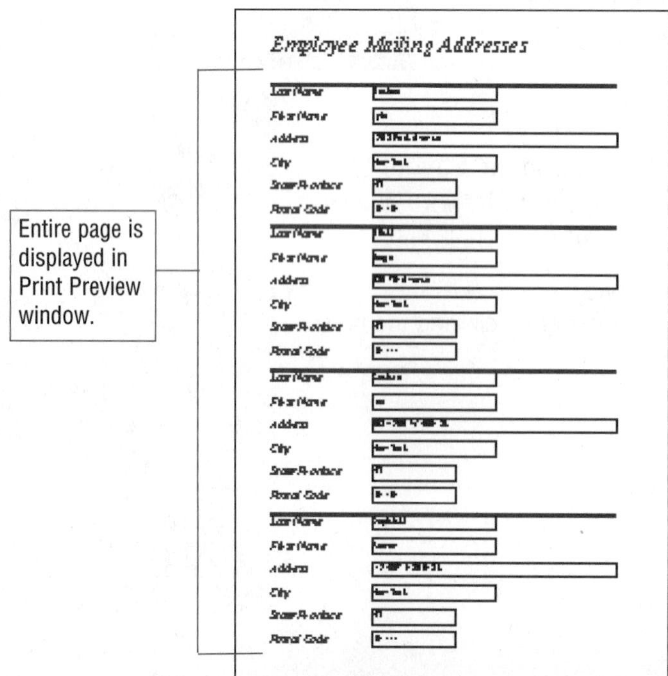

15 Click the Next Page button in the navigation bar to display page 2 of the report.

16 Continue clicking the Next Page button until you have viewed all of the pages in the report.

17 Click the Close button on the Print Preview toolbar.

The Print Preview window closes and the report displays in Design view.

18 Close the Employee Mailing Addresses report window.

Creating a Report in Design View

A report can be created in a blank Design view window, as shown below. Initially, the field list box is blank until a table or query is associated with the report. Double-click the Report Selector button to display the Report Property sheet. Click the Data tab and then click the down-pointing triangle in the Record Source property to select a table or query name. To add fields to the grid, drag the field name from the field list box to the position in the grid where you want the field to appear.

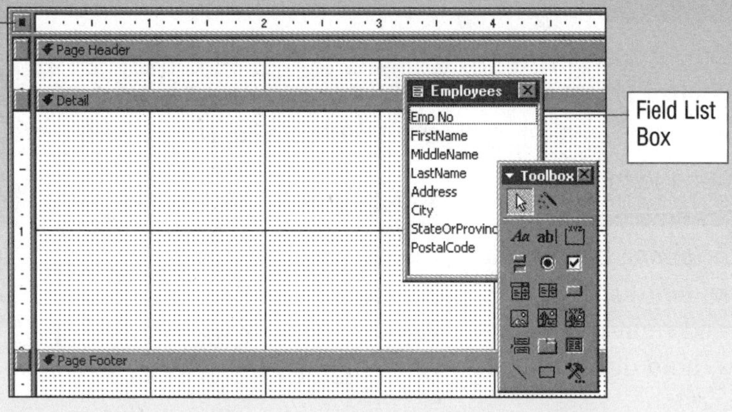

DIRECTOR'S CUT

Create a Report Using Report Wizard

1 Click Reports in Objects bar.
2 Double-click *Create report by using wizard.*
3 Choose table(s) and field(s) to include in report.
4 Click Next.
5 Choose a grouping level and click Next.
6 Choose a field to sort by and click Next.
7 Choose a report layout and click Next.
8 Choose a report style and click Next.
9 Key report title and click Finish.

Resizing Controls in a Report

Once a report has been created using the Report Wizard, the report can be modified by opening it in Design view. A report is composed of a series of objects referred to as *controls*. A report contains a label control and a text box control for each field included from the specified table. The label control contains the field name and is used to describe the data that is adjacent to it in a columnar layout, or below it in a tabular layout. The text box control is the field placeholder, indicating where the data from the table will be printed. The controls can be moved, resized, or deleted from the report.

PROJECT: Some of the controls in the Employee Mailing Addresses report are wider than necessary for the data that will be printed. You will open the report in Design view, resize these controls, and then print the first page only of the report.

steps

1. With WE Employees4 open and *Reports* selected in the Objects bar, right-click Employee Mailing Addresses and then click Design View at the shortcut menu.

   A report contains five sections, as shown in Figure A4.3: Report Header, Page Header, Detail, Page Footer, and Report Footer. The control objects for the fields in the table are displayed in the Detail section. In a tabular report layout, the Page Header section contains the label control objects for the fields placed in the report.

   FIGURE A4.3 Employee Mailing Addresses Report Design View

   Toolbox Palette

   Field List Box

   This control prints the current date.

   This control prints Page x of y.

2. Click the Address text box control object to select it.

3. Position the mouse pointer on the right middle sizing handle until the pointer displays as a left- and right-pointing arrow, hold down the left

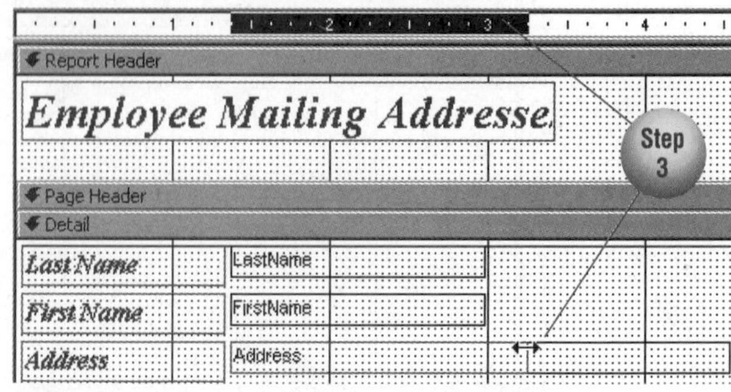

mouse button, drag left until the control is resized to position 3.25 on the horizontal ruler, and then release the mouse button.

4 Resize the City and StateOrProvince controls to position 2.25 on the horizontal ruler.

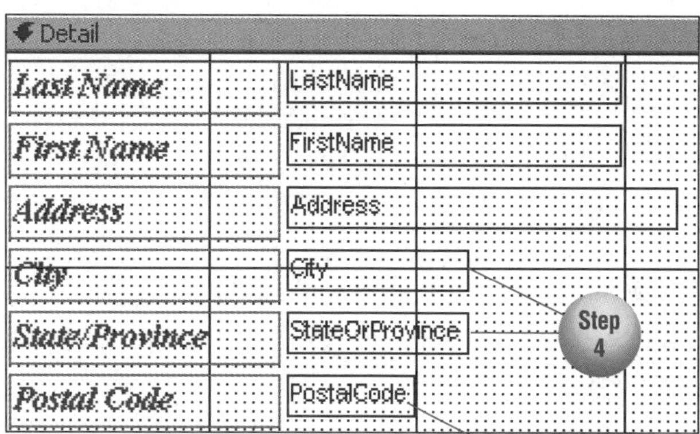

5 Resize the PostalCode control to position 2 on the horizontal ruler.

6 Click Save.

7 Click the Print Preview button on the Report Design toolbar and then preview the report.

8 Click File and then Print, click Pages, key **1**, press Tab, key **1**, and then click OK or press Enter.

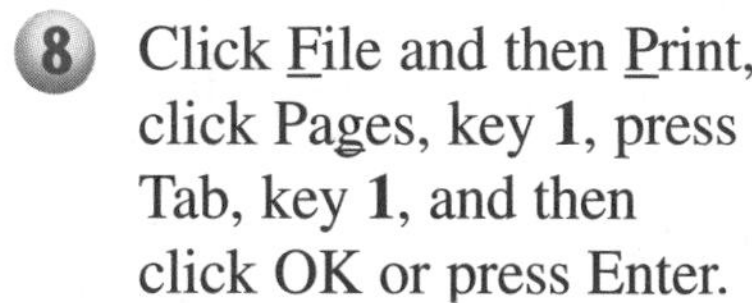

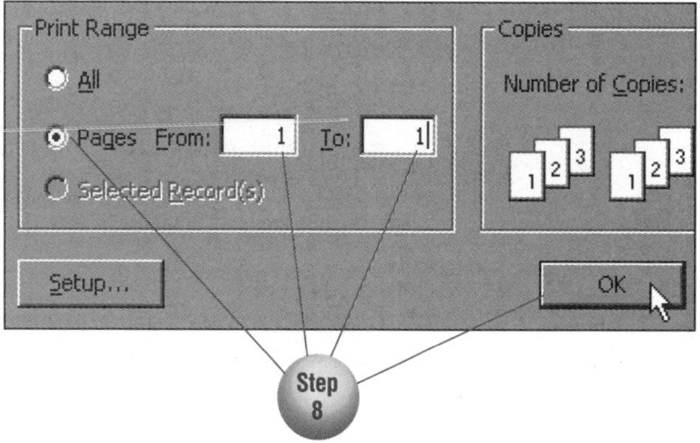

The first page only of the five-page report will print.

9 Click File and then Close to close the Employee Mailing Addresses report.

Take 2

Controls and Report Sections

All of the techniques you learned for moving and deleting controls, and for adding label and text box controls to a form in Design view, can be applied to a report. The five sections of the report are detailed below.

Report Header:	Controls in this section are printed once at the beginning of the report.
Page Header:	Controls in this section are printed at the top of each page in the report.
Detail:	Controls in this section make up the body of the report.
Page Footer:	Controls in this section are printed at the bottom of each page in the report.
Report Footer:	Controls in this section are printed once at the end of the report.

DIRECTOR'S CUT

Resize Control Objects in Design View

1 Right-click report name, click Design View.
2 Click object to be resized.
3 Drag sizing handles to increase or decrease size of object.
4 Click Save.
5 Close the report.

Modifying a Report; Creating a Calculated Control

A calculated control object is inserted to perform a mathematical operation on existing fields in the report. The results are displayed and printed in the report. However, the calculated results are not stored in the underlying table associated with the report. For example, if the table used to create the report is opened in Datasheet view, the calculated results will not appear in a column in the datasheet since a calculated control is not stored as a field.

PROJECT: Worldwide Enterprises estimates that it incurs benefit costs of an additional 20% of an employee's annual salary to cover pension contribution, vacation pay, health insurance, and so on. You will create a report to print a list of employees based on a query and add a control to calculate the estimated benefit cost.

steps

1. With WE Employees4 open and *Reports* selected in the Objects bar, create a new report using the Report Wizard as follows:
   - Add all fields from the Hire Date, Department, and Salaries query.
   - Double-click the *Department* field in the second Report Wizard dialog box to group the entries in the report by department.
   - Sort the report by employee's last name.
   - Choose the block layout in landscape orientation.
   - Choose the Soft Gray style.
   - Key **Employee Benefit Costs** as the title of the report.
2. Click the Close button on the Print Preview toolbar after viewing the report to display the report in Design view.

   The report contains an additional section named Department Header since the report is grouped by the *Department* field.
3. Maximize the report window if it is not already maximized.
4. Click the Emp No label control in the Page Header section.
5. Hold down Shift and then click the Emp No control in the Detail section.

   Both controls are now selected.

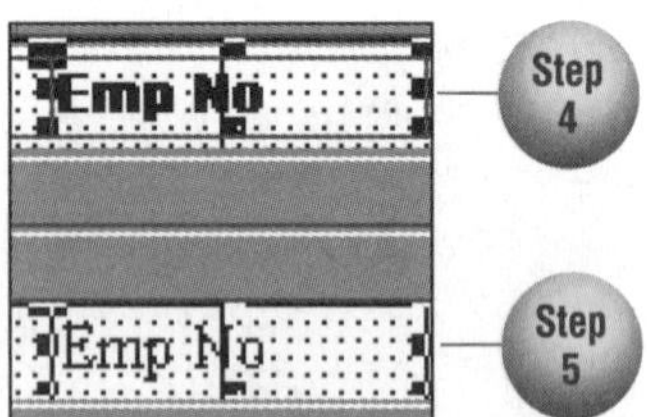

6. Press Delete.
7. Click the Last Name label control in the Page Header section, Shift + click the LastName field control in the Detail section, and then resize the controls to position 3 on the horizontal ruler.

   With both controls selected, dragging the right sizing handle of one control will also resize the other control.

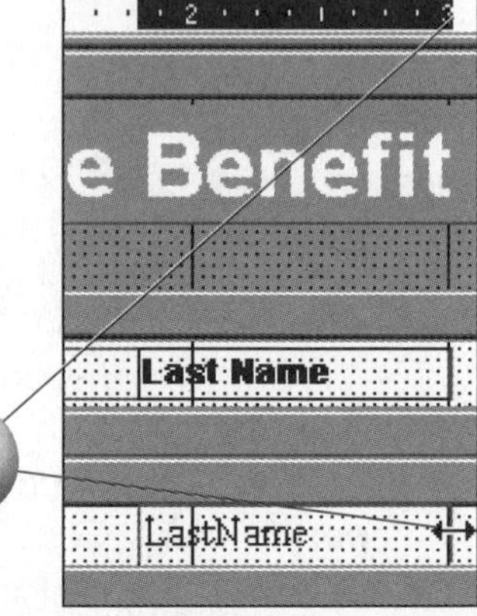

8. Select both First Name controls and then move the controls left to align the left edge at position 3.25 on the horizontal ruler.

Problem ? Can't remember how to move controls? Position the pointer on the control's border until the pointer changes to a black hand and then drag the control to the desired location.

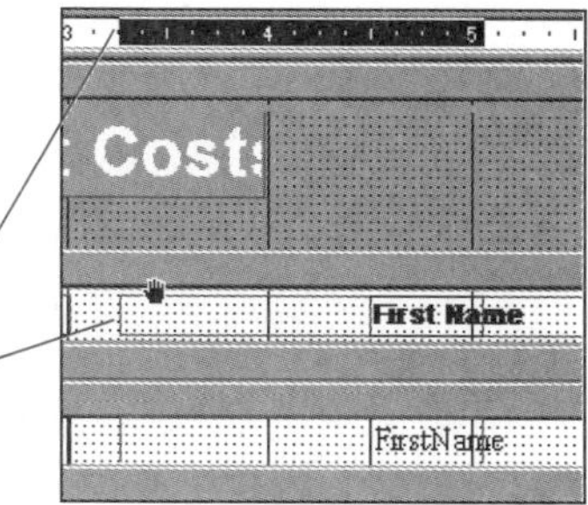

9. With both First Name controls still selected, resize the controls to position 4.25 on the horizontal ruler.
10. Select both Hire Date controls and then move them left to align the left edge at position 4.5 on the horizontal ruler.
11. Select both Annual Salary controls and then move them left to align the left edge at position 5.5 on the horizontal ruler.

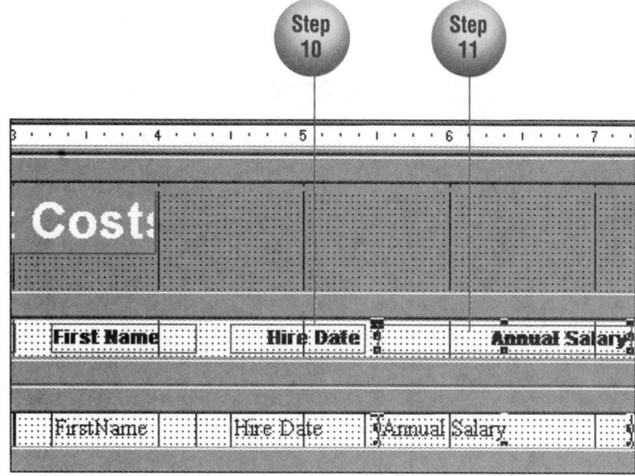

12. Click the right scroll arrow until you can see the right edge of the report.
13. Click the Label object button in the Toolbox palette.

Problem ? Click on the Report Design toolbar if the Toolbox palette is not visible.

(continued)

14 Position the crosshairs pointer with the label icon attached in the Page Header section to the right of Annual Salary, drag to create the outline the approximate height and width shown below, and then release the mouse button.

An insertion point is positioned in the top left corner of the label control.

15 Key **Estimated Benefit Cost** and then click outside the label control to deselect it.

16 Click the Annual Salary label control, click the Format Painter button on the Report Design toolbar, and then click the Estimated Benefit Cost label control. Widen the control if necessary to display the entire label contents.

The attributes for the Annual Salary label are copied to the Estimated Benefit Cost label.

17 Click the Text Box object button in the Toolbox palette.

18 Position the crosshairs pointer with the text box icon attached in the Detail section below the Estimated Benefit Cost label, drag to create an object the same height and width as the label, and then release the mouse button.

19 Click in the text box control (displays *Unbound*), key **=[Annual Salary]*0.2** and then click outside the control to deselect it.

20 Click the label control to the left of the text box control (displays *Text21* [your number may vary]) and press Delete.

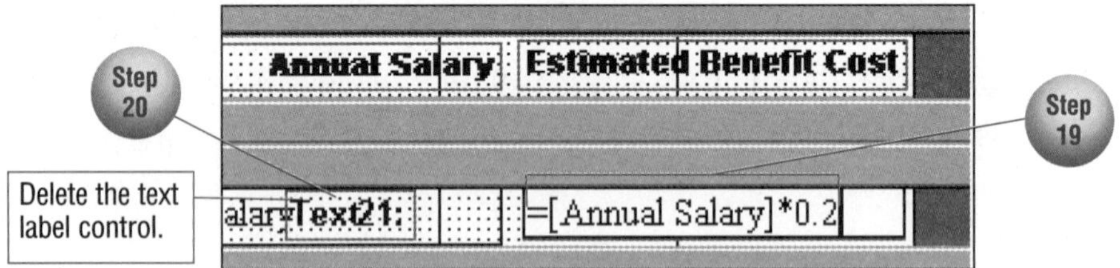

21 Click the Print Preview button to preview the report. If necessary, scroll right to view the right edge of the report.

Notice that the calculated values are aligned at the left edge of the column and the border lines are not surrounding the values as in the remainder of the report.

22 Close the Print Preview window.

23 Click the Annual Salary control in the Detail section, click the Format Painter button on the Report Design toolbar, and then click the calculated control object.

The border attributes are copied to the calculated control object.

24 With the calculated control still selected, click the Properties button on the Report Design toolbar.

25 If necessary, click the Format tab in the property sheet and then change the properties as follows:

- Format property to Currency.
- Text Align property to right.

Scroll down the Format property sheet to locate the Text Align property.

26 Close the Text Box property sheet.

27 Preview the Employee Benefit Costs report. Adjust controls by moving and/or resizing objects as necessary to fine-tune the report.

Employee Benefit Costs

Department	Last Name	First Name	Hire Date	Annual Salary	Estimated Benefit Cost
European Distribution	Couture	Leo	1/17/99	$42,135.00	$8,427.00
	Fraccaro	Valerie	3/15/98	$43,664.00	$8,732.80
	McKnight	Donald	6/22/98	$41,854.00	$8,370.80
	Postma	Hans	1/30/98	$67,850.00	$13,570.00
	Yiu	Terry	4/12/99	$41,328.00	$8,265.60
	Zakowski	Carl	2/9/98	$43,698.00	$8,739.60

Step 27

28 Print and then close the Employee Benefit Costs report. Click Yes when prompted to save changes to the report design.

Report and Section Properties

A property sheet is available for the report and for each section in the report. Open the report or section property sheet to change formats, control page breaks, and so on. To display the property sheet for the report, double-click the Report Selector button ■ at the top left corner of the horizontal and vertical rulers in Design view. To display the property sheet for a section, double-click the section name in the gray section bar. The Format tab in the Detail property sheet is shown at the right.

Section: Detail

Format | Data | Event | Other | All

Force New Page	None
New Row Or Col	None
Keep Together	Yes
Visible	Yes
Can Grow	No
Can Shrink	No
Height	0.2292"
Back Color	16777215
Special Effect	Flat

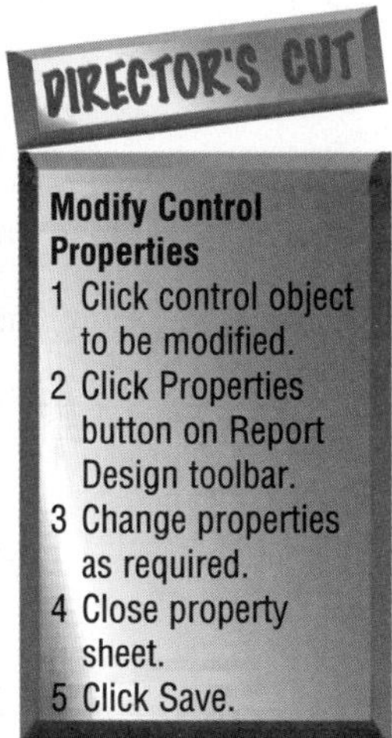

Creating Web Pages

Access tables or queries can be saved as Web pages for viewing on the Internet or on a company's intranet. In Access, Web pages are referred to as *data access pages*—a special type of Web page for viewing and editing Microsoft Access data from the Internet. Data access pages are stored outside the database file. Designing and modifying a data access page is similar to designing forms and reports. Access includes a Page Wizard that can be used to create a data access page.

PROJECT: You will create a Web page for viewing employer pension contributions using the Employer Pension Contributions query.

steps

1. With WE Employees4 open, click *Pages* in the Objects bar.
2. Double-click *Create data access page by using wizard.*
3. Click the down-pointing triangle next to the Tables/Queries text box and then click *Query:Employer Pension Contributions* in the drop-down list.

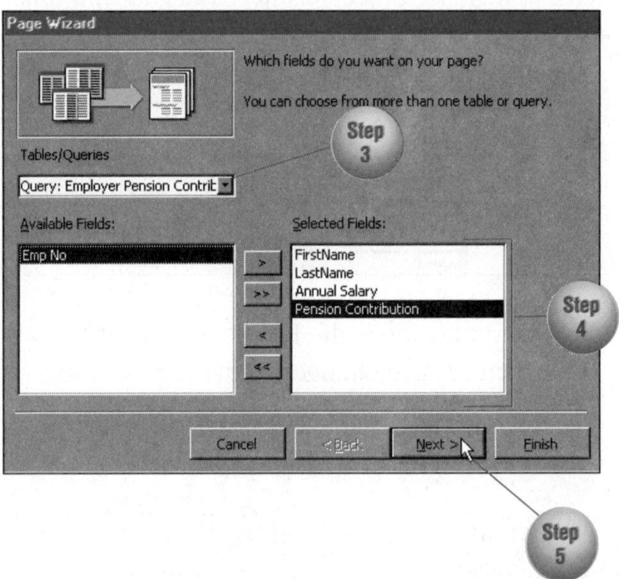

4. Double-click *FirstName, LastName, Annual Salary,* and *Pension Contribution* in the Available Fields list box to move the fields to the Selected Fields list box.
5. Click Next.
6. Click Next at the second Page Wizard dialog box to continue without adding a grouping level to the page.

7. Click the down-pointing triangle next to the first text box in the third Page Wizard dialog box and then click *LastName* in the drop-down list.
8. Click Next.
9. Click Finish at the last Page Wizard dialog box to accept the default title *Employer Pension Contributions*.

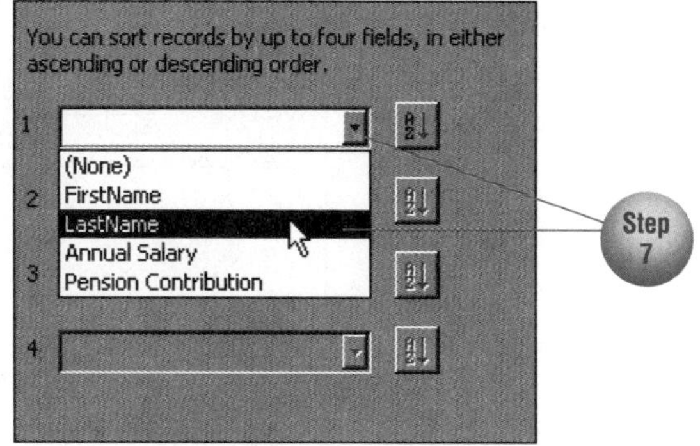

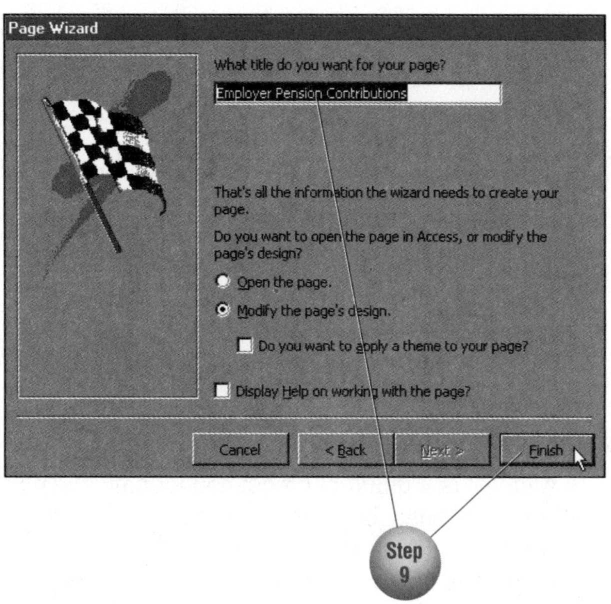

In a few seconds the data access page is displayed in Design view, as shown in Figure A4.4 on page 118.

(continued)

FIGURE A4.4 Data Access Page Design View

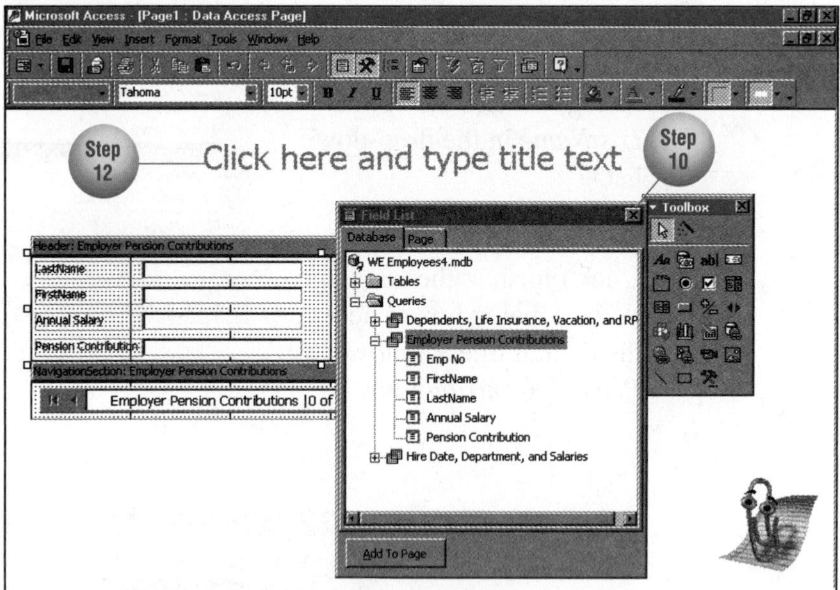

10 Click the Close button in the Field List Title bar window.

11 If necessary, drag the Toolbox palette to the side of the screen.

12 Click in the text *Click here and type title text* and then key **Worldwide Enterprises Pension Contributions**.

As soon as you click within *Click here and type title text,* the text will disappear and will be replaced with the text you key.

13 Click Format and then Theme.

A *theme* is a group of predefined formats and color schemes for bullets, fonts, horizontal lines, background images, and other data access page elements. Choosing a theme saves a considerable amount of time and allows you to create a Web page that has a professional appearance.

14 Click *Blends* in the Choose a Theme list box.

The Sample of theme Blends window displays the selected theme's colors, bullet style, line style, button style, and formats.

15 Click OK.

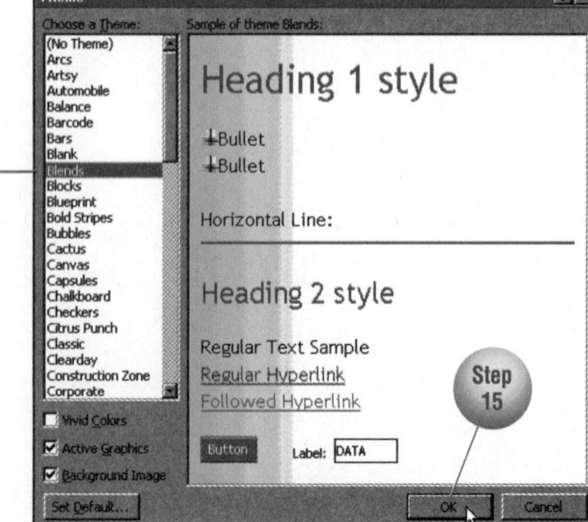

16 Click Save.

17 Key **Pension Web Page** in the File name text box and then click Save.

18 Click File and then Web Page Preview.

The data access page displays in the default Web browser window, as shown in Figure A4.5. (Your screen may vary.)

FIGURE A4.5 Employer Pension Contributions Data Access Page in Web Browser Window

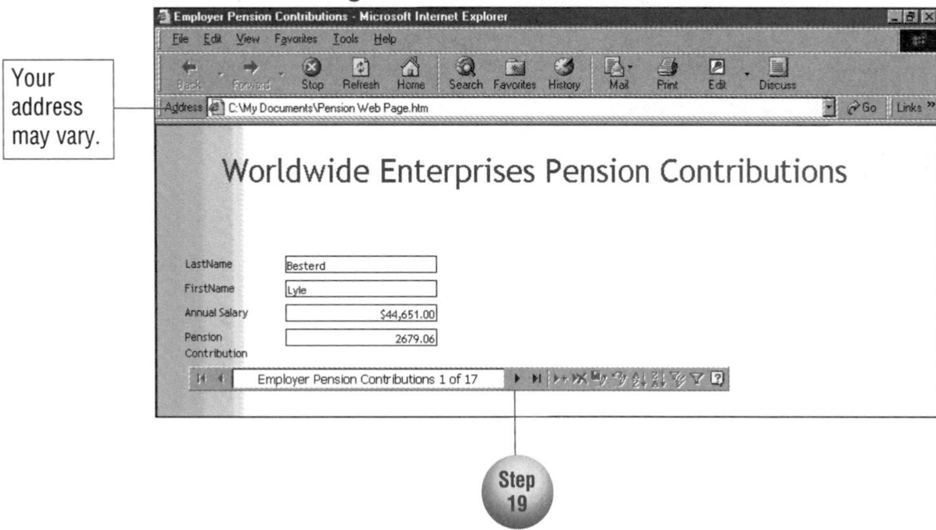

19 Scroll through the records in the data access page in the Web browser window by clicking the Next Record button in the navigation bar.

20 Close the Web browser window.

21 Close the Pension Web Page : Data Access Page window.

Take 2

Using Data Access Pages

When a data access page is created, Access creates a folder in which to store the Web page files. Although the Web pages are not stored directly within the database, the data access page is directly connected to the source database. When a user displays the data access page in the browser, she or he is viewing a copy of the page. Any filtering or sorting that is done to affect the way the data is *displayed* affects only this copy of the page. Changes made to the *content* of the data, however, such as inserting, editing, or deleting field values, are updated immediately in the source database so that everyone viewing the data access page is working with the same information.

DIRECTOR'S CUT

Create a Web Page Using Page Wizard

1 Click Pages in Objects bar.
2 Double-click *Create data access page by using wizard.*
3 Choose table or query and field(s) to include in Web page.
4 Click Next.
5 Choose a grouping level and click Next.
6 Choose a field to sort by and click Next.
7 Key page title and click Finish.
8 Modify page in Design view as required.
9 Click Save.
10 Key Web page file name, click Save.

Inserting Hyperlinks

Hyperlinks can be inserted in data access pages by keying a URL in a label control in the data access page. Access automatically converts the URL to a hyperlink. To hyperlink to other files or Web pages, click the Hyperlink button in the Toolbox palette. Drag to create the outline of a rectangle in the data access page. When you release the mouse button, the Insert Hyperlink dialog box automatically appears. Key the text you want to display for the hyperlink in the Text to display text box and then key the destination for the link in the Type the file or Web page name text box.

PROJECT: You will create a new Web page for displaying employee benefits and then create a link in the page to display the Pension Web page.

steps

1. With WE Employees4 open and *Pages* selected in the Objects bar, create a new data access page using the Page Wizard as follows:
   - Add the *Emp No, FirstName,* and *LastName* fields from the Employees table and the *Pension Plan, Dental Plan, Premium Health,* and *Vacation* fields from the Employee Benefits table.
   - Click Next in the second Page Wizard dialog box to specify no grouping levels.
   - Click Next in the third Page Wizard dialog box to specify no sorting.
   - Accept Employee Benefits as the title of the Web page.
2. Close the Field List window in the data access page Design view window.
3. Key **Worldwide Enterprises Employee Benefits** as the title text.
4. Apply the Arcs theme to the data access page.
5. Click the Hyperlink button in the Toolbox Palette.
6. Position the crosshairs pointer with the hyperlink icon attached to the right of the Pension Plan check box and then drag to create a box the approximate height and width shown.

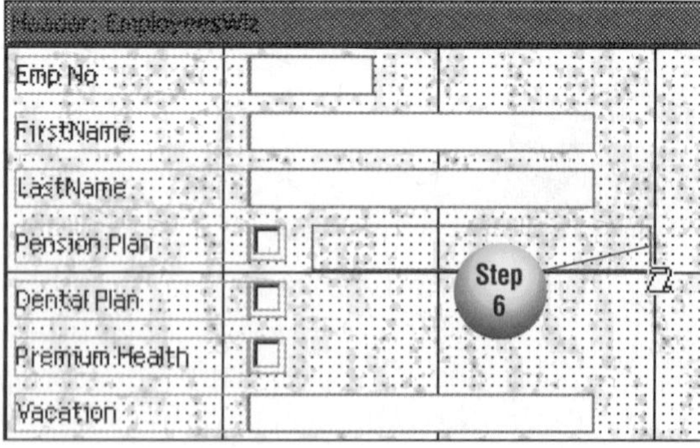

7. Click in the Text to display text box and key **Employer Pension Contributions**.

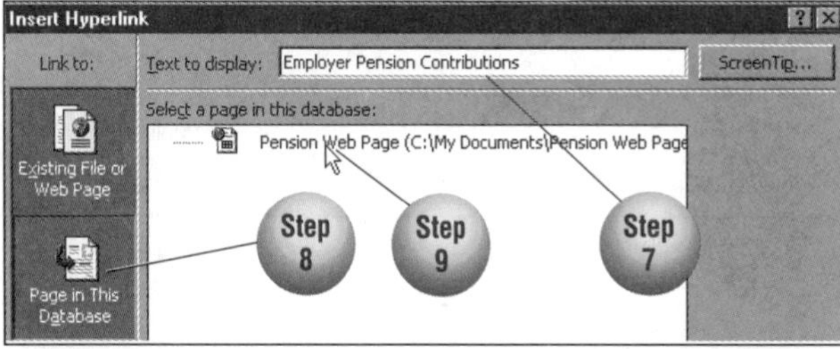

8. Click Page in This Database in the Insert Hyperlink Objects bar.
9. Double-click *Pension Web Page* in the Select a page in this database list box.

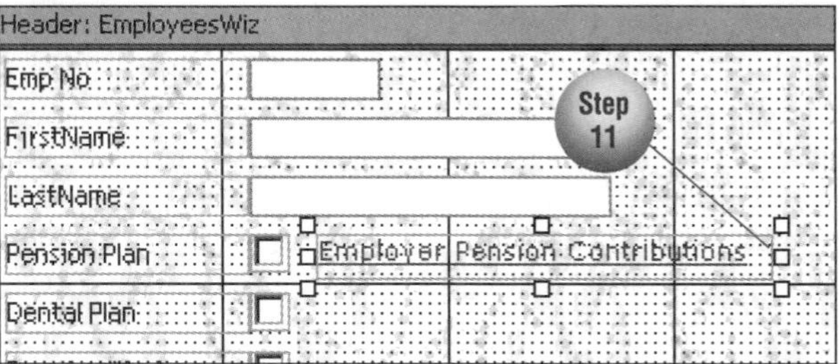

10. Click the down-pointing triangle at the right of the Font Size button on the Formatting (Page) toolbar and then click *8* in the drop-down list.
11. Adjust the size of the hyperlink control as required to display all of the text.
12. Click Save, key **Employee Benefits** in the File name text box, and then click Save.
13. Click File and then Web Page Preview.
14. Click the hyperlink text *Employer Pension Contributions* when the first record displays in the default Web browser.
15. Click the Back button on the Web browser toolbar to return to the Employee Benefits Web page.
16. Close the Web browser window.
17. Close the Employee Benefits : Data Access Page.
18. Close the WE Employees4 database.

E-Mail Address Hyperlinks

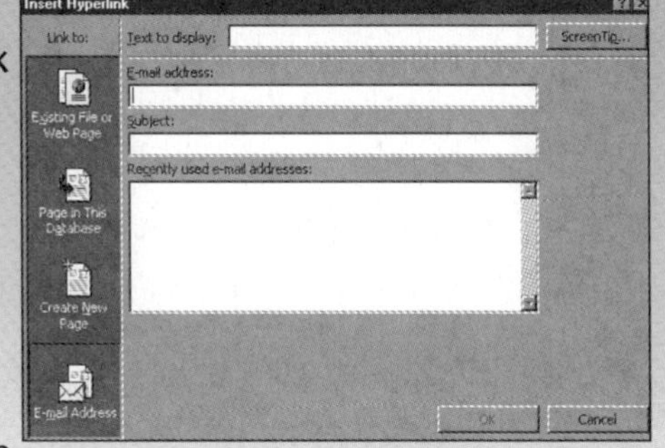

The Objects bar in the Insert Hyperlink dialog box contains an E-mail Address button. Create an e-mail hyperlink to allow users to create an e-mail message with the correct address entered for them. When the user clicks the link, a message window will open in which he or she can key the subject and content of the message and then click Send. When you click E-mail Address in the Objects bar, the Insert Hyperlink dialog box displays as shown above.

Insert Hyperlink
1. Open data access page in Design view.
2. Click Hyperlink button in Toolbox.
3. Drag to create outline of rectangle in the page.
4. Key display text for the link in the Text to display text box.
5. Key file name or URL in the Type the file or Web page name text box.
6. Click OK.
7. Click Save.

Features Summary

Feature	Button	Menu	Keyboard
Delete Columns		Edit, Cut	Ctrl + X
Design view		View, Design View	
Insert Hyperlink		Insert, Hyperlink	Ctrl + K
Page Wizard		Insert, Page, Page Wizard	
Properties Sheet		View, Properties	
Report Wizard		Insert, Report, Report Wizard	
Run query	!	Query, Run	
Simple Query Wizard		Insert, Query, Query Wizard	
Theme		Format, Theme	
Web Page Preview		File, Web Page Preview	

Procedures Check

In the space provided at the right, indicate the correct term or command.

1. This is the name of the wizard used to facilitate creating a query to select records from a table. ____________
2. Key this entry in the Annual Salary criteria row in Query Design view to extract records of employees who earn more than $40,000. ____________
3. Click the check box in this row in the query design grid to prevent a column from being displayed in the query results. ____________
4. A report is composed of a series of objects referred to as this. ____________
5. Click this button in the Toolbox to create a calculated field in a report. ____________
6. This is the name of the wizard used to facilitate creating a Web page for a table. ____________
7. This is the name given to a group of predefined formats and color schemes that can be applied to Web pages. ____________
8. Click this button in the Toolbox to create a link to another Web page or URL. ____________

9. Provide the entry you would key in a blank Field row in the Query Design grid to calculate the total cost of an item given the following information:
   - the total cost is calculated by multiplying the units ordered by the unit price.
   - the units ordered is stored in a field named *UnitsOnOrder*.
   - the unit cost is stored in a field named *UnitCost*.
   - the new column should have the column heading *Total Cost*.

   ____

List the names of the five sections found in a report.

10. ____________________ 13. ____________________

11. ____________________ 14. ____________________

12. ____________________

Identify the features represented by the buttons.

15. ____________________  16. ____________________  17. ____________________

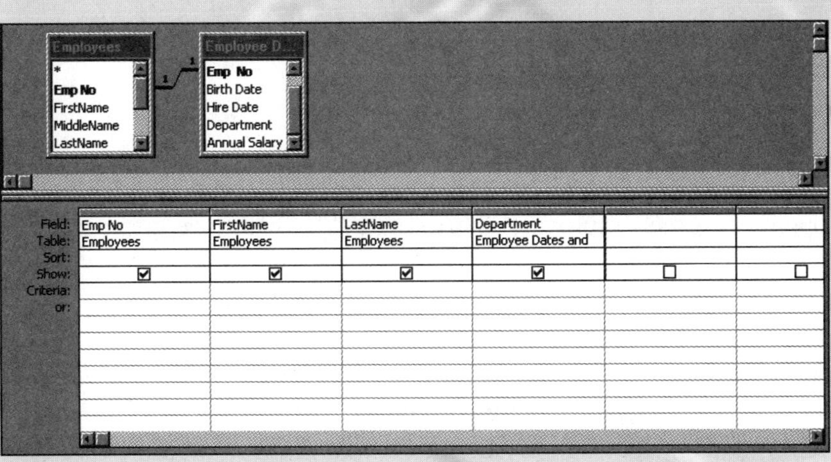

Use the Query Design window shown above to answer questions 18–20.

18. List the steps you would complete to sort the query results by the *LastName* field.

    ____

    ____

19. List the steps you would complete to add the *Annual Salary* field in the Employee Dates and Salaries table to the blank column after *Department* in the query design grid.

    ____

    ____

20. List the steps you would complete to extract records of employees who work in the Overseas Distribution department.

    ____

    ____

Skills Review

Activity 1: Creating a Query

1 Open the WE Employees4 database.
2 Use the Simple Query Wizard to create a detail query that will display the fields from the Employees, Employees Dates and Salaries, and Employee Benefits tables as follows:

Employees	**Employee Dates and Salaries**	**Employee Benefits**
Emp No	*Hire Date*	*Life Insurance*
FirstName	*Annual Salary*	*RPP Eligibility Date*
LastName		

3 Key **Employee Salaries and Life Insurance** as the title for the query.
4 View the query results.
5 Change the page orientation to landscape and then print the query results.
6 Close the Employee Salaries and Life Insurance query.

Activity 2: Sorting; Adding a Criteria Statement; Creating a Calculated Field

1 With WE Employees4 open, open the Employee Salaries and Life Insurance query in Design view.
2 Sort the query results by the *LastName* field in ascending order.
3 Add a criteria statement in the *Annual Salary* field that will extract the records of employees who earn more than $44,000. *(Hint: Numeric fields do not require quotation marks and should not include any currency symbols or commas.)*
4 Create a calculated field in the query that will divide the *Annual Salary* column by 12 to display the monthly salary. You determine the column heading for the calculated field.
5 Format the calculated field to display the monthly salary in Currency format.
6 Use the Save As command to save the revised query as **Employees who earn over 44,000**.
7 Run the query.
8 Change the page orientation to landscape.
9 Preview and then print the query results.
10 Close the Employees who earn over 44,000 query.

Activity 3: Creating and Modifying a Report

1 With WE Employees4 open, use the Report Wizard to create a report based on the Employee Salaries and Life Insurance query as follows:
   - Add all of the fields from the query to the report.
   - Do not include any grouping or sorting.
   - Select the Tabular layout in landscape orientation.
   - Select the Bold style.
   - Accept the default title for the report.

2 Display the report in Design view and then modify the report as follows:
   - Resize and/or move controls so that all column headings and data are completely visible in the report.
   - Insert a label control in the Report Header section that will print the text *Report Design by: Student Name*. Substitute your first and last names for Student Name. Align the control at the right edge of the report and change the font size to 12 point. If necessary, resize the control to display the entire text in the label.
3 Preview and then print the report.
4 Close the Employees Salaries and Life Insurance report. Click Yes when prompted to save changes to the report design.

Activity 4: Creating a Web Page; Inserting a Hyperlink; Using Web Page Preview

1 Use the Page Wizard to create a Web page based on the Employee Salaries and Life Insurance query as follows:
   - Add all of the fields from the query to the Web page.
   - Do not include any grouping or sorting.
   - Accept the default title for the Web page.
2 Apply a theme of your choosing to the Web page.
3 Key **Worldwide Enterprises Salaries and Life Insurance** as the title text in the Web page.
4 Save the Web page and name it Salaries and Life Insurance.
5 Create a hyperlink positioned to the right of the *LastName* field that will display the Employee Benefits Web page when the user clicks the link.
6 Save the Web page, display it in the default browser window, and then view two or three records.
7 Print the Web page.
8 Click the link to view the Employee Benefits Web page.
9 Click the Back button on the browser toolbar to return to the Salaries and Life Insurance page and then close the browser window.
10 Close the Salaries and Life Insurance Web page.
11 Close WE Employees4.

Performance Plus

Activity 1: Creating a Query; Adding Criteria

1 The Bursary Selection Committee at Niagara Peninsula College would like you to provide them with the names of students who have achieved an A+ in all three of their courses.
2 Open NPC Grades4.
3 Create a query that will extract the records of those students who have an A+ in all three courses. Include student numbers, first names, last names, and grades. Sort the query in ascending order by student's last name. *(Hint: Key A+ encased in quotation marks in the Criteria row to indicate the plus symbol is not part of an expression.)*

4 Save the query and name it A+ Students.
5 Run the query.
6 Best Fit the columns in the query results datasheet.
7 Print the query results.
8 Close the A+ Students query.
9 Close NPC Grades4.

Activity 2: Creating a Query and Report

1 Bobbie Sinclair, business manager of Performance Threads, would like a report that lists the costumes rented in August 2002.
2 Open PT Costume Inventory4.
3 Open the Costumes Rented in July 2002 query in Design view.
4 Expand the column width for the *Date Out* field in the design grid to view the entire criteria statement. Write the criteria statement. ______________________________
5 Create a new query based on the Costume Inventory table that will list the fields in the following order: *Costume No., Date Out, Date In, Character, Daily Rental Fee.*
6 Add a criteria statement in the *Date Out* column that will extract the records for costumes rented in the month of August 2002. *(Hint: You can key dates in long form [i.e., August 1, 2002] and without the # symbol. Access automatically converts to an entry similar to the one you viewed in the other query.)*
7 Sort the query results first by *Date Out*, then by *Date In*, and then by *Character* in ascending order.
8 Save the query and name it Costumes Rented in August 2002.
9 Run the query.
10 Create a report based on the Costumes Rented in August 2002 query. Add all of the fields to the report. You determine the layout, style, and title for the report.
11 Add your name in a label object control at the right side of the Report Header section.
12 Print the report.
13 Close PT Costume Inventory4.

Activity 3: Modifying a Report

1 Heidi Pasqual, financial officer of Worldwide Enterprises, has created three reports that print the names and addresses of the distributors. Heidi has noticed that the street addresses are truncated on the report and requested your assistance to correct them.
2 Open WE Distributors4.
3 Open the Canadian Distributors Addresses report.
4 Magnify the report in the Print Preview window to view the information in the *Street Address1* and *Street Address2* columns.
5 Switch to Design view.
6 Resize and move the City, Province, and Postal Code controls to make enough room on the page to widen the address columns.
7 Widen the Street Address1 and Street Address2 controls.
8 View the report in Print Preview.

9. If necessary, switch to Design view and make further adjustments to the size and placement of the controls.
10. Position the pointer on the bottom gray border line for the Report Footer section and then drag the design grid down approximately 0.5 inch. Add a label object in the Report Footer that includes the text *Report Design by: Student Name*. Substitute your first and last name for Student Name. Apply Italic formatting to the label object.
11. Save, print, and then close the Canadian Distributors Addresses report.
12. Make the same changes to the design of the Overseas Distributors Addresses report.
13. Save, print, and then close the Overseas Distributors Addresses report.
14. Make the same design changes to the US Distributors Addresses report.
15. Save, print, and then close the US Distributors Addresses report.
16. Close WE Distributors4.

Activity 4: Creating and Modifying a Web Page

1. Dana Hirsch, manager of The Waterfront Bistro, has been considering posting the inventory purchases information on the company intranet for the executive chef, who is more familiar with Web browser navigation methods than with Access. Dana has asked you to create a Web page from the Purchases table.
2. Open WB Inventory4.
3. Create a Web page using the Page Wizard and adding the fields in the order listed below. Accept all other default settings in the Page Wizard dialog boxes.

Table	Field
Purchases	*Purchase Order No.*
Purchases	*Item No.*
Inventory List	*Item*
Inventory List	*Supplier Code*
Inventory List	*Unit*
Purchases	*Purchase Date*
Purchases	*Amount*

4. Apply a theme of your choosing to the Web page.
5. Key **The Waterfront Bistro Inventory Purchases** as the title of the page.
6. Save the Web page and name it Inventory Purchases.
7. View the Web page in the Web browser window.
8. Scroll through the records in the Web browser window.
9. Print the last record in the page.
10. Close the Web browser window.
11. Close the Inventory Purchases Web page.
12. Close WB Inventory4.

Activity 5: Finding Information on Adding Fields to an Existing Report

1 Use the online help to find out how to add a field to an existing report in Design view. *(Hint: A control that will display data from the associated table is considered a bound control.)*
2 Print the help topic that you find.
3 Open WE Distributors4.
4 Open the Canadian Distributors Addresses report in Design view.
5 Resize and move controls left to make room for the telephone number to print as the last column in the report. You will need a width of approximately 1 inch at the right edge of the form for the telephone number.
6 Add the Telephone field to the report. *(Hint: Cut and paste the label control for the* Telephone *field from the Detail section to the Page Header section after you have added the field. You may have to edit the control after it is pasted.)*
7 Preview the report.
8 Save, print, and then close the Canadian Distributors Addresses report.
9 Close WE Distributors4.

Activity 6: Researching Movies on the Internet

1 Choose five movies currently playing in your vicinity that you have seen or would like to see, and then find their Web sites on the Internet. Look for the information listed in step 3 that you will be entering into a new database.
2 Create a new database named Movies.
3 Create a table named Movie Facts that will store the following information:
   Movie title
   Director's name
   Producer's name
   Lead Actor – Male
   Supporting Actor – Male
   Lead Actor – Female
   Supporting Actor – Female
   Movie category – e.g., drama, action, thriller, science fiction
   Web site address
4 Design and create a form to enter the records for the movies you researched.
5 Enter the records using the form created in step 4.
6 Print the last form only.
7 Design and create a report for the Movie Facts table. Add your name to the Report Header or Report Footer section in a label control object.
8 Print the Movie Facts report.
9 Close the Movies database.

INTEGRATED 2

Word Excel Access

Data in one program within the Microsoft Office suite can be imported and/or exported to another program. For example, you can export data in an Access table to an Excel worksheet or a Word document. One of the advantages of exporting data to Excel or Word is that formatting can be applied using Excel or Word formatting features. Data can also be imported into an Access database file. If you know that you will update data in a program other than Access, link the data. Changes made to linked data are reflected in both the source and destination programs. In this section, you will learn the following skills and complete the projects listed below.

Skills

- Export Access data in a table to Excel
- Export Access data in a table to Word
- Export Access data in a report to Word
- Import Excel data to a new Access table
- Link data between an Excel worksheet and an Access table
- Edit linked data

Projects

Export grades for PRD 112 from an Access table to an Excel worksheet. Import grades for a Beginning Theatre class from an Excel worksheet into an Access database table. Link grades for TRA 220 between an Excel worksheet and an Access database table.

Export data on overseas distributors from an Access table to a Word document. Export data on Canadian distributors from an Access report to a Word document.

Export data on costume inventory from an Access table to an Excel worksheet. Export data on costume inventory from an Access report to a Word document. Import data on costume design hours from an Excel worksheet into an Access table.

Export data on inventory from an Access table to a Word document.

Link data on booking commissions between an Excel worksheet and an Access table and then update the data.

Exporting Access Data to Excel

One of the advantages of a suite program like Microsoft Office is the ability to exchange data from one program to another. Access, like the other programs in the suite, offers a feature to export data from Access into Excel and/or Word. Export data using the OfficeLinks button on the Database toolbar. Access data saved in a table, form, or report can be exported to Excel. The data is saved as an Excel file in the folder where Access is installed.

PROJECT: You are Katherine Lamont, Theatre Arts Division instructor at Niagara Peninsula College. You want to work on your grades for your PRD 112 class over the weekend and you do not have Access installed on your personal laptop. You decide to export your Access grading table to Excel.

steps

1. Open Access and then open the NPC Classes database file.

Problem: You may need to copy the NPC Classes database file to your folder or disk.

2. Click the Tables button on the Objects bar and then click once on PRD112 Grades in the list box.
3. Click the down-pointing triangle at the right side of the OfficeLinks button on the Database toolbar.
4. At the drop-down list that displays, click Analyze It with MS Excel.

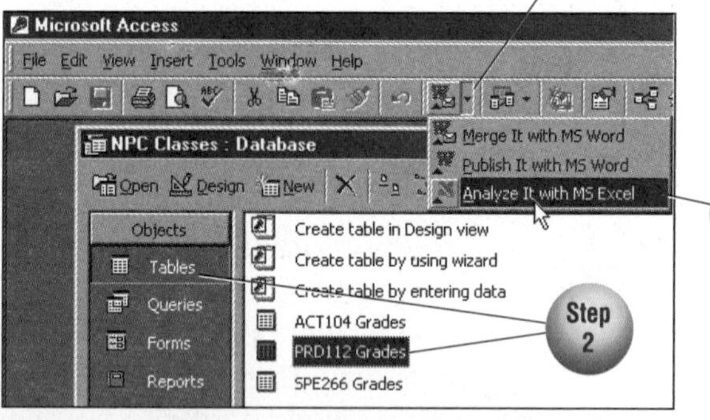

5. When the data displays on the screen in Excel as a worksheet, key the following grades in the specified cells:

D2	=	**B**
D5	=	**A**
D13	=	**D**
D15	=	**C**
D16	=	**D**
D17	=	**B**

	A	B	C	D
1	Student No	Last Name	First Name	Grade
2	111-785-156	Bastow	Maren	B
3	118-487-578	Andre	Ian	B
4	137-845-746	Knowlton	Sherri	A
5	138-456-749	Yiu	Terry	A
6	146-984-137	Rhodes	Tari	C
7	157-457-856	Dwyer	Barbara	C
8	184-457-156	Van Este	Doranda	C
9	197-486-745	Koning	Jeffrey	A
10	198-744-149	Lysenko	Earl	B
11	211-745-856	Uhrig	Andrew	B
12	217-458-687	Husson	Ahmad	A+
13	221-689-478	Bhullar	Ash	D
14	229-658-412	Mysior	Melanie	C
15	255-158-498	Gibson	Kevin	C
16	274-658-986	Woollatt	Bentley	D
17	314-745-856	Morgan	Bruce	B

Step 5

6. Select cells A1 through D17.
7. Click Format and then AutoFormat.
8. At the AutoFormat dialog box, scroll down the list of autoformats until *List 1* is visible and then double-click *List 1*.

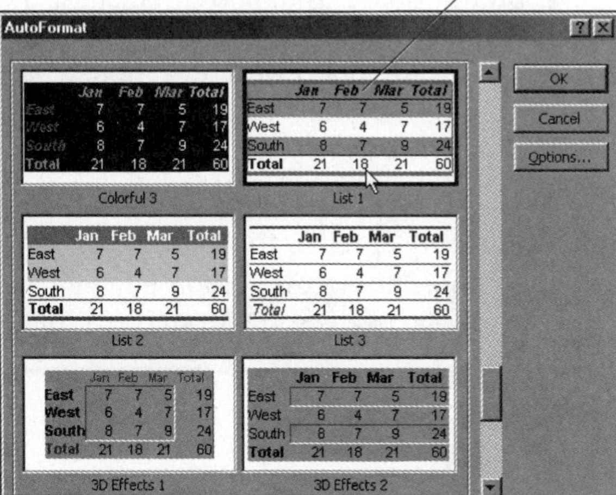

9. Deselect the cells by clicking outside the selected cells.
10. Save the worksheet with the name Int E2-01.
11. Print and then close Int E2-01.
12. Click the button on the Taskbar representing the Access database file NPC Classes and then close the database file.

Exporting to Excel

Three methods are available for exporting Access data to an Excel worksheet. You can export data using the Analyze It with MS Excel option from the OfficeLinks drop-down list as you did in this section. You can save the output of a datasheet, form, or report directly as an Excel (.xls) worksheet or you can export the datasheet as unformatted data to Excel.

Export Access Table to Excel

1. Open database file.
2. Click Tables button in Objects bar and then click desired table.
3. Click down-pointing triangle at right side of OfficeLinks button.
4. Click Analyze It with MS Excel.

Exporting Access Data to Word

Export data from Access to Word in the same manner as you would export to Excel. To export data to Word, open the database file, select the table, form, or report, and then click the OfficeLinks button on the Database toolbar. At the drop-down list, click Publish It with MS Word. Word opens and the data displays in a Word document that is automatically saved with the same name as the database table, form, or report. The difference is that the file extension *.rtf* is added to the name rather than the Word file extension *.doc*. An rtf file is saved in "rich-text format," which preserves formatting such as fonts and styles. A document saved with the .rtf extension can be opened in Word and in other Windows word processing or desktop publishing programs.

PROJECT: Roman Deptulski, the manager of overseas distribution for Worldwide Enterprises, has asked you to export an Access database table containing information on overseas distributors to a Word document. He needs some of the information for a distribution meeting.

steps

1. With Access the active program, open WE Company.
2. Click the Tables button on the Objects bar and then click once on *Overseas Distributors* in the list box.
3. Click the down-pointing triangle at the right side of the OfficeLinks button on the Database toolbar and then click *Publish It with MS Word* at the drop-down list.

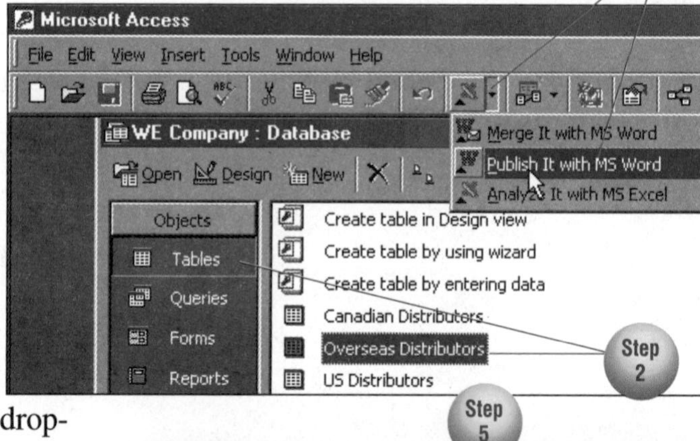

4. When the data displays on the screen in Word, select all of the cells in the two *Street* columns.
5. Delete the selected columns by clicking Table, pointing to Delete, and then clicking Columns.
6. Select all of the cells in the *Postal Code*, *Telephone*, and *Fax* columns. Then click Table, point to Delete, and then click Columns.

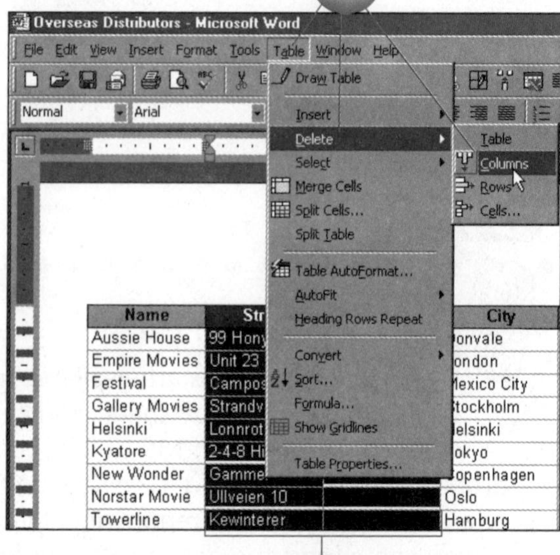

7 The Word Table feature has an AutoFit feature that will automatically adjust the column widths to the contents of the columns. Make sure the insertion point is positioned in a cell in the table and then use this feature by clicking Table, pointing to AutoFit, and then clicking AutoFit to Contents.

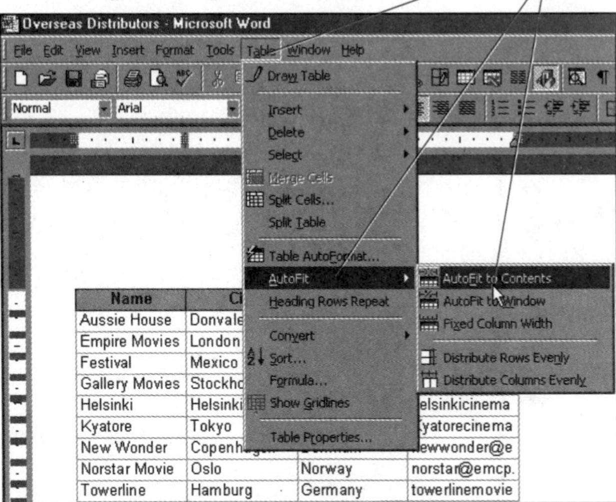

8 With the insertion point positioned in any cell in the table, click Table and then Table AutoFormat.

9 At the Table AutoFormat dialog box, scroll down the list of autoformats in the Formats list box until *List 7* is visible and then double-click *List 7*.

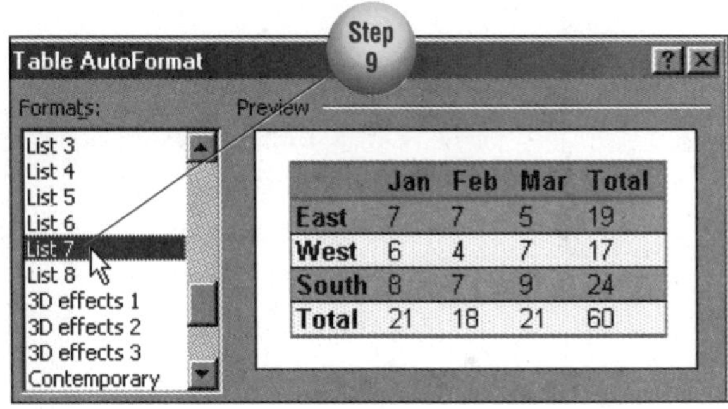

10 Click the Save button to save the document with the same name (Overseas Distributors).

11 Print and then close Overseas Distributors.

12 Click the button on the Taskbar representing the WE Company Access database file and then close the database file.

Adjusting a Table

In this section, you adjusted the Word table to the cell contents. The Table AutoFit feature contains several options for adjusting table contents. These options are:

Option	Action
AutoFit to Contents	Adjusts table to accommodate the table text
AutoFit to Window	Resizes table to fit within the window or browser. If browser changes size, table size automatically adjusts to fit within window
Fixed Column Width	Adjusts each column to a fixed width using the current widths of the columns
Distribute Rows Evenly	Changes selected rows or cells to equal row height
Distribute Columns Evenly	Changes selected columns or cells to equal column width

DIRECTOR'S CUT

Export Access Table to Word

1 Open database file.
2 Click Tables button in Objects bar and then click desired table.
3 Click down-pointing triangle at right side of OfficeLinks button.
4 Click Publish It with MS Word.

Exporting an Access Report to Word

An Access report, like an Access table, can be exported to a Word document. Export a report to Word by using the Publish It with MS Word option from the OfficeLinks drop-down list. One of the advantages in exporting a report to Word is that formatting can be applied to the report using Word formatting features.

PROJECT: Sam Vestering, manager of North American distribution for Worldwide Enterprises, needs a list of Canadian distributors. He has asked you to export a report to Word and then apply specific formatting to the report. He needs some of the information for a contact list.

steps

1. With Access the active program, open WE Company.
2. At the WE Company Database window, click the Reports button in the Objects bar.
3. Click *Canadian Distributors Addresses* in the list box.
4. Click the down-pointing triangle at the right side of the OfficeLinks button, and then click *Publish It with MS Word*.
5. When the data displays on the screen in Word, press Ctrl + A to select the entire document.
6. Click the down-pointing triangle at the right side of the Font button on the Formatting toolbar and then click *Arial* at the drop-down list.

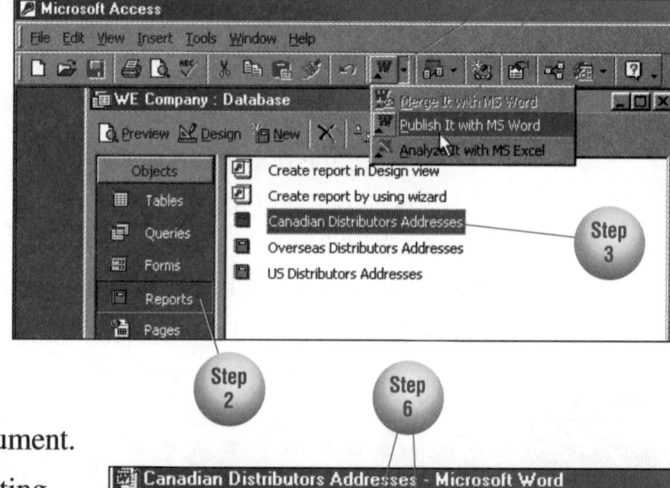

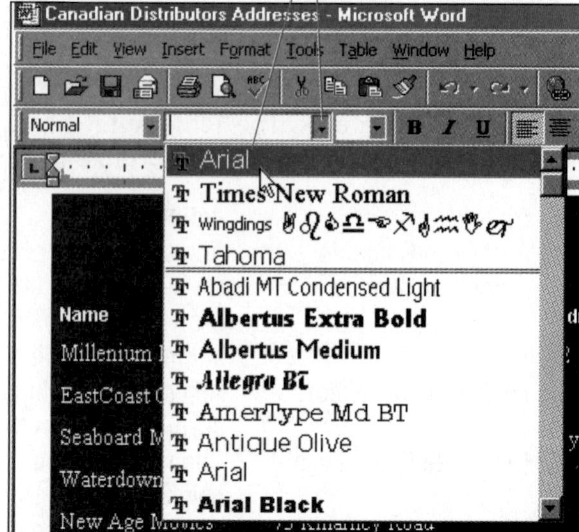

7. With the document still selected, click the down-pointing triangle at the right side of the Font Size button on the Formatting toolbar and then click *10* at the drop-down list.
8. Press Ctrl + Home to move the insertion point to the beginning of the document and then key **Worldwide Enterprises**.
9. Press Enter and then key **Canadian Distributors**.
10. Select *Worldwide Enterprises* and then change the font to 22-point Arial bold.
11. Select *Canadian Distributors* and then change the font to 18-point Arial bold.
12. Click the Save button to save the report with the default name (Canadian Distributors Addresses).
13. Print and then close Canadian Distributors Addresses.

    The Canadian Distributors Addresses document prints in landscape orientation and includes a footer at the bottom of the page that prints the current date.
14. Exit Word.
15. In Access, close the WE Company Access database file.

Merging Access Data with a Word Document

Word includes a Mail Merge feature that you can use to create letters, envelopes, and much more, with personalized information. Generally, a merge requires two documents—the *data source* and the *main document*. The data source contains the variable information that will be inserted in the main document. Create a data source document in Word or create a data source using data from an Access table. When merging Access data, you can either key the text in the main document or merge Access data with an existing Word document. To merge data in an Access table, open the database file, click the Tables button in the Objects bar, and then click the desired table. Click the OfficeLinks button on the Database toolbar and then click Merge It with MS Word. Follow the steps presented by the Microsoft Word Mail Merge Wizard to complete the merge.

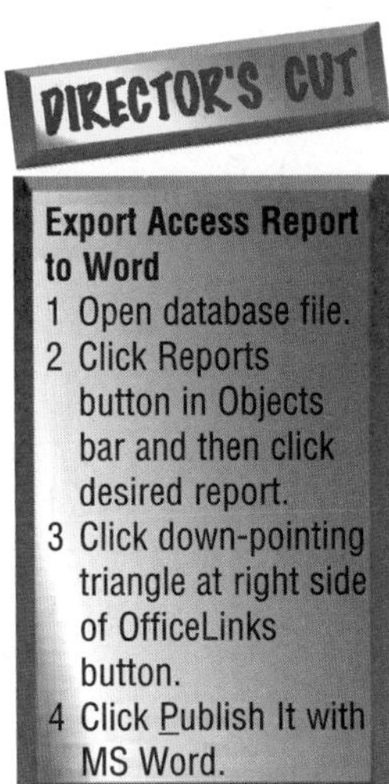

Importing Data to a New Table

In the previous three sections, you exported Access data to Excel and Word. You can also import data from other programs into an Access table. For example, you can import data from an Excel worksheet and create a new table in a database file. Data in the original program is not connected to the data imported into an Access table. If you make changes to the data in the original program, those changes are not reflected in the Access table.

PROJECT: You are Gina Simmons, Theatre Arts instructor, and have recorded grades in an Excel worksheet for your students in the Beginning Theatre class. You want to import those grades into the NPC Classes database file.

steps

1. In Access, open the NPC Classes database file and then click the Tables button in the Objects bar.
2. Import an Excel worksheet by clicking File, pointing to Get External Data, and then clicking Import.
3. At the Import dialog box, change the Files of type option to *Microsoft Excel*, and then double-click *NPC Beg Th Grades* in the list box.

   Your list of documents may vary from what you see in the image at the right.

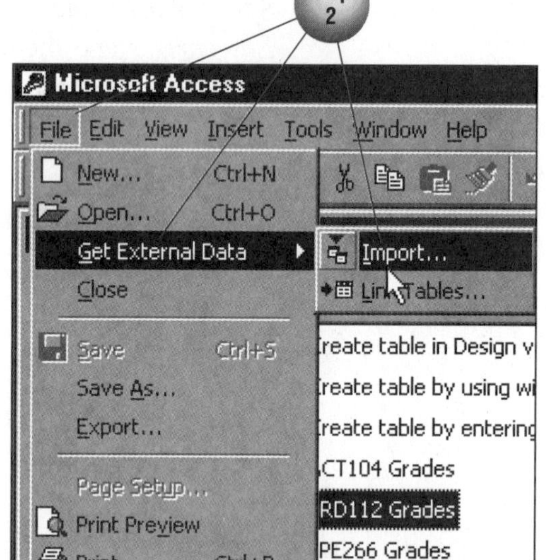

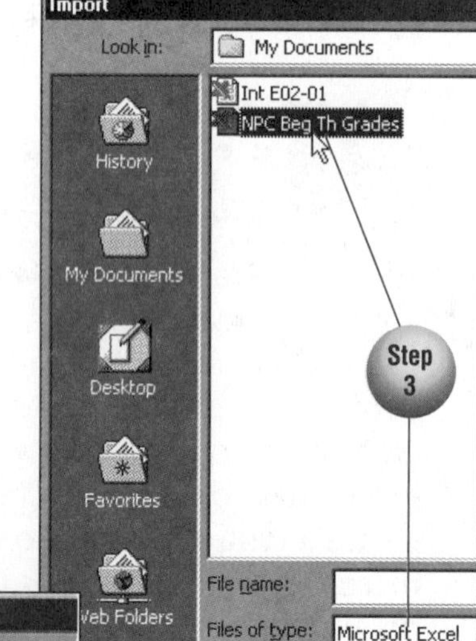

Problem ? If *NPC Beg Th Grades* does not display in the list box, you may need to navigate to another folder. Check with your instructor.

4. At the first Import Spreadsheet Wizard dialog box, click the Next button.
5. At the second dialog box, insert a check mark in the First Row Contains Column Headings option, and then click the Next button.

6. At the third dialog box, make sure the In a New Table option is selected, and then click the Next button.
7. At the fourth dialog box, click the Next button.
8. At the fifth dialog box, click the Choose my own primary key option (this inserts *Student No* in the text box located to the right of the option), and then click the Next button.

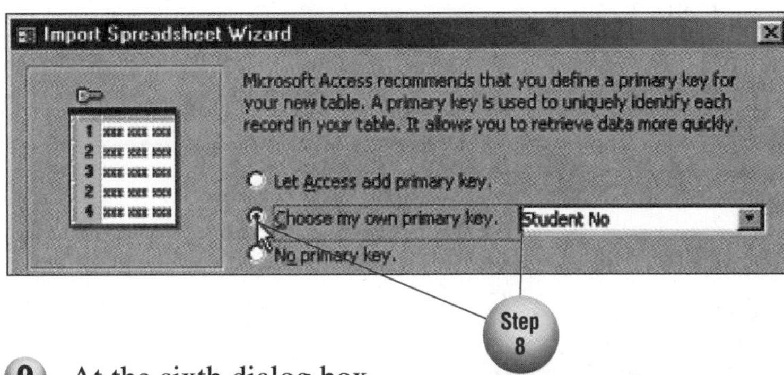

9. At the sixth dialog box, key **Beg Th Grades** in the Import to Table text box, and then click the Finish button.
10. At the message saying the data was imported, click OK.
11. Open the new table by double-clicking *Beg Th Grades* in the list box.
12. Print and then close Beg Th Grades.
13. Close the NPC Classes database file.

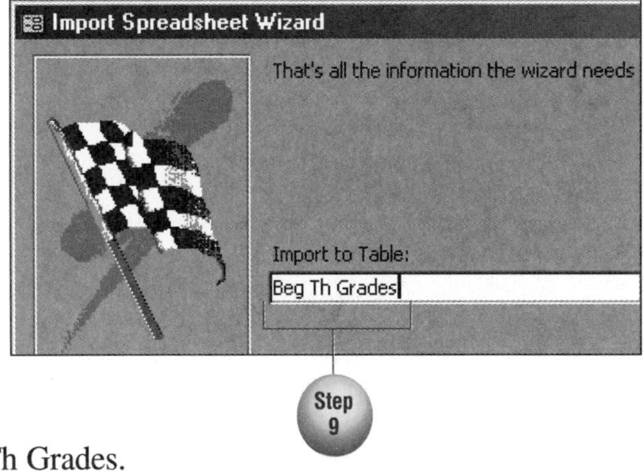

Take 2

Importing or Linking a Table

You can import data from another program into an Access table or you can link the data. Choose the method depending on how you are going to use the data. Import data to a table if you are going to use the data only in Access. Access generally operates faster working with its own tables. Link data to an Access table if the data will be changed or updated in a program other than Access. Changes made to linked data are reflected in both the source and destination programs.

Linking Data to a New Table and Editing Linked Data

Imported data is not connected to the source program. If you know that you will use your data only in Access, import it. However, if you want to update data in a program other than Access, link the data. Changes made to linked data are reflected in both the source and destination programs. For example, you can link an Excel worksheet with an Access table and when you make changes in either the Excel worksheet or the Access table, the change is reflected in the other program. To link data to a new table, open the database file, click File, point to Get External Data, and then click Link Tables. At the Link dialog box, double-click the desired document name. This activates the Link Wizard that walks you through the steps to link the data.

PROJECT: You are Cal Rubine, Theatre Arts instructor at Niagara Peninsula College. You record students' grades in an Excel worksheet and also link the grades to an Access database file. With the data linked, changes you make to either the Excel table or the Access table will be reflected in the other table.

steps

1. Open Excel and then open NPC TRA 220.
2. Save the worksheet with the name Int E2-02.
3. Print and then close Int E2-02.
4. Make Access the active program, open the NPC Classes database file, and then click the Tables button in the Objects bar.
5. Link an Excel worksheet by clicking File, pointing to Get External Data, and then clicking Link Tables.
6. Change the Files of type option to *Microsoft Excel*, and then double-click *Int E2-02* in the list box.

   Depending on your system configuration, you may need to navigate to the folder containing Int E2-02.

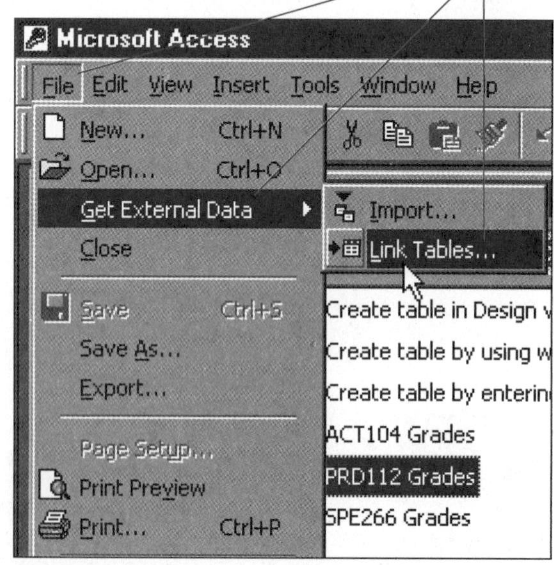

7. At the first Link Spreadsheet Wizard dialog box, make sure Show Worksheets is selected, and that *Sheet1* is selected in the list box, and then click the Next button.

8. At the second dialog box, make sure there is a check mark in the First Row Contains Column Headings option, and then click the Next button.

9. At the third dialog box, key **Linked Grades** in the Linked Table Name text box, and then click the Finish button.

10. At the message stating the link is finished, click OK.

    Access uses different icons to represent linked tables and tables that are stored in the current database. Notice the icon that displays before the *Linked Grades* table.

11. Open the new Linked Grades table in Datasheet view.

12. As you look at the table, you realize that you need to add a student to the end of the list. Add the following new record in the specified fields (see image below):

Student No	*Student*	*Midterm*
138-456-749	**Yui, T.**	**3.25**

Linked Grades : Table

Student No	Student	Midterm
111-75-156	Bastow, M.	3.25
359-845-475	Collyer, S.	1.50
157-457-856	Dwyer, B.	3.50
348-876-486	Ennis, A.	2.25
378-159-746	Gagne, M.	3.00
197-486-745	Koning, J.	2.75
314-745-856	Morgan, B.	3.75
349-874-658	Retieffe, S.	4.00
138-456-749	Yui, T.	3.25

Step 12

(continued)

13. Save, print, and then close the Linked Grades table.
14. Make Excel the active program and then open Int E2-02.

    Notice that the worksheet contains the student name Yui, T., which you added to the Access table.
15. You have finished grading student finals and need to insert the grades in the worksheet. Key the following grades in the specified cells:

D2	=	**2.75**
D3	=	**1**
D4	=	**3.5**
D5	=	**2**
D6	=	**3.5**
D7	=	**2.5**
D8	=	**3**
D9	=	**3.5**
D10	=	**2.5**

	A	B	C	D
1	Student No	Student	Midterm	Final
2	111-75-156	Bastow, M.	3.25	2.75
3	359-845-475	Collyer, S.	1.50	1.00
4	157-457-856	Dwyer, B.	3.50	3.50
5	348-876-486	Ennis, A.	2.25	2.00
6	378-159-746	Gagne, M.	3.00	3.50
7	197-486-745	Koning, J.	2.75	2.50
8	314-745-856	Morgan, B.	3.75	3.00
9	349-874-658	Retieffe, S.	4.00	3.50
10	138-456-749	Yui, T.	3.25	2.50

Step 15

16. Make cell E2 the active cell and then insert a formula to average scores by clicking the Paste Function button on the Standard toolbar.
17. Double-click *AVERAGE* in the Function name list box.

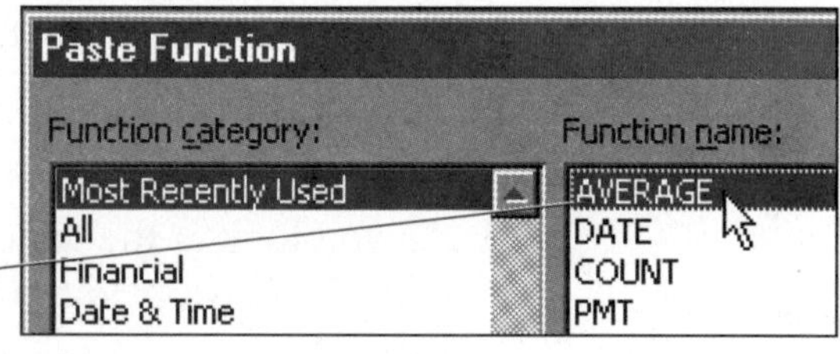

If *AVERAGE* is not visible in the Function name list box, click *Most Recently Used* in the Function category list box.

18. At the formula palette, make sure *C2:D2* displays in the Number1 text box, and then click OK.

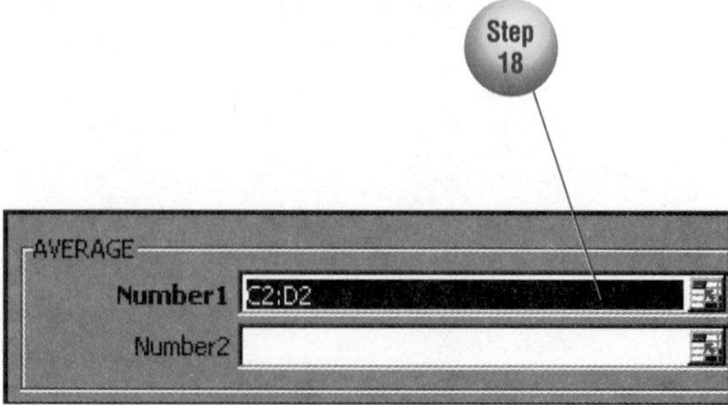

19 Using the fill handle, copy the formula down to cell E10.

	A	B	C	D	E
1	Student No	Student	Midterm	Final	Average
2	111-75-156	Bastow, M.	3.25	2.75	3.00
3	359-845-475	Collyer, S.	1.50	1.00	1.25
4	157-457-856	Dwyer, B.	3.50	3.50	3.50
5	348-876-486	Ennis, A.	2.25	2.00	2.13
6	378-159-746	Gagne, M.	3.00	3.50	3.25
7	197-486-745	Koning, J.	2.75	2.50	2.63
8	314-745-856	Morgan, B.	3.75	3.00	3.38
9	349-874-658	Retieffe, S.	4.00	3.50	3.75
10	138-456-749	Yui, T.	3.25	2.50	2.88

Step 19

20 Deselect the cells by clicking outside the selected cells.

21 Save and then print Int E2-02.

22 Click the button on the Taskbar representing the NPC Classes Access database file.

23 Open the Linked Grades table.

Notice that this linked table contains the final grades and the average scores you inserted in the Excel Int E2-02 worksheet.

24 Save, print, and then close the Linked Grades table.

25 Close the NPC Classes database file and then exit Access.

26 With Excel the active program, close Int E2-02, and then exit Excel.

Take 2

Deleting the Link to a Linked Table

If you want to delete the link to a table, open the database file, and then click the Tables button on the Objects bar. Click the linked table in the list box and then click the Delete button on the Tables toolbar (or press the Delete key). At the Microsoft question asking if you want to remove the link to the table, click Yes. Access deletes the link and removes the table's name from the list box. When you delete a linked table, you are deleting the information Access uses to open the table, not the table itself. You can link to the same table again, if necessary.

INTEGRATED 2 Skills Review

Word
Excel
Access

Activity 1: Exporting Access Data to Excel

1 Open Access and then open the PT Costumes database file.
2 Click the Tables button in the Objects bar and then export the data in the Costume Inventory table to Excel.
3 When the data displays in Excel, make the following changes in the specified cells:

C4	=	Change *110.00* to *120.00*
C5	=	Change *110.00* to *125.00*
C7	=	Change *99.50* to *105.00*

4 Select cells A1 through E17 and then apply an autoformat of your choosing.
5 Save the worksheet with the name Int E2-R1.
6 Print and then close Int E2-R1.
7 Click the button on the Taskbar representing the Access database file PT Costumes and then close the database file.

Activity 2: Exporting Access Data to Word

1 With Access the active program, open WB Supplies.
2 Click the Tables button in the Objects bar and then export the data in the Inventory List table to Word.
3 When the data displays on the screen in Word, apply a table autoformat of your choosing to the table.
4 Move the insertion point to the beginning of the document, press Enter three times, and then move the insertion point back to the beginning of the document.
5 Key **The Waterfront Bistro** on the first line and **Inventory List** on the second line.
6 Select *The Waterfront Bistro* and *Inventory List* and then change the font to 22-point Arial bold.
7 Save the Word document with the default name (Inventory List).
8 Print and then close Inventory List.
9 Click the button on the Taskbar representing the Access database file WB Supplies and then close the database file.

Activity 3: Exporting an Access Report to Word

1 With Access the active program, open PT Costumes.
2 At the PT Costumes Database window, click the Reports button in the Objects bar and then export the *Costume Inventory* report to a Word document.
3 When the data displays on the screen in Word, move the insertion point to the beginning of the document and then key the company name, **Performance Threads**.

4 Press Enter and then key **Costume Inventory**.
5 Increase the size and apply bolding to *Performance Threads* and *Costume Inventory*.
6 Save the Word document with the default name (Costume Inventory).
7 Print and then close Costume Inventory.
8 Exit Word.
9 With Access the active program, close the PT Costumes database file.

Activity 4: Importing Data to a New Table

1 In Access, open the PT Costumes database file and then click the Tables button in the Objects bar.
2 Import the Excel worksheet named PT Costume Hours. (Make sure you change the Files of type option to *Microsoft Excel*, and then double-click *PT Costume Hours* in the list box. Do not make any changes to the first Import Spreadsheet Wizard dialog box. At the second dialog box, make sure there is a check mark in the First Row Contains Column Headings option. Make sure the In a New Table option is selected at the third dialog box. Do make changes to the fourth dialog box and click the No Primary key option at the fifth dialog box. At the sixth dialog box, key **Design Hours** in the Import to Table text box, and then click the Finish button.)
3 Open the new table, Design Hours.
4 Print and then close the Design Hours table.
5 Close the PT Costumes database file.

Activity 5: Linking Data to a New Table and Editing Linked Data

1 Open Excel and then open FCT Bookings.
2 Save the worksheet with the name Int E2-R2.
3 Make Access the active program, open the FCT Commissions database file, and then click the Tables button in the Objects bar.
4 Link the Excel worksheet Int E2-R2 with the FCT Commissions database file. (At the Link dialog box, make sure you change the Files of type option to *Microsoft Excel*. At the third Link Spreadsheet Wizard dialog box, key **Linked Commissions** in the Linked Table Name text box.)
5 Open, print, and then close the new Linked Commissions table.
6 Click the button on the Taskbar representing the Excel worksheet Int E2-R2.
7 Make cell C2 active, key the formula **=B2*0.03** and then press Enter.
8 Make cell C2 active and then use the fill handle to copy the formula down to cell C13.
9 Save, print, and then close Int E2-R2.
10 Click the button on the Taskbar representing the FCT Commissions Access database file and then open the Linked Commissions table.
11 Save, print, and then close the Linked Commissions table.
12 Close the FCT Commissions database file.
13 Exit Access and then exit Excel.

Index